Israel's Jewish Identity Crisis

An important and topical contribution to the field of Middle East Studies, this innovative, provocative, and timely study tackles head-on the main assumptions of the foundation of Israel as a Jewish state. Theoretically sophisticated and empirically rich, this study provides a novel analysis of the interplay between Israeli nationalism and Jewish tradition, arriving at a fresh understanding of the Israeli – Palestinian conflict through its focus on internal questions about Israeli identity. By critiquing and transcending the current discourse on religion and politics in Israel, this study brings to an international audience debates within Israel that have previously been inaccessible to non-Hebrew-speaking academics. Featuring discussions on Israeli jurisprudence, the nation-state law, and rabbinic courts, *Israel's Jewish Identity Crisis* will have far-reaching implications, not only within the state of Israel but on politics, society, and culture beyond its borders.

YAACOV YADGAR is the Stanley Lewis Professor of Israel Studies at the University of Oxford. He has written extensively on matters of Jewish identity, nationalism, secularism, modernity, and tradition in Israel. He is the author of *Sovereign Jews: Israel, Zionism, and Judaism* (2017).

The Global Middle East

General Editors

Arshin Adib-Moghaddam, *SOAS, University of London*
Ali Mirsepassi, *New York University*

Editorial Advisory Board

Faisal Devji, *University of Oxford*
John Hobson, *University of Sheffield*
Firoozeh Kashani-Sabet, *University of Pennsylvania*
Zachary Lockman, *New York University*
Madawi Al-Rasheed, *London School of Economics and Political Science*
David Ryan, *University College Cork, Ireland*

The Global Middle East series seeks to broaden and deconstruct the geograph-ical boundaries of the 'Middle East' as a concept to include North Africa, Central and South Asia, and diaspora communities in Western Europe and North America. The series features fresh scholarship that employs theoretically rigorous and innovative methodological frameworks resonating across rele-vant disciplines in the humanities and the social sciences. In particular, the general editors welcome approaches that focus on mobility, the erosion of nation-state structures, travelling ideas and theories, transcendental techno-politics, the decentralization of grand narratives, and the dislocation of ideolo-gies inspired by popular movements. The series will also consider translations of works by authors in these regions whose ideas are salient to global scholarly trends but have yet to be introduced to the Anglophone academy.

Other books in the series:

Israel's Jewish Identity Crisis

State and Politics in the Middle East

YAACOV YADGAR
University of Oxford

CAMBRIDGE
UNIVERSITY PRESS

CAMBRIDGE
UNIVERSITY PRESS

University Printing House, Cambridge CB2 8BS, United Kingdom

One Liberty Plaza, 20th Floor, New York, NY 10006, USA

477 Williamstown Road, Port Melbourne, VIC 3207, Australia

314–321, 3rd Floor, Plot 3, Splendor Forum, Jasola District Centre,
New Delhi – 110025, India

79 Anson Road, #06–04/06, Singapore 079906

Cambridge University Press is part of the University of Cambridge.

It furthers the University's mission by disseminating knowledge in the pursuit of
education, learning, and research at the highest international levels of excellence.

www.cambridge.org
Information on this title: www.cambridge.org/9781108488945
DOI: 10.1017/9781108773249

© Yaacov Yadgar 2020

First published 2020

Printed in the United Kingdom by TJ International Ltd. Padstow Cornwall

A catalogue record for this publication is available from the British Library.

Library of Congress Cataloging-in-Publication Data
Names: Yadgar, Yaacov, author.
Title: Israel's Jewish identity crisis : state and politics in the Middle East / Yaacov Yadgar.
Other titles: Global Middle East (Cambridge, England)
Description: Cambridge, United Kingdom ; New York, NY : Cambridge University Press, 2020. |
    Series: The global Middle East ; 11 | Includes bibliographical references and index.
Identifiers: LCCN 2019038290 (print) | LCCN 2019038291 (ebook) |
    ISBN 9781108488945 (hardback) | ISBN 9781108715706 (paperback) |
    ISBN 9781108773249 (epub)
Subjects: LCSH: Jews–Israel–Identity. | Zionism. | Nationalism–Israel. | Religion and politics–Israel. |
    Judaism and politics–Israel. | Judaism and secularism–Israel. | Judaism and state–Israel.
Classification: LCC DS113.3 .Y33 2020 (print) | LCC DS113.3 (ebook) | DDC 956.9405/5–dc23
LC record available at https://lccn.loc.gov/2019038290
LC ebook record available at https://lccn.loc.gov/2019038291

ISBN 978-1-108-48894-5 Hardback
ISBN 978-1-108-71570-6 Paperback

To Ester.

Contents

Preface

The idea of writing this book first occurred to me a few years ago when I spent a year as a visiting professor at the University of California, Berkeley. The campus had been teeming with debates, protests, and public controversies surrounding Israel – or, to be precise, Israel's role in the violently conflictual politics of the Middle East. My courses – dealing with the history of Zionism, Israeli political culture, and matters that are usually discussed under the header of 'religion and politics' in Israel – were of obvious interest to many students. But there seemed to be a lingering confusion among my students: Were my courses about this conflict? Would the discussions in my classes – the titles of which suggested a focus on issues that are seemingly internal to Jewish-Israeli history and politics – be of relevance to the matters fiercely debated on campus?

I found this confusion among my students to be a telling testimony to some of the major failings of the dominant discourse on Middle Eastern politics, specifically regarding the conflict between Israelis and Palestinians. My students were echoing a predominant sense of a categorical distinction between matters that are internal to Israeli sociopolitics (i.e., what we would usually call national politics), which are supposedly of only implicit relevance to this conflict, and matters that are international, and bear directly on it. The internal issues – dealing, for example, with Israeli/Zionist national identity, religion, and politics in Israel, Israeli political culture, Jewish identity in Israel, etc. – were seen as only remotely and indirectly influencing the actions taken by Israel in its conflictual relations with the Palestinians and the Arab world at large.

This distinction, which lies at the root of the usual framing of the discussion on a conflict that is commonly (as well as incorrectly and rather insensitively) labeled the 'Jewish-Arab' conflict, assumes the meaning of these names, or sides, to be obvious. It assumes that the meaning implicit in the designation 'Jewish' – which is often synonymized in practice with 'Israeli' – is obvious, an unchallenged given fact of the conflict. Moreover, according to this conventional view this meaning is relevant to the politics of the Middle East *only* in so far as it frames the conflict between the two opposing sides. ('Arab' or 'Palestinian' are consequently seen as the essential opposite of the said meaning.) If debates on the meaning of this Jewishness/Israeliness are acknowledged, they are assumed to be only peripheral to the main binary of Jew versus Arab or Israeli versus Arab/Palestinian.

Another way of putting this is to say that this distinction assumes that the meaning of Israel being a 'Jewish state' is a rather clear and unchallenged issue; that the meaning(s) of Jewish sovereignty, of nationalist (allegedly secular, or at least 'non-religious') Jewish identity, and of the distinction between Jewish politics/nationalism and religion/theology is clear, and essentially unchallenged. Even if it does acknowledge the contested nature of these issues, the predominant discourse does not view them as immediately shaping the 'hard' politics of a violent ethno-national conflict over land and power. It assumes the 'sociology' of Israel to be only remotely of relevance to the politics of the Middle East.

Confronted with my students' confusion, I came to realize that what seemed to me to be an obvious connection – an essential interdependence between the sociology, culture, and internal politics of Israel and the conflict in the Middle East – often went unacknowledged by large swaths of the discursive field in which we all – students, teachers, politicians, activists, and protesters alike – found ourselves. Having studied Israeli sociopolitics extensively, it was apparent to me that we cannot truly understand the one without the other; that a disciplinary distinction between international relations, political science, sociology, and cultural studies may make organizational-institutional sense, but discursively has been caustically misguided.

Searching for reading assignments that would render this interdependence explicit was a frustrating endeavor indeed. A vast field of scholarship on religion and politics in Israel, for example, rarely draws the connection between its immediate subject matter and its implications regarding the Jewish State's self-positioning in the Middle East.

It was easy enough to find books and articles that would acquaint my students with the alleged secularity of Zionist ideology, of the alleged religious-secular cleavage among Jews in Israel, of the history of the controversies on the legal definition of Jewishness in Israel, etc.

But only rarely could I come up with a reading assignment that would tie these in with what was being debated outside of class, on campus, and in the public sphere at large. In the same vein, books that address the conflict – whether critical of the political status quo of Israeli/ Zionist dominance or propagating Zionist apologetics that justify this status quo – tend to focus on the relations between the two conflicting sides, and often fail to problematize the ways in which these rivals negotiate and construct the various aspects of their histories and identities.

Indeed, as a colleague once commented to me in private, debates on secularism, religiosity, and politics in Israel (i.e., among Israeli Jews) sometimes amount to a discursively violent erasure of the very presence of Palestinian-Arabs in Israel, as the dominant discourse assumes the debate to be of no relevance to non-Jews in Israel, while the whole issue of Israel's Jewish identity is constructed exactly around (non-Jewish) Palestinian-Arabs.[1]

This book, then, is primarily an attempt at correcting this lacuna, at least as far as a study of the Israeli side is concerned. I make the connections between the 'internals' of Zionism and Israel and 'the conflict' apparent. This book deals with what is commonly titled 'religion and politics' in Israel: with the meaning of Israeli nationhood and the various ways in which it corresponds with the State of Israel's self-identification as Jewish; with the ways in which this self-identification of the state shapes the state's stance vis-à-vis its non-Jewish, mainly Palestinian-Arab, citizens; with the ways in which this apparent entanglement of 'religion and politics' shapes Israel's position in the Middle East; and with the ways in which the State's claim to Jewish identity shapes Jewish-Israeli nationhood's relations with Jews outside of the Jewish state.

The book tackles these issues, and others derived from them, by refocusing the discussion on the Israeli nation-state's unresolved relationship with its own claim to a nonreligious, or 'secular' Jewish

---

[1] This insight is echoed in Ian Lustick's analysis of the political implications of Israel's immigration politics, which he summarizes as constituting 'Israel as a non-Arab state.' I. S. Lustick, 'Israel as a non-Arab state: The political implications of mass immigration of non-Jews,' *Middle East Journal*, 53/3 (1999), 417–33. In this context see also Y. Yonah, 'Israel's immigration policies: The twofold face of the 'demographic threat,'' *Social Identities*, 10/2 (2004), 195–218.

identity – or, as the title of this books suggest, with Israel's Jewish identity crisis. I argue that this is a key to understanding not only the intricacies of intra-Jewish sociopolitics, but also Israel's positions and actions in international affairs. If we wish to understand the Israeli–Arab conflict we must try and decipher the meaning of Israeli nationhood, and especially the way it understands its own Jewishness.[2]

At the same time, it should be clear to the reader that the main subject of this book is far from being an Israeli or Zionist idiosyncrasy. To a significant extent, this book is about the modern, liberal, so-called nonreligious nation-state as such; it takes Israel as a specific case history that sheds light on the broader issue of the theopolitics[3] of the nation-state. Specifically, the book offers a view into the ways in which the dichotomy between religion and politics serves the allegedly 'secular' state and the limitations of this service.

* * *

Before I introduce my argument in a more comprehensive manner, a quick return to my Berkeley experience may be in place, for it sheds light on the charged nature of the discourse that I will analyze.

One day a guest appeared in my 'Religion and Politics in Israel' class. The young man, in his early 20s, was an Israeli-Jewish cousin of one of my American students. He came to the United States for a family visit, and when he heard about the class, he told me, he had to come and see it for himself. He was happy that his American cousin is learning about Israel and wanted to see what the class is like. The topic of the discussion that day was the implicit-yet-all-too-dominant identification between Israeliness and Jewishness in Israel. We necessarily also discussed the exclusionary, discriminatory implications that this sociocultural fact has for non-Jewish, mainly Palestinian-Arab citizens of Israel, rendering them, by practical definition, Israel's Others. (This is also, of course, a major topic of discussion in this book.) The Israeli visitor, who kept silent during the class itself, approached me afterwards, and in a rather familiar tone kept for insiders, chided me for what went on in class. Surely, these are all facts of the Israeli reality, he said, but they

---

[2] *See* Y. M. Rabkin, 'The problem, Benny Morris, is Zionism,' *The Jerusalem Post*, January 29 (2007).

[3] W. T. Cavanaugh, *Theopolitical Imagination: Christian Practices of Space and Time* (Edinburgh: Bloomsbury T&T Clark, 2003).

do not reflect nicely upon Israel. One has to be careful when talking about such sensitive matters 'to them' (i.e., non-Israeli Americans, in this case), for they, unlike us Israelis, do not see 'the whole picture.'

I understood this to mean, as one so often hears in intra-Jewish-Israeli discussions, that while these, and other elements of our reality, are indeed problematic, often ugly facts of our lives, we nevertheless have to accept them in practice, since 'they,' our alleged enemies, are much worse than us; were it not for this or that discriminatory policy or practice, for example, the state would no longer be, and the fate of the whole Jewish people will be in jeopardy. They, non-Israeli-Jews, do not know this, or they may not care for the state as much as we do. Hence, one has to be careful when talking to them.

Indeed, this has been one of the more profound implications of the establishment of Israel in the shadow of the Holocaust, as the state positions itself as the guarantor of the very survival of Jews worldwide. As such, it is, in an important sense, beyond critiquing. Unjust and misguided as its policies may be, they are nevertheless justified by the menace of the alleged alternative, namely a precarious existence of stateless Jews. This binary, unidimensional and fallacious as it is, nevertheless shadows much of the debate on Israel. One is assumed to be taking a position in this binary, and in it alone: Either one is critical of the state – and hence assumed to be wishing for its demise, or one is supporting the very idea of the state, and hence expected to eventually, almost unreflectively, justify its actions. (Needless to say, this is obviously a simplified image of a complicated field of shifting red line, on both sides of this binary.)

Regrettably for my visitor-cum-critic, I accept neither this binary, nor the statist narrative that propagates it. My position is critical; it challenges the status quo and seeks to shed light on and problematize those unmarked aspects of our political reality, those taken-for-granted significations and meanings, that carry overwhelming political consequences exactly because they go unnoticed, working, as they are, as the infrastructure of the way our very reality is constructed. This necessarily is a disturbing exercise. It brings to the surface arguments, notions, meanings, and other facts of our political world, which may be uncomfortable to acknowledge explicitly, no matter how prevalent they are when working silently 'in the background.' Yet, I believe it is an inescapable fact that without confronting these truths we may never be able to truly understand our reality. Hence this book.

***

I am grateful to the numerous people who have accompanied me in the intellectual journey culminating in this book, and whose ideas must have ultimately also found their place in its pages – whether knowingly and explicitly or unknowingly and implicitly so. Of these I should especially note Brian Klug, who offered his unwavering, carefully attuned and unconditionally supportive engagement with my work, and whose intellectual companionship I cherish. I am also especially grateful to Yakov Rabkin, who not only endured hearing my arguments repeatedly, but also offered his comments on early versions of their textual iteration. The anonymous readers who reviewed the manuscript for Cambridge University Press have offered illuminating critiques and have helped me improve my presentation of my argument in a manner that was impossible for me to achieve without their attentive readings. Kfir Cohen, David Myers, Amnon Raz-Krakotzkin, Eskandar Sadeghi-Boroujerdi, Lena Salaymeh, Yehouda Shenhav, and Yael Zerubavel have all taken part in the gradual formation of my own thoughts on the subjects discussed here, and for this I am indebted to them.

The book was written as my family and I were relocating to Oxford, and it would not have been possible to write it without the heart-warming support of members of the university and its wider community. Among these, I am especially grateful to Raymond Dweck, Louise Fawcett, Martin Goodman, Roger Goodman, Matthew Leigh, Hindy Najman, Eduardo Posada-Carbo, Eugene Rogan, Anna Sapir-Abulafia, and Avi Shlaim. St. Anne's College has been a welcoming, warm academic home to me. I am also grateful to the different institutions in Oxford who provided me with the strong backing that allows for one's thoughts to fruitfully develop: Oxford's School of Global and Area Studies, the Department of Politics and International Relations, The Middle East Centre at St. Antony's College, and the Oxford Centre for Hebrew and Jewish Studies. Working with Cambridge University Press has been a delightfully productive process thanks to the professionalism, accessibility, and generosity of Maria Marsh, Daniel Brown, Mathew Rohit, and Stephanie Taylor. Thanks also to Alta Bridges, who edited the text, and to Yuval Ben-David, who prepared the index.

Introduction
Israel's Jewish Identity Crisis

In his masterful history of Judaism, Martin Goodman leaves the reader with somewhat of a perplexing note, given almost in passing, regarding the (ir-)relevance to the history of Judaism, of what has historically been the most influential segment of Israeli society, namely the secularist, liberal-Zionist elite. As he puts it,

> Many Jewish Israelis, including a vocal elite, are defiantly secular, and it may be questioned to what extent the attitude of such secular Israelis to their Jewish heritage, which is sometimes for them essentially a matter only of status within Israeli society in distinguishing them from Arab Israelis … belongs to a history of Judaism.[1]

This perceptive observation may sound to some readers as quite shocking: it suggests that a dominant element of the Israeli elite has ceased to be part of the history of Judaism. How has this come to be? And what does it tell us about the meaning of Israel's being a – or rather *the* – 'Jewish state'?

This may demand that we also ask: What is the meaning of Israeli nationhood, as distinct from Jewish nationhood? How does an Israeli nationalism correspond with the state's assumed self-identification as Jewish? What does this Jewishness of the state mean in the first place? What, in other words, is the meaning of *Jewish* sovereignty in Israel? How does Israel's self-identification as a Jewish state (confused as this identification may be, even after 70 years of sovereign statehood) shape the state's stance vis-à-vis its non-Jewish, mainly Palestinian-Arab, citizens? Where does it leave non-Jewish, non-Arabs citizens of Israel? How does this apparent entanglement of religion and politics shape Israel's position in the Middle East? And, lastly, how does the state's claim to Jewish identity shape the relations between Jewish-Israeli nationhood and Jews outside of the Jewish state?

---

[1] M. Goodman, *A History of Judaism* (London: Allen Lane, 2017), 437.

This book tackles these questions and others derived from them by refocusing the discussion on the Israeli nation-state's unresolved relationship with its own claim to a nonreligious Jewish identity. These issues all have to do, in other words, with what can be safely termed Israel's Jewish identity crisis. This, I argue, is a key to understanding not only the intricacies of intra-Jewish sociopolitics, but also Israel's positions and actions in international affairs. This is to say that if we wish to truly understand the Israeli–Arab conflict we must (also) decipher the meaning of Israeli nationhood, and especially its Jewishness.

A central argument of this book is that Zionism's and Israel's failure (or lack of interest thereof) to formulate a viable national identity that is independent of what the self-proclaimed secularist Zionist ideology itself has viewed (largely negatively) as Jewish religion renders the state's definition of Jewish politics a matter of 'biological,' quasi-racial exclusionary logic. Zionism, which entails a transition from the understanding of Jewish identity through a dialogue with diverse traditions to a so-called natural definition of this identity in effect conditions the viability of 'Jewish politics' on the existence of a majority of Jews, whose (Jewish) identity is defined and understood primarily as a matter of their 'biological' origin (call, it, then, ethnicity, race, 'blood,' or otherwise; needless to say, this very naming exercise is highly contentious). Compounded by Zionism's notion of an inherent antinomy between Jewishness and Arabness, this nationalist-racial logic marks Israel's minority of non-Jewish Palestinian-Arab citizens a threat to the very existence of the state in its current self-understanding, and (among other things) renders both Palestinian-Israeli and Jewish-Arab identities precarious anomalies.

Moreover, while this exclusionary *nation-statist, political* logic has very little of substance to do with traditional understandings of Jewish identity,[2] it nevertheless carries one critical 'religiously' traditional implication, as it leaves the supposedly secular nation-state inherently dependent on Orthodox interpreters of Jewish ('religious') law for the very definition and preservation of the State's Jewish identity.

---

[2] As I discuss shortly, I do not mean to suggest that Jewish tradition and Jewish law disregard matter of biological descend. Chapter 1 will also present a more detailed account of this matter.

I thus argue that a simplistic view of Zionism and Israel as 'essentially nonreligious'[3] phenomena, which are somehow pushed by religious or Orthodox reactionaries into enforcing Jewish religion on the otherwise secular public, is misguided and misleading.[4] Accordingly, this book highlights the critical importance of a set of legal measures, cultural conventions, and institutional practices, which the simplistic discourse marks negatively as a malignant religious coercion, for the construction and preservation of the supposedly secular nation-state's configuration of power.

The book focuses mainly on certain major, relatively recent case histories of social, political, and cultural debates that have dominated public discourse in Israel as shedding light on some of the main fault lines of Jewish-Israeli nationhood. These cases touch on various elements of Israel's Jewish identity, dealing, among many other things, with the political debate on religious conversions, initiatives to 'anchor' and 'bolster' Israel's Jewish identity by legislative measures and governmental initiatives, debates about the supposed growing role of what critics see as 'religion' in the Israeli public sphere, and the corresponding attempts at propagating and promoting a secularist, non- or even anti-Jewish-Israeli national identity as a hoped-for (and ultimately failed) solution to the identity crisis at hand. While these are seemingly mainly intra-Jewish-Israeli controversies or debates, they in effect deal not only with the Jewishness of Israel, but also, often primarily so, with Israel's contentious position (for want of a better term) in the Middle East.

The book utilizes these case histories also to outline a critique of the secularist discourse on what is commonly viewed as 'religion and politics' in Israel, and to offer an alternative understanding of Israeli sociopolitics. Released from both the secularist epistemology and the theopolitics of the nation-state that establishes and maintains the duality of religious and secular, the book explicates some of the major failings of a secular(ist), liberal-Zionist discourse on Israeli nationhood

---

[3] 'Secular' is too contested a term to be applied naïvely, even in the framework of this simplistic view.

[4] Michael Walzer has recently offered a sophisticated rendition of this argument, by which Israel's or Zionism's 'secular revolution' is impeded by 'religious counterrevolutionaries'; M. Walzer, *The Paradox of Liberation: Secular Revolutions and Religious Counterrevolutions* (New Haven, CT: Yale University Press, 2015).

and the Israeli–Arab conflict. In place of the misleading secularist framework, the book is guided by a 'traditionist,'[5] post-secular epistemology, which facilitates a Jewish critique of the Zionist and Israeli project of reinventing Jewish identity.

Accordingly, as shall become clear in the next chapters, my main (but surely not sole) object of study is the secularist, liberal-Zionist discourse on matters of Israeliness, Jewishness, and Judaism. Not for nothing, *Haaretz*, by far the most important venue for this discourse, figures prominently in the book's references.[6] I would argue that the liberal-Zionist understanding of the matters at hand, brings to the fore – much more so than is the case with other constructions of Jewish-Israeli identity – the Zionist, or Israeli-Jewish identity crisis.

Readers may indeed wonder whether my focus on the secularist and liberal elites, most thoroughly represented in *Haaretz* is justified. Isn't it the case that this is but an elite, small in size by definition, whose influence has been waning? Indeed, as the chapters in this book will show (and see especially Chapter 3), many of the spokespeople of this elite decry exactly that: their small numbers and their decreasing influence. Yet I would argue that there is a strong case for focusing, as I do, on the discourse propagated by this secularist, liberal-Zionist elite. To begin with, this elite is quite clearly a foremost heir of the dominant Zionist ideology that lies at the basis of the Israeli polity. Being part of an elite group does not mean being irrelevant; rather, this group has the luxury of delving into matters that others may experience and live, but do not necessarily discuss explicitly, systematically, and publicly.

---

[5] Y. Yadgar, 'Tradition,' *Human Studies*, 36/4 (2013), 451–70; Y. Yadgar, 'Traditionism,' *Cogent Social Sciences*, 1/1 (2015), 1–17.

[6] The references to *Haaretz* are complicated by two practices of the newspaper: First, it offers 'official' English print and web versions, which are largely based on the Hebrew version(s) of the paper but are not identical to it. Specifically, it does not carry translations of all articles published in Hebrew. As I will note in due course, its translation practices also offer some insights into the matters at hand. Second, its Hebrew web version and print version offer different titles for the same articles. My work here, focused on the Israeli (Hebrew) discourse, is mainly based on the Hebrew text (either in print or web versions). Wherever available, my references would be to the English translation available online, so as to offer the English reader an easier access to these texts. My quotations will rely on the Hebrew version, consulting with the English ones, but not bound by them. The titles in the references are of the web versions, which are more easily accessible.

To put this point more bluntly, this elite has the privilege of in effect being more attentive to some of the logical inconsistencies that characterize not only itself, but the Israeli polity at large. Moreover, the relatively sophisticated and evidently deeply thought observations, critiques, and predications expressed by this elite are interesting – and illuminating – exactly when they nevertheless fail to see some of the most foundational 'unthoughts,' the taken-for-granted assumptions, that underlie their view of political, cultural, and social reality.

But maybe even more important, this elite is the foremost advocate of a secular, liberal nationalism, that would supposedly – by its own account – save the Israeli polity from the malicious influences of benighted religion and illiberal nationalism – two maladies which the secularist elite sees as almost synonymous. This elite refuses to renege on its commitment to liberal and democratic values, while vociferously – at least in the most mainstream part of it – remaining adherent to foundational Zionist ideas, on their implied (although not always thoroughly thought through) appropriations of Jewishness.[7]

For this reason, as I already noted above, liberal-Zionism brings Israel's *Jewish* identity crisis into a sharper relief. Moreover, I would argue that it is exactly this elite's failure to account for this crisis that motivates the rise of those malicious trends, by which Israel is pushed more forcefully into the fold of what John Plamenatz identified as an 'Eastern' version of nationalism.[8] Clearly, these trends understand themselves primarily as concerned with *Jewish* identity, beholden as this notion of Jewishness may be to the nation-statist, Zionist rendition of Jewishness that has been promoted for decades by the secularist

---

[7] There are, of course, voices in the Israeli Left who argue that secularist, liberal-democratic principles are inconsistent with a Zionist commitment. A more recent articulation of this stance was put by Gideon Levy, against the backdrop of the 2019 (first) general election campaign. As Levy puts it:

> Here's an oxymoron: Zionism and the Left. These are two conflicting values that can no longer be upheld simultaneously, and the time has come to recognize this.
> This is the most important reason for the Israeli left's erosion to its current nadir: The left declined because it lost its way. This loss of its way was inbuilt and inevitable. If you remain a Zionist, you can no longer be of the left; if you're of the left, you can no longer be a Zionist.

G. Levy, 'It's Leftism or Zionism – you can't have both,' *Haaretz*, February 10, 2019.

[8] J. Plamenatz, 'Two types of nationalism' in E. Kamenka (ed.), *Nationalism: The Nature and Evolution of an Idea* (London: Edward Arnold, 1978), 22–36.

Zionist elite. In other words, for us to understand what many agree is a growing trend of a continuous Israeli shift toward a less tolerant and more nationalistic interpretation of Zionist ideology, we must first see the crisis to which this trend is but a reaction.

It must be stressed that this does not mean that I see the Jewish identity crisis and its aftermath as affecting only, or even mostly, the Israeli Left. Indeed, as shall become clearer later on, I see the fault lines determining this crisis as a direct outcome of the Zionists' failed attempt to redefine Judaism and Jewishness in terms of a modern European, nation-statist epistemology and worldview. In other words, this is a characteristic of the Zionist field as a whole, and it is not the exclusive territory of the Israeli Left, or of liberal-Zionism at large (for matters of convenience, I allow myself to identify the two here; this is not to suggest that I forget the problematics of suggesting that the Israeli Left is necessarily liberal[9]; I return to the issue of the interplay between the Israeli Left and the increasingly dominant Right in the Conclusion).

Epistemology and Power

Israel's Jewish identity crisis is, to a large extent, a direct outcome of the failed attempt to 'fit' or 'force' Jewish traditions and histories into conceptual, ideological, and political molds that were born out of modern European, Christian history. These molds are characterized by a predominance of a historically and politically situated Protestant epistemology that serves the allegedly secular nation-statist configuration of power, and perpetuates itself as universal, neutral, and suprahistorical.

We may get a better sense of what stands at the basis of this failed attempt by taking a short detour of sorts, and considering an argument made in one of the foundational texts of the Iranian revolution, probably the most influential book published in twentieth-century Iran, by arguably the most interesting of the intellectual forefathers of the revolution, Jalal Al-e Ahmad.

The Persian title of the work, and the central idea at hand, *Gharbzadegi* (originally published in 1962), has been variously translated as

[9] Z. Sternhell, *The Founding Myths of Israel: Nationalism, Socialism, and the Making of the Jewish State* (Princeton, NJ: Princeton University Press, 1998).

'West-struckness,'[10] 'Plagued by the West,'[11] and 'Occidentosis.'[12] The book has established its author's reputation as one of the most influential formulators of the idea that Western dominance, or 'Westernization,' if you like, is nothing short of a malignant disease that has taken over the East, leaving it helpless in the face of the colonial onslaught in its various manifestations.

Among many other things, Al-e Ahmad forecasts Edward Said's *Orientalism*, as he deals not necessarily with the immediate political question, that is the direct or indirect rule of colonial Europe over the governments and resources of the East (manifested by Iran, in this case), but with what I would call the European *intellectual* domination, or colonization, of the East.

Al-e Ahmad narrates a history of *longue durée*, in which two rivals, who used to hold a healthy competition between them, have in recent times taken a more sinister relationship of master and servant. In the past, East and West – both, of course, are only fictitiously coherent constructs – had been rivals competing not only for political domination, but also, maybe primarily, over intellectual superiority. They held a productive dialogue on scientific and epistemological questions, debating the very way we should understand the world and conduct ourselves in it.

But in modern times the West has become master, and the East its servant. Among other things, this is manifested in the way in which the West has been forcing its view of the world, its concepts and ideas, in short: its epistemology, on the East. Thus, if in the past East and West had been equal rivals in a competitive relationship that was beneficial to both sides, now, writes Al-e Ahmad,

We have forgotten the spirit of competition and come to feel in its place the spirit of helplessness, the spirit of worshipfulness. We no longer feel ourselves to be in the right and deserving. (They take the oil, because it is their right and because we cannot stop them; they manage our politics, because our hands are tied; they take away our freedom, because we're unworthy of it.) If we seek to evaluate some aspect of our lives, we do so by their criteria, as

[10] J. Al-e Ahmad, *Gharbzadegi [Weststruckness]*, trans. John Green and Ahmad Alizadeh (Costa Mesa, CA: Mazda Publishers, 1997).
[11] J. Al-e Ahmad, *Plagued by the West*, trans. Paul Sprachman (Delmor, NY: Center for Iranian Studies, Columbia University, 1982).
[12] J. Al-e Ahmad, *Occidentosis: A Plague from the West*, trans. Robert Campbell (Berkeley, CA: Mizan Press, 1984).

prescribed by their advisors and consultants. Thus do we study; thus do we gather statistics; thus do we conduct research. This makes sense insofar as science has universal methods: scientific methods bear the imprint of no nationality.

But what is curious is that we marry just like the Westerners. We pretend to be free just like them. We sort the world into good and bad along the lines they lay out. We dress like them. We write like them. Night and day are night and day when they confirm it. One would think our own values had been abrogated. We even pride ourselves in thus being their one-eyed offspring. One of the two ancient rival wrestlers has been demoted to the position of ring keeper; the other owns the ring. And the ring is filled with lust, stupidity, boasting, and vanity.[13]

Note how domination in its immediate political sense – the stealing of oil, the dictate of the regime, the restrictions on freedom – is closely tied to epistemology, to the very way we understand (or, if I will forecast my argument: *mis*understand) the world, how we interpret (or misinterpret) it, and how we talk about it.

As Al-e Ahmad suggests, I would like to question the way in which concepts, ideas, worldviews, and political interests which have been prevalent in Europe were 'imported' into Jewish traditions or histories, and to shed some light, I hope, on the political implications of this importation.

More specifically, I would like to discuss the ways in which the foundational political ideas of the modern, European nation-state were 'imported' or 'applied' to the Jewish-European framework, and from there spread over to the Jewish world at large. These foundational concepts primarily include the modern, post-Westphalian notions of the nation-state: that is, nationalism and sovereignty, together with their counterparts, which were usually understood in the same conceptual framework as the very opposites of nationalism and the sovereignty of the nation-state, namely religion and its derivatives.

Zionism, Jewish 'Religion,' and Sovereignty

So, let us discuss the Israeli here-and-now, and, as suggested by Al-e Ahmad, make sure to examine both the historical and epistemological roots of this sociopolitical reality.

---

[13] Al-e Ahmad, *Occidentosis*, 43–4.

What I refer to in this book as Israel's Jewish identity crisis can be seen as a direct outcome of what is often called the project of 'modernizing,' 'secularizing,' and 'politicizing' Judaism. This project has been, to a large extent, motivated by a dual negation:

First, it would negate the argument, originally developed by central European Jews in the eighteenth century, that Judaism is 'only' a religion, which is nonpolitical by its very nature.[14] Put positively, the counter-argument developed mostly in nineteenth-century Europe (by both European nationalist anti-Semites and Jewish nationalists) is that Judaism is in essence primarily a political entity, as the term is understood in the context of the European, 'secular' nation-state. It sees 'religion' and 'politics' through the same Protestant toolkit,[15] understanding religion to be private, apolitical, and irrational by nature (as opposed to the secular, rational, and public realm of politics), but argues that Judaism cannot, and should not, be reduced to mean 'only' a matter of religion. Instead, it would call for religion to be relegated to the sidelines of the wider (and more authentic, it would argue) meaning of Judaism as a 'secular,' political nationality.

Second, the same nationalist, political project would negate what it calls Jewish 'exile,' which it defines, once again using the European conceptual toolkit, as a nonmodern, malignant case of ahistorical and apolitical religiousness, a (Jewish) life outside of history, which is marked primarily by the deformity of lacking sovereignty.[16]

This dual negation figures prominently in the history of the Zionist and Israeli construction of the meaning of Jewish politics, and I will further my discussion on it later. What I wish to stress at this point is that in its height, this double negation would bring about the phenomenon of Zionist ideological pioneers, who are so vehemently opposed to any notion of Jewishness, that they would prefer not to be called Jews at all (they would usually prefer 'Hebrew' as the adjective of their

---

[14] L. F. Batnitzky, *How Judaism Became a Religion: An Introduction to Modern Jewish Though* (Princeton, NJ: Princeton University Press, 2011).

[15] W. T. Cavanaugh, *The Myth of Religious Violence: Secular Ideology and the Roots of Modern Conflict* (New York: Oxford University Press, 2009); B. Nongbri, *Before Religion: A History of a Modern Concept* (New Haven, CT: Yale University Press, 2015); T. Fitzgerald, *Discourse on Civility and Barbarity* (New York: Oxford University Press, 2007).

[16] A. Raz-Krakotzkin, 'Exile, history and the nationalization of Jewish memory: Some reflections on the Zionist notion of history and return,' *Journal of Levantine Studies*, 3/2 (2013), 37–70.

nationalism; more recently the same sentiment has taken the form of advocating Israeli national identity as precluding Jewish 'sectarianism'). This would ultimately feed the aforementioned sense of alienation from – and resentment toward – Jewish history prevalent among the elite of a state that self-identifies as Jewish, whatever the meaning of this self-identification may be.

Yet at the end the Zionist movement and its culmination in the nation-state of Israel have nevertheless focused on the construction, perpetuation, and upholding of a *Jewish* national identity, encouraging a conflicted, sometimes explicitly inconsistent, sense of the very meaning of Israeli politics as Jewish nation-statehood. Zionism's and Israel's failure to construct and maintain a viable national identity (call it 'Hebrew,' 'Israeli,' or otherwise)[17] that is independent from a 'religious' (and specifically Orthodox-rabbinical) determination of this identity has thus rendered the state's definition of Jewish politics and Jewish sovereignty a problematic matter, to say the least.

Zionism and the Meaning of Jewishness

One way to begin and clarify the murky relationship between Israeliness and Jewishness, or between Israeli politics and the notion of Judaism, Jewish politics, and Jewish nationhood is to highlight the major change – indeed, this may amount to an historical revolution that sometimes goes uncommented on – in the way Zionism approaches the very idea of Jewish identity.

Zionism entails a transition from the understanding of Jewish identity through a dialogue with diverse traditions to a so-called natural, or ethnic, definition of this identity. Echoing nationalist anti-Semitic notions of Jewishness (that were especially prevalent in Eastern Europe, where the Zionist movement took much of its formative ideological shape), it would claim that at root, Jewishness is primarily a matter of 'blood' and 'biology,' i.e., something that one is born with and not – or only secondarily so – something normative, cultural, or practical that one carries as her tradition.

---

[17] This has culminated in the state's and the Israeli Supreme Court's denial of the very existence of an Israeli nationality, both insisting the true essence of Israeli, Zionist politics lies in the notion of Jewish nationalism. See Chapter 4, and Y. Yadgar, *Sovereign Jews: Israel, Zionism, and Judaism* (New York: SUNY Press, 2017), ch. 7.

Understood 'biologically,' Jews – the primary reference point, as opposed to Judaism, which is relegated to the role of the derivative of Jews' actions – are thus defined, however abstractly, not by what they do (or should to, aspire to do, etc.) but 'by what they are.'[18] To understand what is entailed in this shift from history or tradition to biology or 'blood,' let us consider the traditional view and contrast it with the Zionist revolutionary view:

It may be safely asserted (all reservations regarding the futility of such generalizations notwithstanding) that historically or traditionally Judaism, however understood, preceded the Jew. Judaism has been that which defines the Jew. A Jew, in other words, has been understood to mean someone who 'does' (or is expected to 'do') Judaism. Needless to say, the actual meaning of this normative practice or observance has in itself gone through obvious historical changes and has been continuously debated. Yet the principle relationship between Judaism and the Jew has been rather clear. As put by Leon Roth in his discussion of the biblical notion of a 'holy nation':

Judaism is not to be considered in terms of the Jews but the Jews in terms of Judaism. Judaism is not what some or all individual Jews happen as a fact to do. It is what Jews should be doing (but often are not doing) as members of a holy people. Judaism comes first. It is not a product but a programme and the Jews are the instruments of its fulfilment.[19]

As Roth stresses, this would also mean that one's 'being' a Jew has nothing of substance to do with the biological chance of her origin: 'When it is said that the Jewish people is the bearer or carrier or transmitter of Judaism, the phrase 'Jewish people' has to be understood in the widest sense. In principle, the tie constituting this people is not one of 'race' or 'blood.'"[20]

Now, clearly, Judaism does not lack a focus on matters of what we may call biological heredity. As I will discuss in Chapter 1, this is manifested primarily in rabbinical notions of matrilineal descent and the collectivity of 'the seed of Israel' (*zera' yisrael*). These are, to a large

---

[18] As put by Yakov Rabkin, *A Threat from Within: A Century of Jewish Opposition to Zionism* (London: Zed Books, 2006), 6: 'Secularism revolutionized Jewish identity, turning a once normative concept, Jewishness, into a purely descriptive one. Traditional Jews can be distinguished by what they do or should do; the new Jews by what they are.'

[19] L. Roth, *Judaism: A Portrait* (New York: Viking Press, 1968), 16.

[20] Roth, *Judaism: A Portrait*, 16.

extent, derivatives of a dominant narrative by which the Jews all over the world form an extended family, with shared roots that are not only (although clearly primarily) historical and traditional, but also 'biological.' (This narrative or myth is the material from which some advocates of nationalism would construct the edifice of the archaic, historical 'ethnic' root, which allegedly lies at the core of modern nationalism, hence legitimizing the clearly modern phenomenon's claim for historical validity.)

Yet, there is a critical difference between this familial myth of the collectivity (narrated by a group that has been historically a small 'family' among 'other families') and the uses of 'blood' heredity, or biological descent in the context of the modern nation-state. First, even in the most committed rabbinical narrations of this story, it is a manifestly mythical sense of the *spiritual*, not biological, 'essence' that is thought of as having passed through the generations of this extended family, hence as defining it. Second, and clearly more importantly, this narrative has traditionally *not* been used as a *political* notion or criterion for a designation of a 'nation' in the modern, nation-statist understanding of the term.

The difference I am stressing here, then, is that between a familial notion of heredity – a fundamental trait of human life per se – expanded as it may be to form the basis of a shared 'essence' or group identity, and the political construction and uses of such a notion in the specific historical context of nationalism and sovereign nation-statehood, with its concern for majority and minority among the nation-state's population.

Thus, for example, in Maimonides's rendition of the idea discussed here, the biblical notion of 'kingdom of priests and a holy nation' far outweighs the familial sense of kinship. As Roth puts it, this 'nation,' or 'family,' is read by Maimonides as 'in intention infinitely expandable;

Its outer limits are every human being. Born Jews start indeed with an advantage; but the advantage is communicable to others ... Thus ideally the community or 'body' of Judaism is coterminous with the whole of mankind. It is not confined to those born Jews or to those inhabiting a particular parcel of earth; except in so far as being born into a tradition and living in an environment in which it is practiced, makes that tradition more 'natural' and therefore more easy to follow.[21]

[21] Roth, *Judaism: A Portrait*, 100.

In any event, as Roth insists, the rabbinical, traditional notion of Judaism has viewed Judaism as preceding the Jew, and ultimately as defining the Jew. The Zionist idea, rebelling against this tradition, which it has marked as anachronistic religion, would proclaim that (to paraphrase this time a plethora of Zionist writers, from Y. Ḥ. Brenner to A. B. Yehoshua)[22] the Jew precedes Judaism: 'Judaism is not an autonomous entity, but contingent on the activity of Jews ...Judaism has no essentialist features of its own. Judaism is Judaism because it is the Jews' cultural creation, and only its being such a product determines its being Judaism.'[23]

The defining, foundational element shaping the very core of this Jewish nationalism, then, is not a sense of a dialogue with some normative tradition and history (these will surely come into the picture in some readings of the Zionist idea, but only secondarily so), but an a priori sense of some so-called natural and biological determinant of Jewish identity. As Aḥad Haʿam (himself propagating a 'cultural' notion of Zionism, in which a certain sense of knowledge of – and dialoguing with – Jewish tradition has certainly been foundational) put it, noticeably agreeing with the basic premise entailed in this shift toward a 'natural' definition of Jewish identity, 'these new Jews ... see Jewish nationality solely as a matter of the racial sentiment [*regesh hageza*ʿ].' Furthermore, the impetus of this sentiment is read primarily in nationalist terms, as its main, if not sole message is 'the duty of love for their people and work for its exultation.'[24]

Furthermore, as Aḥad Haʿam's interlocutors, espousing a *political* sense of Zionism (as opposed to his 'cultural' or 'spiritual' sense of the ideology) would argue, this must mean that Judaism has no essential features of its own (Aḥad Haʿam, it must be noted, would strongly

---

[22] Y. Ḥ. Brenner, *Ketavim* [Writings] (Tel Aviv: Sifriyat Poʿalim and Haqibutz Hameuḥad, 5738/1978), 1214; A. B. Yehoshua, 'The meaning of homeland,' *The A. B. Yehoshua Controversy: An Israel-Diaspora Dialogue on Jewishness, Israeliness, and Identity* (New York: Dorothy and Julius Koppelman Institute On American Jewish-Israeli Relations American Jewish Committee, 2006), 7–13.

[23] As summed by A. Sagi, *To Be a Jew: Joseph Chayim Brenner as a Jewish Existentialist* (Continuum, 2011), 111–12.

[24] Aḥad Haʿam (Asher Ginzburg), *ʾAl Parashat Derakhim* [On a crossroad], vol. 2 (Berlin: Judischer Verlag, 5690), 80.

refute this argument[25]). This would imply that the survival of Judaism, which has worried Jews for generations, is no longer a matter of critical relevance; the critical issue is the survival – and empowerment – of Jews. Judaism, in this reading, is everything that Jews – or, to be precise, national Jews, Zionists – do. Whether this creation of Jews corresponds with traditional understandings of Judaism or not is irrelevant. What is relevant is that it is the outcome of the doings of Jews.[26]

Jewish Sovereignty or the Sovereignty of Jews?

The notion that the Jew precedes Judaism in effect conditions the viability of 'Jewish politics' in Israel on the active preservation of a 'biological,' 'racial,' or 'ethnic' (as aforementioned, all of these adjectives are politically charged; common Israeli political parlance would usually choose 'demographic') Jewish majority, leaving other meaningful aspects of Jewish politics unattended. In other words, read politically, in the context of a Zionist sovereign nation-state, this idea has been understood to mean that the 'ethnic' or 'biological' makeup of Israeli society is a precondition of the state's upholding of its very *raison d'etre*: As long as the state maintains a majority of Jews among its citizens, the state and its politics, regardless of their specific actions, guiding values, or general outlooks should be considered 'Jewish,' as in 'done by Jews.'

Israel, in this understanding, is 'only,' or 'simply' a state of Jews. It is not, in other words, a 'Jewish state' in the sense of answering to some normative sense of Judaism. This, indeed, has been a rallying cry of secularist liberal-Zionists to this day. They, as we shall see shortly, would argue, or at least imply, that the only viable meaning of Jewish sovereignty is that it is a sovereignty held by Jews. Anything beyond it would amount to a pathological introduction of a 'religious' criteria into the otherwise healthily secular body politic of the nation-state.

---

[25] Ahad Ha'am's thought is obviously much more complex and nuanced than this brief discussion might suggest. For a careful consideration of his thought and its contemporary relevance see Brian Klug's introduction to Ahad Ha'am (Asher Ginzburg), *Words of Fire: Selected Essays of Ahad Ha'am* (Widworthy, UK: Notting Hill Editions, 2015).

[26] G. Shimoni, *The Zionist ideology* (Hanover, NH: Brandeis University Press, 1995), 269–332; Yadgar, *Sovereign Jews*, 65–160.

The understanding of Israeli politics and sovereignty as Jewish (only) by virtue of the 'ethnic' makeup of its population would demand, of course, that there is some basic trait (a 'natural,' or even 'biological' one, at that), that defines the Jew a priori, before we consider any humanly constructed notions such as tradition, religion, ideology, etc. (namely, 'Judaism'). This quite obviously brings about a political-practical need for a clear definition of Jewishness, as in one's being a Jew hence as belonging to the in-group, the national unit in the name of which the state exercises its sovereignty.

Yet it is quite clear that Zionist ideology and the allegedly secular (at least 'in principle') nation-state embodying it have failed to offer such a rational, natural ('biological' or otherwise), secular definition of Jewishness. Instead, Zionist ideologues have offered a largely tacit notion of an intrinsic, unescapable Jewishness, that would in effect render the matter of Jewish identity more mythical than natural: Tautologically, they would argue that a Jew, simply, is a Jew; that Jewishness is something unarticulated (and, in most readings, impossible to be articulated) that someone is born with. One does not choose it, nor can one rid oneself of her Jewishness; It is in one's 'blood.'[27]

This tautology, which has dominated pre-state Zionist ideology and shaped much of the Zionist ideologues' discussions on Jewish identity, proved insufficient in the framework of a nation-state that self-identifies as the state of Jews. At the same time, as I noted earlier, the history of the Zionist idea and the State of Israel also shows that both the ideology and its political realization have failed (if they ever really strove to do so) to offer a full-fledged definition (i.e., a meaningful political construct that goes beyond the matter of one's origin or 'blood') of Jewish national identity that would be independent from (traditional, religious, or Orthodox) rabbinical readings of Judaism.

This brought to life a 'practical,' political solution, by which the state endows the Orthodox-rabbinical establishment with the role of ethnonational gatekeeper, in effect making a 'religious' identity a precondition of national belonging, as the state has given up on the authority over setting the limits of – and determining the mechanism for – belonging to the very national group in the name of which it exercises sovereignty. At the same time, this mainstream, dominant political-Zionist ideology and the political culture it has nurtured in the

[27] Yadgar, *Sovereign Jews*, 65–160.

State of Israel have zealously rebelled against that same rabbinical authority and against 'religion' in general, representing these as mere symptoms of the malady of exile.

Ultimately, this stance has brought to life one of the more challenging aspects of Jewish-Israeli, Zionist nationhood: the unresolved tension between, on the one hand, the sense that Jewish history, or even tradition (not to say 'religion'), embodies a fundamental justification for the Zionist claim to sovereign nation-statehood (which entails, of course, a violent fight over a land inhabited mostly by non-Jews), and on the other hand the motivating rebellion against this Jewish history/tradition as a core impetus of the Zionist project. Indeed, in Y. Ḥ Brenner's apt phrasing, the central, existential question hovering over the national movement of these 'new' Jews such as himself, who are motivated primarily by a Nietzschean rebellion against their Jewish past if not against Jewishness per se, has been 'how shall we [Zionist, Jews] become not-us?'[28]

The establishment of the sovereign nation-state of the Jews transformed the meaningful identification of what Jewishness is from a cultural matter to a politically existential one: it bore directly on the state's survival as the nation-state of Jews. This was specifically true since the state, following the logic of mainstream Zionist ideology, viewed itself as secular; it could not explicitly, self-consciously rely on what it viewed as religious elements of Jewish identity for its own identification or constitution as Jewish. Instead, it allowed itself to be 'forced' to implement, as a matter of ad hoc solutions, a narrow, quite deformed interpretation of Judaism for the purpose of upholding a clear distinction between a Jewish majority and a non-Jewish minority among its subjects.

The state chose not to (or maybe it was unable to, given its indebtedness to secularist epistemology and ideology) focus on maintaining a sovereignty that is *Jewish*, that is, a sovereignty that dialogues with Judaism as a constituting tradition, but rather to maintain the sovereignty of *Jews*. Indeed, as I mentioned earlier, a dominant secularist liberal-Zionist reading has insisted that the secularity of the state means that it does not identify as Jewish at all (i.e., that the state does not carry a so-called religious identity of its own; that its sovereignty

---

[28] Brenner, *Ketavim*, 1296.

cannot be meaningfully Jewish); Rather, it is 'simply' a state of those identified as Jews.

Yet, as anyone who is even slightly familiar with Israel would know, this is not the prevailing sense in the country. The notion that Israel is indeed a *Jewish* (usually accompanied by 'and democratic,' of course) state has been a staple of Israeli political discourse throughout, and of quasi-constitutional legislation in recent decades. Moreover, if we judge contemporary Israeli political culture by the recent debates on the newly legislated (at the time of writing) Basic Law: Israel the Nation-State of the Jewish People – a bill that seeks to constitutionally 'anchor' Israel's 'Jewish identity' (see Chapter 2) – the emphasis on Israel's Jewish identity is so great so as to sideline the state's commitment to democratic principles.

The Politics of Israel's Jewish Identity Crisis

This tension lies at the core of some of the more pressing (and illuminating) debates that have dominated the Israeli political sphere. Let us consider the questions raised by some of these debates in brief, if only to illustrate the nature of the issues raised by the crisis at hand. These debates (a more detailed discussion of which forms the backbone of this book) have all to do with Israel's struggle to understand the meaning of its Jewishness; they all deal, in other words, with Israel's Jewish identity crisis.

One such debate has to do with the issue of religious conversion. Reading the news from Israel, one may indeed be perplexed: Why is the so-called secular, liberal media, as is public debate in general (a public who is overwhelmingly non-Orthodox by self-definition), so preoccupied with the intricacies of the Orthodox interpretation and practice of Jewish law on matters of (religious) conversion into Judaism? Why have competing interpretations of Jewish (i.e., 'religious') law on matters of conversion become a locus of ('secular') political contestation? And why has the (non-theocratic) state itself been actively involved (utilizing, among other state institutions, the military itself) in the mass conversion – as a matter of religious, Orthodox practice – of non-Jews (provided they are not Arabs) into Jewish religion? And how does this correspond with the status of non-Jewish Palestinian-Arabs in Israel?

Or take, as another example, the abovementioned controversial Basic Law: Israel the Nation-State of the Jewish People, which seeks to enshrine and 'anchor,' constitutionally so, the State of Israel's 'Jewish identity': Why does the law assert Israel's identity as the nation-state of the Jewish people by negating and prohibiting recognition of other peoples' (read: Palestinians') similar claims for nationhood? Does a declarative-constitutional Jewishness of the state necessarily amount to an explicit commitment of the state to prefer Jews and their interests over non-Jews? Does the law in actuality explicate that Israel's proclaimed wish to be both Jewish and democratic is unachievable, as it makes the state's Jewish identity superior to its commitment to democracy? Maybe most importantly – how had it come to be that the law, proposed and advanced by so-called secular members of Israel's parliament, who adhere to a secularist Zionist discourse, relies, at least in part, on Jewish tradition and Jewish law – i.e., what is commonly referred to by the same secularist discourse as Jewish religion – for the preservation and maintenance of the (Jewish) identity of the supposedly secular nation-state? And why would parties representing Orthodox and Ultra-Orthodox Jews oppose such a bill?

And take, as a last example, the challenge posed to mainstream (secular) political-Zionism by a vocal minority of Israelis who adhere to a non- or even anti-Jewish Israeliness. Combined with a growing sense among secularist Israelis of an encroaching religious presence in practically all realms of life, the idea of a (Zionist or otherwise) Israeliness that is wholly released from the shackles of Jewishness/ Judaism clearly exposes the fault lines of the Israeli sense of Jewishness. The state's reaction to this challenge, in which Israel vehemently denies the viability of an Israeli national identity, must be counted as one of the most intriguing aspects of Jewish-Israeli nation-statehood.

Beyond 'Religion and Politics' in Israel

Clearly, all of these issues have to do with the inherent tension at the core of the Zionist construction of Jewish nationalism. [29] Furthermore,

---

[29] I am relying here on my previous work, especially Yadgar, *Sovereign Jews*;
Y. Yadgar, 'Overcoming the 'religion and politics' discourse: A new
interpretation of the Israeli case,' *Journal of Religion and Society*, 16 (2014).

as I suggested earlier, the confusion surrounding these debates also has to do with the application of historically and politically situated (that is, modern European, Christian) conceptual toolkits as if they were ahistorical, universal, and overall neutral.

At root, all of these debates touch on the inherent tension, or contradiction, between, on the one hand, a secularist discourse and conceptual framework, born out of the history and politics of the modern, European nation-state, which designates secular/rational politics and religion into separate realms of human life, and, on the other hand, the particularities of Zionist and Jewish histories, which do not obey this framework's expectations.

The predominance of a Western discourse on 'church and state' (and of 'religion and politics') brings to life the almost naïve assumption that 'Jewish religion' and 'Israeli politics' are two separate, essentially distinguishable realms that tend, for some historical and political reasons, to be entangled, intertwined, and confused. This is manifested by an assumption shared by many commentators that Israeli society and politics are essentially dictated by the (secularist) epistemological tension between religion and politics and by the sociocultural cleavage between secular and religious Jews in Israel. This view tends to see the former (i.e., modern, Jewish-Israeli secularity and secular Israelis) as committed to liberal-democratic (secular) values and the latter (i.e., Jewish 'religion' at large and religious Israeli-Jews in particular) as manifesting a worldview that necessarily amounts to a preference of antidemocratic values, culminating in a hoped-for Jewish theocracy.

To reiterate: the attractive power of this discourse on Israel lies in the fact that it echoes – or rather mimics – a well-established (historically and politically situated, European, largely Protestant) secularist discourse; it applies or implants this discourse – or rather its epistemology and ontology – with their particularistic roots and history, onto the Jewish, Zionist and Israeli cases. Yet, as a growing body of literature has convincingly established, this dominant, secularist discourse on religion and politics (even before we consider the Jewish and Israeli/Zionist cases) is flawed; applied as a universal conceptualization of human sociopolitical evolution it is misleading and distorting. It assumes its main concepts (primarily the duo of religion and the secular) to be suprahistorical and universal, while they – or the way we commonly understand and use them today – are in effect the products of a specific, historically situated configuration of power (which they, in turn, serve).[30]

The application of these secularist epistemology and discourse to the Jewish and Israeli/Zionist cases is doubly misleading. It both perpetuates the interests hiding behind its dominance (in a nutshell: the configuration of power beneficial to the modern, sovereign nation-state), and ties the histories of Jews (and of Judaism) into the conceptual bed of European, Protestant modernity.

Obeying the dictates of this discourse, the debate on religion and politics in Israel perpetuates the misconception that Zionism has been an essentially secular project. This misconception breeds a historical narrative that assumes that Israel is a secular, liberal, and democratic nation-state – just like any other (ideally) Western liberal democracy – which for this or that reason (primarily, the representational and coalitional structure of the Israeli regime, which allegedly endows the so-called religious parties with the ability to extort compromises and concessions from the secular majority) is forced or coerced to pass and enforce laws that impose Jewish religion on the public sphere and on the private lives of the Israeli citizens.

This, essentially, is the idea encapsulated in one of the foundational institutions – or, indeed, traditions – of Israeli politics, namely the (in) famous status quo (on religious/secular matters), which is, to judge by most popular and academic accounts of it, a kind of an armistice between two contesting parties: The 'secular camp' (which is committed to establishing an enlightened, secular, liberal and democratic regime, in which religion is excluded from public matters), and the 'religious camp' (which is committed to the enforcement and coercion of Jewish law onto the state and its citizens).

As I have argued in my previous work,[31] this (mis)understanding of the status quo fails to appreciate the ways and the degree to which the supposedly secular state relies on what it itself views as religious

---

[30] Cavanaugh, *The Myth of Religious Violence*; Nongbri, *Before Religion*; Fitzgerald, *Discourse on Civility and Barbarity*; T. Asad, *Genealogies of Religion: Discipline and Reasons of Power in Christianity and Islam* (Baltimore, MD: Johns Hopkins University Press, 1993); T. Asad, *Formations of the Secular: Christianity, Islam, Modernity* (Stanford, CA: Stanford University Press, 2003); E. S. Hurd, *Beyond Religious Freedom: The New Global Politics of Religion* (Princeton, NJ: Princeton University Press, 2015).

[31] Yadgar, *Sovereign Jews*, ch. 9.

tradition (and on an Orthodox establishment it had endowed with the role of determining this tradition) for preserving its 'Jewish character,' hence its very sovereignty as the nation-state of the Jews, or even as a Jewish nation-state. This narrative fails, in other words, to appreciate the reliance of the theopolitics of the ('secular') state on ('religious') theology.

Questions of Tradition(s)

One of the more fruitful ways to transcend this discourse's narrow horizon and to engage in an examination – a construction, even – of its alternatives, is to identify the matters at hand not as an issue of religion and politics in Israel, but rather as a (quintessentially political) issue of our relations with our traditions.[32]

In other words, I would propose that we engage in a critical Jewish (as in attentive to the messages entailed in the histories and traditions of Judaism) reading of the unresolved, charged nature of the State of Israel's approach to the numerous histories of Jewish communities, histories that are manifested in the Jewish traditions that preceded the Zionist project and its culmination in the State of Israel.

This, then, is the central issue to be addressed: How does the nation-state's theopolitics – constituted, as it is (symbolically, at least), on an invented or recreated national tradition – approach Jewish traditions that preceded it and continue to live alongside it?

The problem with these Jewish traditions is that they do not fit easily, if ever, into commonly used categorical frameworks, which originate in modern Western discourse such as nation, ethnicity, race, and, maybe most importantly, religion. Let us ignore for a moment, even if only for the sake of argument, the tendency to view these categories, borne as they are from a specific European-Christian history, as if they were a universal language of human life, which is necessarily also applicable to the histories of Jewish communities. What is critical to note is that in many meaningful senses – by the discourse's own logic – Judaism might both and at the same time answer to each and every one of these terms/categories, and to neither of them. This is so since Jewish traditions are comprehensive ways of life that touch on various dimensions of human experience, which are

---

[32] For an expanded discussion of the concept of tradition see: Yadgar, 'Tradition.'

sometimes labeled (in the context of modern European, secularized discourse) under one of the abovementioned categories, while at others they are labeled under another.

Bearing this in mind, I would like to offer now a short assessment of three critical issues that are seen in a new light once we forego the misleading secularist epistemology and discourse on religion and politics. These deal with the role of Jewish traditions in (a) the shaping of the Zionist project, (b) the shaping of the Israeli public sphere, and (c) the formation and development of Jewish identities in Israel.

Zionism and Jewish Traditions

One of the more fruitful ways to understand Zionism is to forego its identification as a project of secularizing Judaism through the invention of a national tradition; predominant as such a description is, it fails both to be clear as to the very meaning of this secularization and to account for the obviously 'religious-like' elements in Zionist nationalism. [33] Attempts at preserving the religious-secular dichotomy in the case of Zionist ideology and practice (as in the cases of other nationalist ideologies or movements), by reference to Zionism as embodying a 'civil religion' (and even 'secular religion' in some formulations) are unhelpful, as they leave the very rationale for making this distinction (i.e., between 'real' religion and secular imitations of it, titled as 'civil religion') obscure.[34]

Instead, as I suggested earlier, Zionism is better understood when viewed as a forceful counterreaction to another act of invention, which preceded Zionism: the transformation of Judaism into a religion. This 'invention' of Judaism as a religion (as the term is understood in the modern, European, Protestant framework, i.e., as a personal matter of spirituality and belief that is by definition apolitical) originated in Europe, mostly in Germany and France, from the eighteenth century onwards. It sought to reinterpret Jewish traditions so as to render them applicable to the allegedly universal category of 'religion,' in effect claiming that Judaism cannot and should not be read in terms of (political) nationalism.

---

[33] The following is a necessarily schematic summation of an argument that I am making in more detail in Yadgar, *Sovereign Jews*, 67–160.

[34] Cavanaugh, *The Myth of Religious Violence*, 110–20.

The original formulation of the idea that Judaism *is* a religion – exactly that which is labeled under this title and nothing beyond it – is usually accredited to Moses Mendelssohn. Its further development and articulation (mostly by other German Jewish philosophers) brought about the formation of Reform Judaism, encouraged the shaping of the historical positivist interpretation of Judaism (better known today as Conservative Judaism in the US), and, ultimately, facilitated the shaping of modern Orthodoxy and Ultra-Orthodoxy as counter reactions to the reform interpretation of the implications of this idea.[35]

By making Judaism a religion, European Jews sought to solve the tension in their potential identification as members of an alien, foreign nation living among (non-Jewish) host nationalities. It enabled Jews, as the famous term of phrase states, to become 'German (or French, or otherwise) nationals of the Mosaic faith': loyal citizens and subjects of the nation-state who differ from the majority only in the limited, politically insignificant realm of religious faith.

Zionism sought to negate this argument, and the whole project of political and cultural assimilation it entailed. The driving ideological force of the Zionist movement has been fundamentally based on a competing argument, which also used the European political discourse of the time: Judaism, so argues the Zionist idea on its various formulations, is a nationality – it is about *national* identity. Mainstream, political-Zionism, the ultimately triumphant stream of Zionist ideology, would further argue that this Jewish nationalism must be expressed and realized in the political framework of a nation-state, in which the true meaning of Judaism as a nationality will be reincarnated.[36]

---

[35] Batnitzky, *How Judaism Became a Religion.*

[36] This, of course, is not to suggest that all Zionist ideologues – or Jewish nationalists – have taken a political stance by which the establishment of a nation-state of Jews is the ultimate aim of Zionism. Prominent figures such as Heinrich Graetz, Peretz Smolenskin and Moshe Leib Lilienblum, have instead offered a 'spiritual' interpretation of the national idea. As works by Dmitry Shumsky and Arie Dobnov show, prior to 1948 there were strong alternatives advocated, primarily among them was an imperial framework in which to place the Zionist polity. Ultimately, though, a nation-statist rendition of Zionist ideology has been triumphant, and has shaped the Israeli polity in its image.
See D. Shumsky, *Beyond the Nation-State: The Zionist Political Imagination from Pinsker to Ben-Gurion* (New Haven, CT: Yale University Press, 2018); A. M. Dubnov, 'Notes on the Zionist passage to India, or: The analogical

This nationalism – which, as mentioned before, many Zionist thinkers preferred to label Hebrew, not Jewish, betraying their uneasiness with their own claim to Jewish identity – was thus presented as a broader frame of meaning, which incorporates Jewish religion but is surely not dictated by this religion, nor is it identical to it.

This understanding of Jewish identity also stands at the very ideological, politico-cultural foundation of the State of Israel, which is commonly identified – and since the legislation of the aforementioned Basic Law, also quasi-constitutionally so – as the (supposedly secular, or at least 'not religious') state of the Jewish nation.

As in other cases of emerging nationalist movements, the Zionist project has also involved a wide-ranging endeavor of constructing a national tradition; Zionism was required to instill the notion of a national Jewish identity with a positive meaning, and Zionist ideologues were required to rewrite Jewish history, that is: to reinterpret Jewish meaning and subjects throughout history, so as to render these consistent with the nationalist metanarrative of a collective identity, and to generate a political conflation between territory and identity (whether ethnic, national, linguistic, etc.).

Needless to say, Zionism has found the building blocks for this rewriting in Jewish histories and traditions. But it had arrived at this move while already deeply immersed in the context, or discourse, of the secularization of Judaism (a move that first gained shape with the movement called the Jewish Enlightenment, or *haskala*).

That is to say: this project of a national, political rewriting of certain traditions was, from the outset, based on the false distinction between Jewish religion and other, essentially secular, dimensions (political, national, cultural, linguistic, and so on) of Judaism. Moreover, prevalent streams in Zionist ideology tended to view this same religion as oppressing the national vitality and as the root cause for what they viewed as the decline of the Jewish people in exile, i.e., in the state of lacking sovereignty.

How, then, has Zionism constructed its position vis-à-vis Jewish traditions that had preceded it (and were, so the mainstream argument has claimed, besmirched by the stain of religiosity)? Several leading Zionist thinkers (one may count Theodore Herzl among them) chose

imagination and its boundaries,' *Journal of Israeli History*, 35/2 (2016), 177–214.

largely to ignore or pass over this question, focusing instead on the notion of Jewish political power by way of imagining the Jews' polity as a sort of a European nation-state – indeed, a German speaking one, at that (to deduce from Herzl's *Altneuland*) – that is governed by Europeans of Jewish descent.

Others, who were fiercely critical of this neglect – foremost among whom was, of course, Aḥad Ha'am, who flung at Herzl the accusatory (rhetorical?) question (in paraphrase), 'what exactly is Jewish about your *Judenstaat*?'[37] – viewed the Zionist project as primarily obligated to secularize Judaism, that is to reinterpret Jewish traditions so as to make them consistent with a rationalist, modernist, utilitarian world-view, which will be (in the mainstream political reading of Zionism) the basis of the (secular) nation-state of the Jews.

This notion of reinterpretation fed the self-image of those socialist-Zionist ideologues who arrived in Ottoman and later Mandatory Palestine with the declared aim of rewriting the meaning of their Jewish (or Hebrew) identity. These pioneering role models, most of whom had received a traditional Jewish education and were driven by a sense of rebellion against the authority of the way of life into which they were born, had an intimate, unmediated familiarity with certain Jewish traditions (mostly east-European ones), and they sought to reinterpret parts of these traditions.

They did so from a confrontational, aggressive position. Thus, to give but one of the most familiar examples, they rewrote the ritual of the Passover Seder and Haggadah, so as to render these consistent with their ideology and worldview: They took God out of the Haggadah, and replaced Him, in the role of the savior, with Labor, Land, or even Vladimir Ilych Lenin.[38]

It should be noted that this aggressive confrontation with Jewish tradition – abrasive as it may be – nevertheless manifests a certain type of conversation with tradition, which is based on a familiarity with it. A rebellion against authority is also an acknowledgment of it, and it is surely based on a familiarity with it.

But once the ideological enthusiasm had ebbed, and the unmediated familiarity with tradition was lost, the children and grandchildren of

---

[37] Aḥad Ha'am (Asher Ginzburg), 'Altneuland,' *Hashiloaḥ*, 10/6 (1902).

[38] M. Tsur, 'Pesach in the land of Israel: Kibbutz Haggadot,' *Israel Studies*, 12/2 (2007), 74–103.

these ideological pioneers were left with a sour residue of resentment toward what they were taught to think of as tradition and religion, while they were largely ignorant of the contents of these objects of their derision.[39]

They have, of course, remained identified as Jewish. Politically speaking, this part of their identity has been constitutive, overpowering every other ideological or normative commitment they might have. But the positive meaning of this identity, beyond the fact that they have been committed to the establishment of a nation-state for Jews, which is 'their' state became increasingly vague. The dialogue between them and their Jewish traditions became gradually mute.

The Jews' State vs. the Jewish State

The establishment of the State of Israel did not resolve this tension, which could be described – to go back to Goodman's observation quoted in the opening of this chapter – as an alienation of the very elite of the Jewish state from Judaism itself. As I mentioned earlier, the state – or its rulers, among which this elite has been obviously predominant – seems to have eventually chosen to focus primarily on the constitution of a Jewish majority over a non-Jewish, Palestinian-Arab minority as the principal condition for its existence as the State of the Jewish people; the state put relatively few resources into answering the question of how to converse with, and reinterpret, the Jewish traditions of the communities that constitute this majority.

In the famous contest between two possible translations of the very title of Herzl's *Judenstaat*, this Zionist elite chose to focus on the establishment of a *State of Jews*, not necessarily on the constitution of a *Jewish State*. Indeed, as I noted earlier, this seems to be the core understanding of the meaning of Israel's sovereignty among liberal, secularist Zionist circles, who vehemently oppose the aforementioned Basic Law, as well as other attempts by the Israeli government to 'strengthen' Israel's Jewish identity (a problematic matter on its own; see Chapter 3).

---

[39] As early as 1942, Berl Katznelson acknowledged and expressed concern about the distancing of Yishuv youth from the Jewish tradition. See U. Ben-Eliezer, *The Making of Israeli Militarism* (Bloomington: Indiana University Press, 1998), 98.

But even such a limited understanding of Jewish politics – this, simply, is politics of a modern, European-like nation-state, run by people of Jewish origins – is required to address certain issues of Jewish identity in order to run this nation-state that identifies as the State of the Jews.

Most obviously, the state is required to decide who counts as a Jew and who does not – to outline, in other words, the borderlines and definition of that nation in the name of which it functions. Ultimately, the allegedly secular state chose not to carry this task (it is quite clear that Zionism has been unable to provide a full-fledged, self-sufficient 'secular' definition of Jewish identity). Instead, it has outsourced this critical task to those it in effect designates, by force of its sovereignty, as the official representatives (or interpreters) of Jewish religion – namely, rabbis and politicians who adhere to a conservative, Orthodox interpretation of Jewish tradition. The latter function as the nation-state's gatekeepers, both by being assigned with the responsibility to decide who counts as a Jew (utilizing 'religious' criteria to do so), and by being given a monopolistic authority to manage the Jewish citizens' personal matters of marriage and divorce, essentially preventing marriages between Jews and non-Jews in Israel, thus preserving the distinction between these two primary groups.

I should reassert here that the State of Israel has never attempted to build an Israeli national identity that would be liberated, so to speak, from what the secular outlook itself understands as Jewish religion. Instead, the state has focused on the construction of a *Jewish* national identity, which although highly problematical is nevertheless distinct in one critical respect: It is a national identity reserved for Jews only. Non-Jewish minorities in Israel (primarily, of course, the sizable minority of Palestinian-Arab citizens of the state) cannot – by definition – partake in this national identity.

In addition, the state has viewed the diversity of Jewish traditions, which immigrant communities carried with them to the newly established state, as a threat to national unity, and devoted its resources and attention to the abusive project of the 'melting pot,' which, as its name suggests, viewed these traditions as objects that should be dissolved in order for another, newly constructed national tradition to gain hold.

Needless to say, the state still espouses a notion of a distinction between Jewish religion and Jewish (secular) nationality. Yet the political and legal debates surrounding the paradoxes (or dilemmas) that this distinction creates have clearly demonstrated that the state, as well as the culture it has built, remain loyal to the notion that these two categories (religion and nationalism) are essentially identical. This idea stands at the core of the national school curriculum and it feeds a series of laws, which enforce a certain, notoriously narrow, interpretation of Jewish tradition (mainly, if not solely, in terms of practice, or rather the prohibition of certain practices) on the public sphere, aimed as they are to preserve the 'Jewish character' (*sivyon yehudi*) of the state and its public sphere.

This, then, is the key to understanding the Israeli 'status quo.' It is not, at least not primarily so, a matter of a compromise and a submission of the secular majority to the whims of the religious minority; rather, it is an expression of the reliance of the state – who is, it should be stressed, still ruled by representatives of that same nonreligious majority – on a narrow, so-called religious interpretation of the meaning of Jewish traditions for the purpose of regulating the public sphere and administrating national politics.

It is worth stating this explicitly: The secular majority needs this religious coercion more than any other party in this relationship. This coercion is what secures the maintenance and preservation of this majority's Jewish identity in a nation-state that identifies as the State of the Jews. Being a Jew in Israel means belonging to the majority, which enjoys a privileged position in every aspect of life; whoever is Jewish enjoys a political, symbolic, and cultural capital that is reserved for Jews only. And were it not for the state's enforcement of its narrow interpretation of Judaism on the public sphere, most members of this majority would have been left lacking a possibility to positively understand the meaning of their Jewish identity. The state, in other words, enforces so-called religion on the public sphere, and guarantees by it the distinction between Jews and non-Jews, as well as the privileging of the former over the latter.

Israeli-Jews' Jewish Identity beyond the Cleavage Discourse

A focus on the issue of the individuals' and her collective's attitude toward their tradition also sheds new light on the matter of Israeli-Jews' Jewish identity. Primarily, it exposes the negative and distorting influence of the 'cleavage' discourse, which tends to view the binary distinction between secular and religious as the constitutive axis of Jewish identities in Israel.

Take, for example, the secular majority. The positive meaning of its secularity is so enigmatic (largely since so many of those identifying as *ḥiloni*/secular also report on a rather substantial religious observance) as to have encouraged the surveyors running the most comprehensive poll on Jewish beliefs and practical observance among Israeli-Jews to replace the label 'secular' in their questionnaires with the negative designation 'not religious.'[40]

Needless to say, the problem begins with that same cleavage discourse, which gives birth in the first place to such baseless polar images, by which a religious Jew is someone who strictly observes each and every small iota of Jewish law, while secular is someone who is completely indifferent to Jewish observance. Instead, we would be better advised to adopt a traditionist point of view, one that raises the question of Jewish-Israelis' attitudes to their Jewish traditions, to decipher the meaning of Jewish identities in Israel.

I have already suggested above that the formation of mainstream Jewish-Israeli *ḥiloniyut* (which is not characterized by an ideological commitment to secularism) may be seen as an outcome of the waning of dialogue between individuals (or their reference groups) and their traditions. These *ḥilonim* (or 'secular by default'[41]) Israeli-Jews have assigned (mostly passively so) the state and its institutions with the role of maintaining their Jewish identity: The state's institutions educate their children to know certain aspects of Jewish history as their history, they 'force' on them the Jewish (or Hebrew) calendar, they compel them to recognize Shabbat as their day of rest, and they make it difficult for them to marry non-Jews (to mention but some of the facets of this 'religious coercion').

The key to understanding Jewish-Israeli secularity or *ḥiloniyut*, then, is its inability to conduct a meaningful dialogue with the Jewish

[40] S. Levy, H. Levinsohn, and E. Katz, *A Portrait of Israeli Jews: Beliefs, Observance, and Values of Israeli Jews, 2000* (Jerusalem: Avi Chai and the Israel Democracy Institute, 2002).

[41] C. S. Liebman and Y. Yadgar, 'Secular-Jewish identity and the condition of secular Judaism in Israel,' in Z. Gitelman (ed.), *Religion or Ethnicity? Jewish Identities in Evolution* (New Brunswick, NJ: Rutgers University Press, 2009), 149–70.

traditions from which it has emerged. This lack has been acknowledged by an important minority of certain intellectuals and elite
circles, and it is the driving force behind what is sometimes dubbed
the 'Jewish renaissance,'[42] which revolves mainly around a mostly
textual (at least for the time being) endeavor to get reacquainted with
the raw materials of these traditions.

A lack of dialogue with tradition is not reserved for secular Israeli-
Jews alone. A negation of such a dialogue has also become the
founding ideology of Jewish Ultra-Orthodoxy, which prefers to view
its relationship with tradition as a dictation or blind obedience, surely
not as a conversation. The Ultra-Orthodox view seems to be that
tradition is set and sealed, and we are to obey it. This stance is of
course riddled with an unhealthy dose of self-denial. It denies the
dynamic nature of tradition and ignores the fact that even the greatest
conservative is forced to continuously and incessantly interpret the
meaning of tradition's 'dictation,' consequently updating the meaning
of this tradition.[43]

Religious Zionism, which views itself as committed to a reinterpretation and updating of its Jewish tradition, conducts this reinterpretation under the heavy shadow of its commitment to a foreign
European tradition (that is, modern nationalism) and to synthesizing
two alien organs. Religious Zionism tends to view the nation-state, or
its political theology, in the colors of 'religious' theology, in a move
that tends to stain and distort the latter while blindly obeying the
former.

At times it seems that Jewish-Israeli *masortim* or traditionists – who
are mostly Mizrahim and tend not to accept the dichotomous distinction of 'either secular or religious' as the constitutive axis of their
Jewish identity – are those who engage in the most challenging dialogue with their Jewish traditions. But they do so without proper
institutional support, and are constantly and harshly criticized for
what both religious and secular Israeli-Jews depict as the inconsistent
nature of the *masorti* way of life.

---

[42] Y. Sheleg, *The Jewish Renaissance in Israeli Society: The Emergence of a New Jew* (Jerusalem: Israel Democracy Institute, 2010).
[43] A. Sagi, *Tradition vs. Traditionalism: Contemporary Perspectives in Jewish Thought* (New York: Rodopi, 2008).

Structure of the Book

The issues discussed above form the main themes of the discussion that follows. These are obviously intertwined and the attempt to mechanically disengage them from each other may result in either an incomplete argument or a repetitive presentation of a more comprehensive one. In order to allow for the further exploration of these themes without (I hope) falling into either of these traps, I have chosen to anchor my discussion in each of the following chapters on certain controversies or debates – all of which have been preoccupying public discourse in Israel for quite some time now – and through these to try and disentangle some of the main threads of the wider fabric of the Israeli-Jewish identity crisis.

Chapter 1 begins this exploration by focusing on the political controversy surrounding religious conversions in Israel. I find the public debate on *giyyur* (conversion to Judaism) to be touching on some of the basic tenets of the Zionist and Israeli construction of Jewish nationality, while at the same time hiding them by framing the debate along the lines of a secular-religious tension. The chapter outlines the main contours of the debate and the historical and political roots of the current public concern – if not outright panic – surrounding the matter. I also discuss the guiding logic of certain attempts at solving the political problem at hand by introducing a religious reform of sorts, that is dictated by theo*political* considerations. Ultimately, the chapter highlights the prominent yet denied role of a 'blood-centered,' and 'biological'/racial notion of Jewish identity on which the secularist Zionist sense of Jewish nationalism is based.

Chapter 2 hangs on the debate surrounding the recently legislated Basic Law: Israel the Nation-State of the Jewish People to explore the contours – and the limits – of the latest and most assertive attempt at formulating a positive definition – or at least a meaningful explication – of Israel's Jewishness. The chapter traces some of the main threads of the discussion on the meaning of Israel's Jewish identity, the ways in which the bill attempts to positively affirm this Jewishness of the state, and the challenges to it. The bill and the fierce debates surrounding it, I argue, quite clearly betray the fact that there has been a genuine disagreement regarding the very basic notion of Israel's identity as a Jewish state, both inside and outside the state. Clearly, the political discourse surrounding the matter has gained a unique character as a *debated,* sometimes controversial, premise lying at the core of not only the negotiations between Israel and the Palestinian authority, but also the very foundation of Israeli sociopolitics.

Chapter 3 shifts its focus to the liberal-Zionist, secularist discourse on Zionism, Judaism, and secularism. It begins with a discussion of a wider debate over the introduction of 'Jewish identity' programs in Israel, and a growing concern regarding an alleged encroaching process of 'religionization.' The second part of the chapter retraces the contours of a specific public debate on the meaning, value, and future of Israeli secularism. These public debates all manifest the problematic nature of Israel's very claim to Jewish identity, and the critical ways in which it is fed by the Israeli–Palestinian conflict.

Chapter 4 considers attempts to formulate a notion of non-Jewish or even anti-Jewish-Israeli nationalism as a potential solution to Israel's Jewish identity crisis. I argue that these formulations and especially the negative reaction to them coming from the mainstream of Israeli political culture and the state's institutions illuminate the degree to which Israeli nation-statehood is indebted to a sense of Jewishness for its very viability. This debate thus sheds light on the Israeli predicament of being unable to run away from its Jewish identity crisis.

The Conclusion of this book will discuss some of the ways in which Israel's unresolved Jewish predicament, compounded by the state's assertive self-positioning as the center of Jewish life worldwide and as the foremost embodiment of Jewish politics, tends to encourage a reconfiguration of the meaning of Judaism. This reconfiguration may be beneficial to the nation-statist arithmetic of majority vs. minority, but is harmful to Judaism as traditionally understood. In light of this, the Conclusion will also outline what I would suggest could be viable paths for a comprehensive Jewish political thought that does not necessary obey the demands of the theopolitics of the nation-state.

I shall begin, then, with the *political* issue of *religious* conversion.

1 | *The Politics of Religious Conversion and the Limits of Zionist Nationhood*

One of the intriguing curiosities of the human sciences, and especially the branch of the social sciences, is the endurance of the religious-secular binary. Although this conceptual dualism, on the epistemology and the ontology that nourish it, has been critically deconstructed and shown to be misleading and confusing, the discourse it entails seems to endure. Indeed, in significant realms of the fields of scholarship, the very idea of universal and ahistorical categories of 'religion' and 'secular' is seen as wrong not only in the sense that it does not correspond with sociohistorical reality, but also in the ethical sense, as a primary example of the sinister working of power/knowledge. In these academic realms – let us call them, for the sake of simplicity, the 'post-secular' – the main research question has to do with the motives behind the enduring presence of this misleading duality. One dominant, powerfully convincing answer focuses our attention squarely on the configuration of power that maintains this binary, namely the modern nation-state. As put by William Cavanaugh:

[T]he attempt to say that there is a transhistorical and transcultural concept of religion that is separable from secular phenomena is itself part of a particular configuration of power, that of the modern, liberal nation-state as it developed in the West. In this context, religion is constructed as transhistorical, transcultural, essentially interior, and essentially distinct from public, secular rationality. To construe Christianity as a religion, therefore, helps to separate loyalty to God from one's public loyalty to the nation-state.[1]

Cavanaugh directs our attention to the ways in which the construction of the state as secular works to legitimize state violence. The secular(ist) discourse constructs the power – and violence – of the Western, modern, liberal nation-state as rational and legitimate by

[1] Cavanaugh, *The Myth of Religious Violence*, 59.

33

virtue of it being the opposite of so-called religious violence (which is, by this categorical definition, irrational and illegitimate). By legitimizing – or purifying – state violence, the duality of the secular and the religious enables the secular to preserve its self-image as enlightened, contrasted with the benighted religious. Viewed more broadly, the working of this duality entails the legitimation of a whole array of sociopolitical practices that would otherwise be deemed unenlightened, illegitimate, and unethical.

The current chapter demonstrates, among other things, how this duality, being constantly constructed and deconstructed, affirmed and violated, functions to enable the nation-state to act on racial logic, while preserving its self-image as enlightened, secular, and liberal.

The matter at hand has to do not with violence (well, at least not directly so), but with the application of race and racial distinction. I argue that the admittedly murky yet persistent sense of a fundamental distinction between matters that are secular and of-the-state's and matters that are religious and are not-of-the-state's, which dominates the political (and, to a large degree also the social sciences) discourse in Israel, functions to allow the state to be fundamentally and essentially based on a racial logic of belonging and otherness, while celebrating itself as democratic, liberal and enlightened (as is expected from a secular entity). This is enabled by a division of labor that puts the 'burden' of maintaining and applying the racially logical criteria of inclusion and exclusion on those identified as religious (people, institutions, parties, and so on).

Furthermore, this division of labor itself is justified as being a compromise between the two sides (the secular and the religious), in which the secular is allegedly forced to concede to the demands of the religious, a concession that entails the secular's supposed endurance of the suspension of its enlightened, liberal-democratic principles (that would, of course, delegitimize the application of a race-based policy of inclusion and exclusion). Yet, this racially logical principle of inclusion and exclusion stands at the core of the allegedly *secular* ideology on which the nation-state is established and in the name of which it exercises its sovereignty. In this, the Israeli case proves to be an explication of Peter van der Veer's observation regarding 'the immense importance of the demands of the state, of questions of citizenship and subjecthood for the understanding of conversion both in Europe and in the colonies.'[2]

---

[2] P. van der Veer (ed.), *Conversion to Modernities* (London: Routledge, 1995), 10.

Why the Issue of Conversion?

This convoluted sense of application and denial of both the racial logic of inclusion and exclusion and of the distinction between the secular and the religious (as well as that between religion and politics) is revealed in what must be termed the *political* controversy over *religious* conversion in Israel. (As can be deduced from my previous comments, I find the use of the terms 'religion' and 'politics' as if they mark distinct universal categories to be misleading. My use of these terms echoes their prevalent presence in the Israeli political/public sphere, which, as I have already noted, maintains this distinction while constantly invalidating its main sense.)

An observer unfamiliar with the Zionist, Israeli politics of Jewish identity may indeed be perplexed when confronted with the spectacle of this ongoing controversy over conversions. Why is the political sphere in its entirety so preoccupied with the intricacies of the Orthodox rabbinical establishment's interpretation of what is collectively seen as a *religious* and essentially private act of conversion into Judaism (which the official institution overseeing the conversions – the Orthodox Rabbinate – clearly views as synonymous with an individual conversion into Jewish religion, as in accepting and observing the dictates of religious law in its Orthodox interpretation)? Why does the state – whose law, if not essence, is deemed secular, or at least 'nonreligious,' and for which 'Hebrew' law (the common codename for Jewish, 'religious' law) functions merely as a source of inspiration, devote so many resources and so much attention to the rabbinical – Orthodox – interpretation and practice of religious conversion? Why would a non-theocratic state, who often celebrates itself as 'the only democracy in the Middle East' designate certain organs of the statist machinery as agents whose responsibility is the (religious) education and ultimately the successful conversion of non-Jewish citizens – excluding (one is tempted to add 'of course'; but this taken-for-granted sense of exclusion must not evade our critical gaze) Palestinian-Arab citizens of the Israeli democracy? Furthermore, why is it that of all state organs that may fit to carry this task, it is the military that plays a central role in the preparation of young Israeli citizens (recently drafted to serve in the military regardless of their religious identity, as the 'secular' law of the nation-state demands) for the process of religious conversion? (This already baffling practice may be deemed even more confounding if we take into account the fact that the act of conversion itself is overseen and determined by an Orthodox rabbinical establishment whose members in large part belong to a community of (Ultra-) Orthodox Jews who are largely exempt from the draft, deeming the military an ethically and religiously corrupting institution.)

A Narrative of an Historical Compromise

Reading reports and analysis of the controversy may exacerbate the misunderstanding more than it would clarify the matters at hand, especially if we – or our hypothetical observer – do not share some of the foundational (racial, national, ethnic, religious – call it as you wish) notions of inclusion and exclusion on which the Zionist sense of Jewish politics is built. Such prevalent analyses and reports clearly suggest that the 'problem' at hand has to do mostly with Israeli citizens whose origin is in the countries of the former USSR. Why, our hypothetical observe may wonder, would the growing number of 'ex-Soviet Israelis who were Jewish enough to get in, but who are not Jewish enough for the rabbis' be considered 'Israel's time bomb'?[3] Why would the 'tripartite split' in Israel's population entailed in this demographical change – that is, the fact that 'the population is now beginning to divide into three parts: halakhic Jews and Arabs, but also 'others'' – be considered an existential threat to the State of Israel? Why would the state – who endowed these immigrants with almost immediate citizenship based on their sometimes rather distant familial relation to Jews as the application of the Law of Return, which is celebrated as an outmost expression of the Zionist cause[4] – view

---

[3] The quotes are from a report in *The Economist*, 'Who is a Jew?' January 11, 2014. Yedidia Stern, who was interviewed for the report, is the speaker credited in the report with the term 'time bomb.' Stern holds a prominent role in the Israel Democracy Institute's project on religion and state in Israel.

[4] The Law of Return grants almost automatic citizenship to people whom the state deems Jewish (the definition of which is left, by legal precedent and political practice, largely to the Orthodox rabbinical establishment), but also to non-Jewish children or grandchildren of Jews or the spouses of these children/ grandchildren. See: R. Gavison, *The Law of Return at Sixty Years: History, Ideology, Justification* (Jerusalem: The Metzilah Center for Zionist, Jewish, Liberal and Humanist Thought, 2010); Y. Weiss, 'The monster and its creator – or how did the Jewish nation-state became multi-ethnic,' *Theory and Criticism*, 19 (2001), 45–70.

their presence 'outside' of the Jew vs. Arab binary (manufactured and maintained by the same ideology guiding the state) as a menacing reality?

Our hypothetical observer – especially if she has been raised on the Western tradition of political thought – may be forgiven if taking this controversial and perplexing political reality to be a confusion of two distinct spheres of human activity, namely the secular, political matter of citizenship (and civil rights) and the religious matter of conversion, which is limited, by currently prevalent Western definition, to one's private realm. She would also very easily find a prominent, almost 'commonsensical' (as in expressing a sense, a meaning, that seems to be most common in the Israeli discourse) explanation, or excuse, for this apparent confusion of the religious and the secular: that the 'religious' (people, parties) are to blame. The political (hence: 'secular') sphere, embodied by the nation-state, is forced, indeed, coerced, to concede to what are ultimately 'religious' demands, imposed on it by Orthodox representatives of the domain of religion. While a numerical minority, the religious parties take advantage of the parliamentary coalitional structure of Israeli politics, and exercise unproportional power in forcing the secular majority to obey certain religious edicts, including the definition of Jewish identity.

This, so the dominant narrative goes, naturally causes some apparent inconsistencies in the secularist, liberal-democratic politics of the sovereign state. As the afore-quoted report from *The Economist* notes, the 'formula' by which the 'who is a Jew' question (a central issue for the application of the *civil* Law of Return) is given a strictly Orthodox-religious answer according to which one's maternal ancestry determines the answer, regardless of one's self-identification, practice, ideology, or belief, 'has uncomfortable racial undertones.' Moreover, this less-than-ideal reality is not denied, but rather 'privately acknowledge [d]' by 'some Jewish leaders,' who ultimately dismiss it as 'caus[ing] no harm to others.' Most importantly, the onus of responsibility, or blame, for this 'uncomfortably racial' legal practice is put on the 'religious.' As the magazine's report sums the historical-political narrative:

For many Israelis, the rabbis are the problem. In a concession designed to widen support for the new state, when Israel was founded its secular rulers left matters of marriage, divorce and burial in the rabbinate's hands. It decides who is eligible for these rites, as well as carrying them out.[5]

This framing of the conversion debate is part of a foundational narrative of Israeli politics. It tells the story of a 'primordial' concession dating back to pre-statehood Jewish politics in Mandatory Palestine, which has been further instituted as a dominant political practice in the newly established nation-state of the Jews. The concession – a secular suspension of certain foundational values for the sake of keeping the religious at bay and preserving national unity – has thus become a staple of sociopolitical reality. It is, to a large degree, an articulation of Israel's understanding of the very notion of 'Jewish politics,' in which a secular Zionist majority is coerced by a religious (formally non-Zionist) minority into passively observing certain religious dictates, including, in the case of the matter at hand, the definition of who is a Jew.

In light of the dominance of this narrative in the mainstream academic discourse on Israel (and its echoes in the press), one may easily conclude, expect even, that were it not for the coercion of the state and the secular majority of Israelis by the minority of religious Jews and their Orthodox rabbinical elite, things will be fundamentally different. This discourse suggests that without this coercion the quasi-racial take on Jewish identity, on its 'uncomfortable' tones (that is, its inconsistency with a secular, liberal-democratic notion of citizenship and civic belonging) – a 'blood-centered' bent that is said to be necessarily entailed in the Orthodox understanding of Jewish belonging – would be barred from the politics of the Israeli nation-state and its public sphere. The State of Israel, which is often taken to belong to the modern, Western world of liberal-democratic nation-states would surely not choose to institutionalize a practice of, ultimately, racial distinction (or discrimination) in applying its power to endow (or deny) people with citizenship and in setting the criteria for national inclusion and exclusion.

But how are we to understand the endurance of this quasi-racial practice? The answer offered by the same mainstream narrative (and echoed in *The Economist* report quoted above) is quite simple: the practical logic of realpolitik demands that the state – and liberal,

---

[5] *The Economist*, 'Who is a Jew?'

secular(ist) Zionism along with it, concede to the religious constituency, which is, almost by definition (that is, in the view of religion from a secular-Enlightenment point of view) archaic, illiberal, undemocratic and discriminatory (in this case, even racially so). 'They' impose their racism on 'us'; They are religious, which means that by definition they do not adhere to our enlightened values, principles, and worldview; were it not for them, we would not be coerced into enacting policies of racial distinction and, ultimately, discrimination; but reality is different; it dictates that we concede to their demands, at least with regards to this matter, which 'they' see as fundamental.

This division of labor is not limited to the issue of conversion. It lies at the basis of the dominant discourse on religion and politics in Israel, often captured under the title of the 'status quo' on matters of 'religion and state.'[6] This discourse portrays a basic division of labor between the 'religious' minority (and the parties representing it) and the state (which is dominated and run by representatives of the 'secular,' Zionist parties) that is based on a principle compromise of the two quarreling sides. Note that the very notion of 'accommodation' and 'compromise,'[7] captured by the enduring political metaphor or myth of the 'status quo,' entails an otherwise-unarticulated sense of the ultimate contradictory goals of the two sides: a religious yearning for a theocracy and a secular nation-statist yearning for a liberal democracy. And thus, we are expected to believe that while the religious side must cope with a political reality of Jewish sovereignty that is not a theocracy, the secular must cope with a less-than-ideal modern liberal democracy, which, one is forced to assume, would have nothing to do with religion per se, were it not for the Orthodox coercion and extortion. In the name of national unity and out of political necessity the two sides 'concede' and maintain a delicate balance between these two contradictory motivational forces.

---

[6] Practically every work on 'religion and politics' in Israel discusses the 'status quo.' For mainstream assessments of it, see: E. Don-Yehiya, *Religion and Political Accommodation in Israel* (Jerusalem: The Floersheimer Institute for Policy Studies, 1999); A. Cohen and B. Susser, *Israel and the Politics of Jewish Identity: The Secular-Religious Impasse* (Baltimore, MD: Johns Hopkins University Press, 2000); D. Barak-Erez, 'Law and religion under the status quo model: Between past compromises and constant change,' *Cardozo Law Review*, 30 (2008), 2495–508. For an expanded, critical consideration of this narrative of the 'status quo' see Yadgar, *Sovereign Jews*, ch. 9.

[7] Don-Yehiya, *Religion and Political Accommodation in Israel.*

Interestingly, a supposed 'founding document' of the status quo arrangement,[8] the alleged outline of the historical compromise, does not refer to the issue of conversion. But the discourse at large surely designates the practiced division of labor, in which the state relies on the (Orthodox) Rabbinate for determining the individual's Jewish identity, as a matter of the same framework of accommodation. Titled under the 'Who is a Jew' issue, the political practice that lies at the core of the 'controversy' over conversion is seen fully inside the discourse of compromise and accommodation.[9] Depicting the Orthodox Rabbinate as coercing the state to adopt a halakhic definition of Jewish identity, it leaves rather unarticulated the state's preferred alternative.

Yet, as is the case with the 'status quo' at large, it is quite difficult to believe that a dominant socialist-Zionist, vehemently anti-rabbinical, anti-Orthodox and antireligious leadership (personified in David Ben-Gurion and institutionalized by the various incarnations of the Mapai, or Labor party) would be forced by a weak minority of Orthodox Jews (Zionist and non-Zionist alike) to forego a fundamental notion of Zionist ideology itself. Indeed, the history of the Israeli political parties and governing coalitions abounds with cases in which the dominant Mapai reshuffled its coalitions, sending certain parties to the benches of the opposition and joining others – exercising, that is, its dominance – in the face of political pressure by the smaller parties. If the issues discussed had indeed been of critical importance to the governing secularist, socialist-Zionist party, why would it have been so hard pressed to concede to a clearly weaker religious sector?

The State of Jews and the Definition of a Jew

A critical point that may go unacknowledged in the heat of debate on this alleged religious coercion is the fact that this 'bridging' or 'mix-up' between what is seen as an essentially 'religious' matter of one's Jewish identity (by way of conversion, in this case) and the politics of the nation-state fulfills a crucial role in the very maintenance of this state as the nation-state of Jews. 'Religious' conversion is a political matter of

---

[8] See: M. Friedman, 'And this is the history of the status quo,' in V. Pilovsky (ed.), *The Transition from Yishuv to Statehood 1947–1949: Continuity and Changes* (Haifa: Herzl Institute, 1990), 47–79.

[9] See, for example, Don-Yehiya, *Religion and Political Accommodation in Israel*, 6.

the highest importance since it is *politically* constituted as virtually the only way for a person to join the (political) community of those with whom the state is identified – that is, Jews. The Orthodox Rabbinate may be viewing itself as preoccupied primarily, if not exclusively, with the application of Jewish ('religious') law, but the underlying political reality clearly marks the rabbis as the (sole) gatekeepers who mark, uphold, and maintain the boundaries of national, political inclusion (and, of course, exclusion).

Like other nationalist movements, Zionism has put much efforts into narrating a historical narrative that promotes the nationalist world-view and the reimagining of the collectivity of Jews by way of con-structing a collective memory that promotes the nationalist outlook. These, indeed, have won much academic attention in recent decades. Yet Zionist ideology has put relatively little efforts in offering its own definition of the subjectivity that carries this history and memory, namely: the Jews. More specifically, in terms of the current discussion, it is a fact that often goes unnoticed that Zionist ideology at large and the Zionist nation-state in particular have never put much effort, if at all, into devising a nonreligious path to inclusion in the national-political community of Jews. While proclaiming a secularist world-view, mainstream Zionist ideology and the state following its cue have left this most crucial aspect of the (secular) national project – namely, the marking of the boundaries of the very nation for which the state speaks – unarticulated, and have in effect upheld the Orthodox claim for a so-called religious definition of Jewish identity. At the very core of the supposedly secular, or at least 'nonreligious' nation-state lies, then, a 'religious' foundation.

This is exactly where the 'purifying' effect of the secular(ist) dis-course that I have referred to above can be clearly traced: this discourse enables the state to rely on this 'uncomfortably racial' logic – which appears to be, in the final count, quite central to the nation-statist arithmetic of majority and minority – yet to also preserve its image as enlightened, liberal, modern, and democratic (i.e., the value systems that ought to make a 'blood-centered' notion of inclusion and exclu-sion unpalatable). The secular-political can thus endow the 'religious' with the role of an ethnonational gatekeeper, voice discomfort with the allegedly unsecular, (benighted, racial) reality it itself has created (remember that 'the rabbis' blamed in *The Economist* report for this unpalatable illiberal reality are acting by the force endowed to them by the state; they are state employees, their authority constituted by the *secular* law of the state), and, ultimately, preserve itself as a nation-state constituted on a 'blood-centered' arithmetic of majority and minority, inclusion and exclusion.

This, indeed, is an interpretation that goes against the grain of the commonsensical view of Israeli politics, yet I would argue that it holds major keys to understanding not only Israeli, but also Middle Eastern politics, for it pertains directly to the ways in which Israeli political culture understands the meaning of Jewish sovereignty, or the sovereignty of Jews. What is commonly presented as an accommodation between religious and secular Israeli-Jews is in actuality a foundational element in the Zionist, secularist construction of the very meaning of Jewish sovereignty and Jewish politics itself. It derives directly from the Zionist 'natural' understanding of Jewish identity – the idea that Judaism is something one is born with, a trait of 'blood' – and its limited nature in terms of instilling this very Jewishness with positively meaningful content.

Self-defining as a nonreligious (i.e., national, secular) understanding of Jewish identity and collectivity, Zionist ideology has in actuality celebrated its reliance on a quasi-racial notion of identity or belonging – a notion which Zionist ideologues presented as a more genuine, natural 'fact' of Jewish nationhood. We have already seen the Zionist ideologues' triumphalist sense of the new, modern Jewish nationalism as entailing an incarnation of a 'new' type of Jews: national (as opposed to traditional, religious, and 'old') Jews, who are 'secular' or 'liberated' from the shackles of anachronistic religious tradition, and define their relation to the Jewish people and to their Jewish identity not on a traditional-religious worldview but rather on the more substantial 'natural' fact of their ethnic kinship; What Aḥad Ha'am succinctly coded as the 'racial sentiment [*regesh hageza'*]'[10] instilled in them by nature.

As I have discussed in detail elsewhere, this is a foundational notion of the so-called secularity of Zionist ideology in its various branches. A similar, dominant sense of the quasi-racial basis of Jewish identity was prevalent among all streams of the ideology. It united, in a sense, vehement ideological rivals. Thus, for example, one of the most

---

[10] Aḥad Ha'am (Asher Ginzburg), *'Al Parashat Derakhim*, 80.

outspoken critics of Aḥad Haʿam's 'essentialist' sense of Judaism and Jewish identity, Y. Ḥ. Brenner, has insisted on shifting the focus away from 'Judaism' and toward 'Jews,' claiming that 'Judaism' is whatever a Jew does – even if this may entail an explicit negation of foundational notions of Jewish tradition. The agent, by virtue of her ('biological,' ethnic, racial) identity determines the cultural, national 'identity' of her creation. This logically implies that there must be a (rather metaphysical) sense of a 'biologically inherited' Jewish identity, which defines one as Jewish a priori to one's being in the world, merely by virtue of being born 'a Jew.' Other ideologues further developed this biological sense of identity, struggling to coincide their sense of personal choice (as rebels against tradition) with a predetermination of their identity by their Jewish 'blood line.'[11]

This dominant ideological tone has been further amplified with the establishment of the State of Israel, which has historically interpreted or constructed the meaning of its 'Jewish sovereignty' to be identical to – and dependent on – the rule of Jews. In other words, while the positively meaningful implications of Israel being a 'Jewish state' have historically remained vague (see also Chapter 2), the state has mainly focused on establishing a majority of Jews in its population as a necessary (and sufficient) condition for it upholding its very constitutive logic. As long as Jews are a majority, Israel can view itself as a state of the Jews, as a 'Jewish state' even, however detached its policies, law, practices, etc., may be from traditional notions of Jewishness. This, of course, necessitates an a priori 'definition' or distinction between Jews and non-Jews, a matter which, as I've mentioned earlier, has been historically put by the state in the hands of the rabbinical establishment.

In other words, it may be argued that it is not the Orthodox interest or coercion that yields a Zionist, nationalist (i.e. 'secular') reliance on, ultimately, 'blood,' but rather that the very nationalist, Zionist take on the meaning of Jewish nationhood – and, ultimately, sovereignty – that demands a 'natural' (which clearly verges on the racial) threshold for determining political, national inclusion and exclusion. What is commonly dubbed 'religious coercion' is in effect a primary political, statist tool for the construction and maintenance of a majority of Jews, in the name of which the state exercises its sovereignty. It is, in other words,

[11] Yadgar, *Sovereign Jews*, chs. 4–6.

the tool with which the nation-state of the Jews manufactures a *Jewish* majority, in whose name it exercises it sovereignty and yields its power.

'Who Is a Jew' and the Nation-State of Jews

While a detailed history of the political debate over how to decide who should count as a Jew is beyond the limits of my current discussion,[12] the basic fact that the State of Israel has made it its business to register and ultimately decide its citizens' religious and national identity should be clearly noted. As I have suggested above, this practice bears directly on the state's notion of Jewish politics, as Israel views itself primarily as the nation-state *of Jews*; It is required, or so hold the dominant ideology and political culture, to distinguish Jews (whose state it is) from non-Jews (who may enjoy nominal civil rights, if they are citizens of the state, but cannot claim to partake in its *Jewish* nationality/ nationalism).

Nominally, the bureaucratic procedure at hand echoes the Western, modern nation-statist notion of a categorical distinction between nationality (that is, one's political identity) and religion (or one's religious identity, a supposedly private, apolitical matter). In practice, however, the two categories are taken to be identical in the case of Jews; In the eyes of the Zionist state, Jews' political identity is dictated by their religious identity (this principle, it should be stressed, does not apply in the case of non-Jews). As I have already suggested above (and shall discuss in more detail below), this practice – which stands at the core of the ongoing controversies over conversions – betrays the Zionist failure to construct a meaningful national, political Jewish identity that is independent of what secularist-Zionist thought itself views as archaic religious identity.

As determined by the courts and reaffirmed by political debates, mainly surrounding the Law of Return, the Israeli political 'common sense' views it impossible for one to be of Jewish nationality while practicing (or even nominally belonging to) a religion other than Judaism. Thus, for example, a non-Israeli person born Jewish and then converting to Christianity would not be allowed to register as a Jew

---

[12] For a political-legal consideration of the history of the 'Who Is a Jew' issue, see: Gavison, *The Law of Return*.

under the category of nationality when immigrating to Israel, and will not be able to gain the almost automatic citizenship granted to Jews by the Law of Return; Since she has left Jewish *religion*, she is no longer considered to be of the Jewish *nation*, even though she was born a Jew.[13]

I have also already alluded to the fact that following an early political debate and what seemed to be some confusion regarding the state's understanding or definition of one's Jewish (*national*) identity, it has been decided that the matter of determining one's 'religious' Jewish identity, to which one's Jewish nationality is essentially bound, is to be decided by members of the Orthodox rabbinical elite. It has thus been judicially and politically established that one's belonging to the Jewish *nation* – a supposedly 'secular' matter of political identity – is to be decided by rabbinical gatekeepers, who apply Jewish (i.e., 'religious') law for determining this matter.

To put this in the rather straightforward manner of the technicalities of the ways in which the state handles its own Population Registry and applies its power to endow citizenship and civil rights: Immigrants whom the state deems to be of the Jewish religion are registered as 'Jewish' under both religion and nationality (regardless of the nationality and citizenship they held prior to immigrating). For immigrants who are not Jewish (but are granted citizenship by virtue of them being children/grandchildren of Jews or the spouses of these, as dictated by the Law of Return), the state's practice is different: they are registered as non-Jewish under religion (i.e., in the majority of cases of immigrants from the former USSR, 'Of No Religion,' or 'Christian,' etc.), and their registered nationality is determined by their previous citizenship or place of birth (i.e., Russian, Ukrainian, etc.); while Israeli citizens by virtue of the Law of Return, they are not viewed as members of the nation whose state Israel is. Once such a person converts – following the religious procedure – she is automatically registered as Jewish under both religion and nationality; Her religious conversion

---

[13] This was most clearly explicated in the case of Brother Daniel (Shmuel Oswald Rufeisen), a Polish-born Jew (by birth and upbringing) who converted to Christianity. His request to be granted Israeli citizenship under the Law of Return was refused by the Israeli government. The court upheld this decision, determining that any Jew converting to another religion would lose their preferential access to Israeli citizenship. M. Zilberg, *Rufeisen* v. *Minister of the Interior, PD 16(4) 2428,* (1962). See also Gavison, *The Law of Return.*

implies also a national one, and now she is considered to be a member of the political group that is the Jewish nation.

As noted above, the state does not offer (or allow, for that matter) a 'national' or 'secular' path for joining the Jewish nation; One's only option, were it the case that she wishes to join in Jewish nationality (in technical terms, this means to be registered as 'Jewish' under nationality; in more symbolically essential terms, it means that she becomes part of the nation embodied by the State of Israel), is through the 'religious' gate, by the approval of rabbinical, Orthodox gatekeepers. Also of importance in this regard is that the state does not recognize 'Israeli' as a viable national identity (this matter shall be expanded in Chapter 4). Israel is, by its own Zionist self-understanding, a nation-state of *Jews*, not of Israelis.

Now, critically, the State of Israel is determined to increase the number of Jewish nationals in its population. In light of this, it devotes much attention and resource to encouraging non-Jewish citizens (who are also non-Arab, a point that entails the key to understanding the whole matter) to convert – in the religious sense of the term. This may sound confusing, or even paradoxical, given that a central postulate of Zionist ideology is a categorical distinction between religion and nationality. The main impetus of the Zionist idea is the claim that Judaism is primarily, essentially a nationality, which is political (hence also 'secular') in essence; Judaism, in other words, is not merely a matter of apolitical religion.

Why, then, would the state insist on a 'religious' gateway for joining in the Jewish nation? And why would it be so heavily invested – to the point of making this a 'national mission'[14] – in encouraging non-Arab non-Jewish citizens to become Jewish in the first place? What is there in the presence of a sizable minority of non-Jewish immigrants – loyal citizens of the Israeli polity by any conceivable measure – that makes them viewed as 'plac[ing] Jewish coherence and Jewish identity in this country [i.e., Israel] at risk'[15]?

To answer this, we must keep in mind, first, that the state's political interest is heavily invested in the preservation of a national Jewish majority. This has to do with the fact that the state self-identifies

[14]   M. Kravel-Tovi, *When the State Winks: The Performance of Jewish Conversion in Israel* (New York: Columbia University Press, 2017), 1.

[15]   N. Fisher, *The Challenge of Conversion to Judaism in Israel: Policy Analysis and Recommendations* (Jerusalem: The Israel Democracy Institute, 2015), iii.

primarily as the nation-state of the Jews, and only secondarily, somewhat remotely, as a *Jewish* state, i.e., as embodying a meaningfully
Jewish politics. (Indeed, as will be discussed in Chapter 2, the very
constitutional/legal meaning of Israel being a Jewish state, and not
'merely' a state of Jews, is a heavily contested matter.) According to
this guiding logic, which traces back to the foundations of the Zionist
idea, as long as people identified as Jews run the state, and its population is majority Jewish, its politics *are* Jewish – regardless of the
contents of or meaning manifested and promoted by this politics. This,
in other words, is a political manifestation of the notion that anything
that a Jew does is Jewish, regardless of her act's relation to Jewish
traditions, values, and meaning. The identity of the agent predeter-
mines the nature of her act. In individual terms, this makes one's
Jewish biological ancestry, or 'blood' – the historical chance of one's
birth – a prerequisite for her identification as a Jew and her acts Jewish.
In public, political terms it makes the preservation of Jews as a majority a prerequisite for the political body they constitute to be considered
Jewish.

This entails that the state is essentially dependent on the preservation
of a majority of Jews for its very existence in its current self-formation.
By the state's own constitutive political-Zionist logic, its *raison d'être* is
secured only insofar as people it identifies as (*nationally*) Jewish compose the vast majority of its population. The political organization that
self-identifies as the nation-state of the Jews would no longer exist, by
its own logic, were those it identifies as Jews to lose their status as a
majority. This is set primarily in opposition to a Palestinian-Arab
minority, who by the state's own self-definition cannot partake in the
(Jewish) nationality it embodies, and whose own political, national
self-determination is seen as threatening the very existence of the Israeli
state. Needless to say, this feeds a constant fear of a 'demographic
threat,' namely a natural increase in the number of Palestinian-Arab
non-Jews and a tipping of the balance between these two groups.
Hence the Zionist sense that the very existence and natural increase
in the number of Palestinian-Arabs (who are citizens of Israel) is an
existential threat, that should be countered by an ongoing political
mission of increasing the number of Jews.

Yet, the state itself lacks the ability to determine one's national
Jewish identity. As I mentioned earlier, Zionist ideology and the State
of Israel have been unable, or unwilling, to construct what Zionist

thought itself would view as a healthy political, secular (at least as in independent from religion) definition of national Jewish identity. Ideologically, pre-state Zionist thinkers tended to dismiss the issue (what makes one a Jew? What makes their own anti-rabbinical national worldview a *Jewish* one?) as irrelevant, echoing anti-Semitic notions that Jewishness is something one is born with, a metaphysical essence of sorts, that cannot be annulled, nor does it require active upholding. These secularist thinkers, who were primarily concerned with defending their anti-rabbinical stance, would argue, tautologically, that a Jew is a Jew. No further elaboration is needed.[16]

In liberal-democratic political terms this secularist-Zionist sense of Jewish identity would seem to mean that Jewish identity is given to one's self-understanding. And indeed, once the state had been established and defined itself as embodying the sovereignty of Jews, this has been a view upheld by certain functionaries in the state's bureaucracy.[17] But it has been rather swiftly defeated by the wider political and judicial establishment and the political culture they have nurtured. The view that ultimately triumphed, and seems to enjoy widespread support among Israeli-Jews, presumes 'that there is something objectively distinctive about the boundaries of the Jewish public, which is not just a matter of the sincere statements of someone who views himself as belonging to it or wishes to belong to it.'[18]

Procedurally, the state decided to leave the task of determining one's Jewish identity for the Orthodox rabbis, whose understanding of Jewish identity is not necessarily, or only secondarily (from a national, secular point of view, at least), political.

This entails somewhat of a paradox, for lack of a better term: For these Orthodox rabbis, Jewish identity means primarily knowledge of Jewish law, acceptance of its authority, and observance of this law (which touches on all aspects of life) – in short, an observance of what secularist-Zionist thought would view as Jewish religion. The conversion process they oversee (the more mythical-mystical aspects of it, manifested in the formal procedure of ritual baptizing, and, in the case of males, circumcision or symbolic bloodletting, notwithstanding) is primarily a process of learning Jewish 'religion' and accepting its authority; It has very little to do with what Zionist ideology, or Israeli

---

[16] For an elaborated discussion of this matter, see: Yadgar, *Sovereign Jews*, ch. 5.
[17] Gavison, *The Law of Return*, 98.
[18] Gavison, *The Law of Return*, 97–8, 165ff.

political culture (or, for that matter, even a 'commonsensical' notion of nationalism) would take as the primary meaning of a national Jewish identity, such as knowledge of the Hebrew language, the political history of Jews, and the civic working of the Israeli state, as well as active participation in public, national life.

The paradox entailed herein is that Zionist thought tended to view Jewish religion – the onus of this conversion process – as a malaise, a debilitating exilic yoke put on the back of the Jewish nation, which inhibits, instead of invigorating, the nation's political agency. The political culture upheld by the state thus encourages the non-Jew (who is not a Palestinian-Arab) to become a Jew, as in a member of the Jewish nation, directs her to the Rabbinate for this act of conversion, and dismisses the essential meaning entailed in the rabbinic process as archaic religious mambo-jumbo, that has nothing to do with modern, national, political Jewish identity, which is often manifested in the notion of 'Israeliness.' No wonder, then, that an insightful ethnographer titles the whole procedure as a series of 'winks.'[19]

In passing, I should note that a more substantially meaningful definition of Jewish politics, or of collective Jewish political identity and agency, such that would culminate in an understanding of the state as 'Jewish' – as in manifesting or embodying a meaningfully charged sense of a Jewish 'essence' (whatever this may be) – is in principle liberated from the demographic concerns that so preoccupy the state of Jews. Thus, for example, a state/polity that would have a 'Jewish' constitution (again, the meaning of which is far from being clear), which is accepted and upheld by the state's citizens, regardless of their racial, religious, ethnic, or national identity, would not necessarily be dependent on a Jewish majority for its existence; it would remain Jewish as long as its 'Jewish' constitution is upheld by its citizens and institutions, composed of a Jewish majority or otherwise.[20] This, of

---

[19] Kravel-Tovi, *When the State Winks*.

[20] This is echoed, for example, in the legal decrees governing the Jewish (Messianic, at that) kingdom-to-come, as formulated by Maimonides. The presence of non-Jews – '*benei Noah*' (Noahites) in the traditional phrasing – in the Jewish polity (which is ruled by Jewish law) is not seen as threatening the Jewish meaning of this polity, and they are not required to convert. All they are required to do is to observe the seven provisions governing Noahite Law. *Mishne Torah*, 14, Kings and Wars, 10.12; see also H. Kreisel, 'Maimonides political philosophy,' in K. Seeskin (ed.), *The Cambridge Companion to Maimonides* (New York: Cambridge University Press, 2005), 213.

course, is a highly speculative argument, that must be left here in evident vagueness. (The project of developing a substantively mean-ingful sense of modern Jewish politics has yet to be accomplished.[21]) But what this exercise does achieve, even in its immature state, is an explication of the difference between a grounding of the state's own 'Jewish identity' on substantive frameworks of (Jewish) meaning – i.e., it being a 'Jewish state' – and on the demographic, racialized, makeup of its population – i.e., it being a 'Jews' state.' In other words, it is Israel's (and Zionism's) choice of focusing on the 'origin' of the population for determining its sovereignty as a 'Jewish' sovereignty, that traps it in an existential, demographic anxiety.

On the Practical Meaning of Conversion

This is the background against which the 'statist-religious institutional practice,'[22] that ultimately endows the converts with a new political identity, should be understood. The historical and procedural context of this practice is not atypical of Zionist and Israeli political culture, in that the legal basis and procedural outline of the process are rather vague and lack a coherent grounding in the state's law. Surprisingly enough, there is no law in Israel that explicitly endows the Chief Rabbinate, and specifically the rabbinical courts of conversion appointed by the Rabbinate with the role of overseeing conversions. The process is dictated by a directive instituted by the British colonial regime, which was adopted by the newly established state in 1948. This directive, which assigns the authority over matters of conversion to the respective religious institutions, does not even specifically authorize the Rabbinate to appoint the rabbinical courts of conver-sions, that in practice oversee, monopolistically so, all Jewish conver-sions in Israel; 'but in practice this has been how the Rabbinate acted for many years.'[23] Only after a legal battle during the 1990s, as a result

---

[21] See Julie Cooper's comprehensive critique of the field of Jewish political thought: J. E. Cooper, 'The turn to tradition in the study of Jewish politics,' *Annual Review of Political Science*, 19 (2016), 67–87.

[22] Y. Goodman, 'Citizenship, modernity and belief in the nation-state: Racialization and de-racialization in the conversion of Russian immigrants and Ethiopian immigrants in Israel,' in Y. Shenhav and Y. Yonah (eds.), *Racism in Israel* (Jerusalem: Van Leer Jerusalem Institute, 2008), 386.

[23] Fisher, *The Challenge of Conversion to Judaism in Israel*, 33.

of which the Israeli Supreme Court curtailed the authority of the rabbinical courts for conversion, has the state's government officially authorized them to oversee conversions.[24]

The convoluted relation between the state and the 'religious' establishment is captured most clearly by the institutional murky division of labor in matters of conversion. The Israeli government has a dedicated division of *civil* service (located at the prime minister's office, under the direct responsibility of the PM) for conversion to Judaism. This division describes its 'vision' as 'assisting those seeking to convert to Judaism, working out of a sense of national mission and public responsibility for the realization of the vision of the prophets.'[25] Yet, as already noted, the government itself endowed the Rabbinate with the authority to oversee the actual procedure of conversion. This means that the civil service – the state, that is – assists the potential converts by preparing them for an otherwise 'wholly religious' (as in lacking a distinctly political, civil element) rabbinical, Orthodox course of study and ultimately ritual conversion.

The state thus 'uses the services of rabbis and religious bodies ... to carry for it an active and vigorous process of social assimilation through the conversion of the new immigrants';[26] Yet it must be noted that other than the mythical if not mystical sense of the convert ultimately becoming a part of the Jewish people/ethnos/race/blood, the crux of the religious process of conversion has little to do with what the predominant political culture in Israel sees as the essence of the social belonging, or inclusion of the individual among the Jewish majority. It has, in other words, very little to do with how many, if not most Israelis understand the meaning of their Jewishness. (This may be the point to remind the reader that a majority of Israelis self-identify as nonreligious,[27] and that the predominant political culture views Israeliness as an essentially secularized identity.)

---

[24] Fisher, *The Challenge of Conversion to Judaism in Israel*, 33.

[25] State of Israel, 'About the Conversion Administration.' Prime Minister's Office's website, goo.gl/pHL7yW.

[26] Goodman, 'Citizenship, modernity and belief in the nation-state,' 386.

[27] A. Arian and A. Keissar-Sugarmen, *A Portrait of Israeli Jews: Beliefs, Observance, and Values of Israeli Jews, 2009* (Jerusalem: Israel Democracy Institute and Avi Chai Foundation, 2011); Levy, Levinsohn, and Katz, *A Portrait of Israeli Jews*.

Now, given that the state is also seen as secular in essence, this division of labor is bound to bring about some tension. Anthropological studies of the actual conversion process depict an image of state employees metaphorically holding the hands of prospective converts, trying to guide and assist them as they are sent into a largely alien Orthodox world of study and practice:

The conversion process extends over a year, in which the candidates must study mostly about the [Jewish] holidays, daily practice, dietary rules and family purity [i.e., rules pertaining to abstention from physical contact during the menstrual period]. Several [state run] seminaries fulfil this function ... The students attend classes twice a week. They receive written material and are examined on it from time to time. The process is conveyed by a religious governmental administrative officer, who is called 'messenger of the rabbinical court' ... The administrative officer works in cooperation with the special rabbinical court for conversion. He meets the candidates for conversion, explains the process to them, assigns them to study classes, and attends to their advancement. It is [this officer] who decides if the candidate is ready for the final phase of conversion – the appearance in the rabbinical court.[28]

This rabbinical court, following the Orthodox interpretation of Jewish law, interrogates the candidate in order to establish her motives for conversion, as well as the depth of her knowledge of (Orthodoxly halakhic) Jewish life. Note that this culmination of the process is wholly within the realm of rabbinic ('religious,' Orthodox) interpretation of Jewish identity, with its almost absolute focus on practical observance, which, as aforementioned, has very little to do with how most Israeli-Jews understand their Jewishness (especially in terms of it being a *national* identity). An Israeli observer gives the following description of this proceeding:

The rabbinical court invites the candidate for a profound conversation on Judaism in general and on [the candidate's] practical commitment to observe the religious commandments in particular ... [The rabbis-judges] focus on the psychological change – that is, the knowledge, motivation and behaviour – but also on the sociological change. That is, they seek to also clarify if the candidates have changed their social location and joined a religious

---

[28] Goodman, 'Citizenship, modernity and belief in the nation-state,' 386–7; See also Kravel-Tovi, *When the State Winks.*

community (for example, whether they have registered their children to religious educational institutions).[29]

Note that the change of social location that the rabbis-judges seek in effect expects the converts to partake in the social life of a minority within the Jewish-Israeli population (according to survey data, 'religious' Jews compose roughly a fifth of the Jewish-Israeli population). They do not seek to see the converts integrating among what we may call (confusing as the labeling may be, especially given an essential identification between Israeliness and Jewishness in Israeli political culture) the 'Israelis'; rather, they want them to become Orthodox *Jews*. The candidates for conversion are thus expected to gain intimate knowledge of the Orthodox, religiously observant way of life.

As I noted earlier, the one part of the conversion process that strikes a note with the predominant (Zionist, Israeli, secular) view of Jewish identity has to do with the convert's 'becoming' part of the Jewish people. The rabbinical reasoning describes the convert as not only accepting a Jewish lifestyle, but also becoming part of the Jewish people, a divinely elected collective, a manifestation of what we may call a metaphysical essence. As a typical rabbinical answer puts it, while the non-Jew does not have a *neshama* (typically understood as a 'soul,' but here denoting membership of the divinely Chosen People), once she converts to Judaism she 'receives a *neshama* to a certain degree,' while her 'status is considered as wholly Jewish.'[30] It is this last part of the answer that the Israeli political culture focuses on: the conversion process is that which makes the non-Jew part of the Jewish collective. Lacking a 'secularly' national, 'modern' path for joining the nation embodied by state, the latter relies on this 'religious,' explicitly metaphysical and 'nonrational' ritual for setting the boundaries of national inclusion and exclusion.[31]

---

[29] Goodman, 'Citizenship, modernity and belief in the nation-state,' 387.

[30] B. Moṣafi, 'Question #1655,' *Doresh Ṣion* (blog), goo.gl/pnbXHi.

[31] I must note that my discussion here focuses on the allegedly secular nation-state and its logic. The interests of the Orthodox rabbinical establishment in cooperating with the state is a different matter, that merits a separate consideration.

Preserving the (Zionist) Dichotomy of Jew vs. Arab

In the 'blood-centered,' ethnonationalist discourse of secular Zionism the conversion process resolves the tension surrounding the non-Jews–non-Arab's 'problematic' stance outside of the constitutive (Zionist, nationalist) binary of Jew vs. Arab. This is testified to most clearly in the afore-quoted report from *The Economist*. It is worth requoting here, in more detail this time, for it sheds light on the critical issue of how conversion is seen as resolving an existential threat (in terms of identity), of disrupting the friend–enemy[32] or self–other[33] binary. Subtitled under 'Israel's time bomb,' the report explains:

> The biggest problem comes from the clashing consequences of two great ruptures in 20th-century history: the Holocaust and the collapse of the Soviet Union. Under Israel's Law of Return, anyone who has, or whose spouse has, at least one Jewish grandparent can claim citizenship ... The wave of immigration from Russia in the past two decades means the discrepancy between these two standards has become glaring.
>
> There are now several hundred thousand ex-Soviet Israelis who were Jewish enough to get in, but are not Jewish enough for the rabbis ... The population is beginning to divide into three parts: halakhic Jews and Arabs, but also 'others.' This tripartite split, says Yedidia Stern, a jurist at the Israel Democracy Institute, a think-tank, 'is a time bomb.'
>
> Some Israelis want to keep immigrants in the fold by making conversion easier. The response of liberals ... is to try to prise apart synagogue and state.
>
> The long-term choice for Israelis appears stark: between a different model of Jewishness or a different kind of Jewish state – in which intermarriage, hitherto regarded by Israelis as a diaspora woe, becomes, in a peculiar and unexpected way, a worry for them as well.[34]

Two notions entailed in this report are worth explicating, or stressing: First, the issue or 'danger' of intermarriage is nothing new in a historically Jewish context. Indeed, the concern over individuals' marriages to non-Jews, and the Jewish community's approach to those, has been a staple of Jewish history and politics per se. The assumption that the state should be able to 'safeguard' Jews from this predicament, as to allow them to not think about it, does betray the national logic of

---

[32] Z. Bauman, *Modernity and Ambivalence* (Oxford: Polity Press, 1993).

[33] A. Triandafyllidou, 'National identity and the 'other,'' *Ethnic and Racial Studies*, 21/4 (1998), 593–612.

[34] *The Economist*, 'Who is a Jew?'

ethnonational 'purity' of the state's population, but it fails to explain why the current problem is unique from a historically Jewish point of view.

Second, and more importantly, this framing of the issue at hand clearly shows that the Israeli, Zionist (as distinct from the historically Jewish) anxiety over conversion has to do primarily with the interest of the state in preserving its self-definition as the nation-state of Jews. It is, in other words, first and foremost a *political* matter of the (secular) nation-state, and only secondarily of 'religious' importance. Let me explain:

The Israeli concern is borne directly out of the Zionist, *nationalist* outlook of striving for a complete confluence of territory and identity, which leads in more practical and less aspirational terms to the arithmetic of majority–minority. This nationalist logic demands, of course, the national exclusion of the 'significant Other,'[35] but it is also – maybe more importantly for the matter at hand – wary of those 'other Others,' non-Jews/non-Arabs, who do not fall inside the primary friend–enemy binary. This, indeed, has to do with the modernist, national logic of inclusion and exclusion more than anything else. It is a (Jewish, in a Zionist reading of the term) manifestation of the modern attempt to uphold the opposition between friend and enemy which is 'born of the horror of ambiguity.'[36]

The relatively successful implementation of this modernist binary in Israel meant that for some fifty years of nation-statehood the construction of the sizable minority of Palestinian-Arabs as the ultimate, significant Other – that is, as belonging to the 'enemy' camp – largely annulled, in practice, intermarriages between those whom the state views as Jews and (Palestinian-Arabs) non-Jews in Israel. This, in a sense, may be seen as a modern, national take on a historically Jewish practice of clearly demarcating a distinction between Jews and Gentiles, and attempting to preserve the cohesion of the former group by distancing it – socially, culturally, etc. – from the latter. Yet while the Jewish practice at hand has been a minority's strategy in face of an often-overwhelming non-Jewish majority, the Israeli-Zionist case, framed as a nation-statist matter, dramatically tips the scale.

[35] Triandafyllidou, 'National identity and the 'other."
[36] Bauman, *Modernity and Ambivalence*, 25.

The nation-statist logic demands that the Jews be not only separate from non-Jews, but also outnumber them.

It is precisely the anxiety over preserving this demographic balance, in which friend, i.e., 'Jews' outnumber enemy, i.e., 'non-Jews' that ultimately caused the 'problem' at hand. Indeed, 'problem' may be an understatement; the 'demographic' balance is clearly seen in Israel as an existential matter. This anxiety is what led the Israeli government to aggressively court Soviet Jews and proactively encourage the immigration of those eligible for an immigrant visa based on their relation to Jews.[37] Among other things, this has created a severe disruption of the friend–enemy binary by introducing a sizable minority of 'strangers' into the foray:

> [The stranger] calls the bluff of the opposition between friends and enemies as the *compleate mappa mundi*, as the difference which consumes all differences and hence leaves nothing outside itself. As that opposition is the foundation on which all social life and all differences which patch and hold it together rest, the stranger saps social life itself. And all this because the stranger is neither friend nor enemy; and because he may be both.[38]

Note that the debate over conversion (in the framework of the politics of the nation-state) is rather oblivious to the political, civil, or religious practices and beliefs of those 'strangers.' This debate assumes that their active participation in either Jewish life and culture or Israeli politics and civic life does not solve their 'strange-ness,' as it does not dissolve them into one of the binary poles of friend vs. enemy – since the latter is ultimately constituted on 'blood.' According to the discourse from which this debate nourishes, only the 'strangers'' transformation to Jews – i.e., members of the Jewish people, as in becoming (through conversion) carriers of the mythical markers of Jewish ethnos/ blood/race – solves the disruption caused by their presence outside of the binary. (Needless to say, alternative options – such as their leaving the scene or becoming members of the 'enemy' group – are too contradictory to the very fundamentals of the discourse at hand to be taken seriously into consideration.)

---

[37] Similarly, during the late 1980s and early 1990s Israel has exerted diplomatic pressure to have friendly governments such as Germany and the USA curtail immigration of Soviet Jews in order to channel them to Israel. Yonah, 'Israel's immigration policies.'

[38] Bauman, *Modernity and Ambivalence*, 55.

This, indeed, may be seen as a mirror image of the picture depicted in the above-quoted report, where the reporter stresses the uncomfortable racial tones of the Orthodox rabbinical understanding of conversion. As the reporter notes, 'Gentiles might be surprised that for Jews by birth this traditional test [of one's Jewish identity] makes no reference to faith or behavior.'[39] If one is born Jewish (that is, carries the 'Jewish blood' by virtue of being born to a mother who also carries this same essence), one's religious, political, and civic practices and beliefs are irrelevant to one's Jewishness. She may be not only indifferent to, but, as was the case of many founding fathers of Zionism, even actively working against the fundamentals of Jewish practice and belief and would still be considered Jewish.

My point, then, is that the same may be said of the *political* criteria put into practice in Israel: It does not make a difference whether the 'stranger' is a loyal citizen of the state or even an ardent philo-Semitic adherent of Zionist nationalism; her very presence outside of the binary friend–enemy (read: Jew–Arab) is seen as menacing; Similarly, once the ambiguity of her presence is resolved, as she is converted and counted with the Jews, her (national, secular, political) beliefs and practices do not make a difference; she is now counted with the Jewish majority, even if she may be wholly indifferent to the politics of the nation-state and atheistic regarding its theopolitics.

This is further highlighted by the fact that inside the confines of the rabbinical jurisprudence, whom the state endows with the task of demarcating the line separating 'friends' from others (by converting the 'strangers' and making them 'friends,' that is: Jews), the considerations are of a wholly different scale: For the rabbis, the positively meaningful manifestation of one's joining Jewishness must take the form of practice and knowledge. Consider, by way of example, this ethnographic depiction of the routine working of the rabbinical court of conversion:

The candidates [for conversion] are required to answer concrete questions [such as:] 'What holidays do we celebrate on this month?,' 'What is the counting of the Omer?,' 'What happened on Mount Sinai?,' 'How do you

---

[39] *The Economist*, 'Who is a Jew?' It should be noted here that this is only partially true. Halakhicly, in terms of one's participation in the Jewish community, such as one's eligibility to give testimony in a rabbinical court, practice plays a decisive role.

make tea on Shabbat?' ... In addition, the candidates should prove that they wholeheartedly wish to join the Jewish people. The Court investigates the candidate's sincerity and degree of willingness with questions such as 'Why do you wish to be a Jew?' ... or by 'warnings' such as 'Do you know it is hard to be Jewish?' ... Most important [for the rabbis-judges] is the religious observance and the religious formation of the body, and only afterwards the understanding or knowledge. The rabbis-judges wish to make sure that the knowledge reflects daily practice, and not just study and memorization. Moreover, the judges of the rabbinical court are not satisfied with proof of knowledge and motivation and changes to body and behavior of the individual but [also] expect a wider change: they wish to include the converts and their family in a religious community, mostly of the kind that they themselves belong to.[40]

A Secular Alternative?

The tension between the modern fantasy of strict, 'clean' binaries and the just as modern reality of the continuous disruption of these binaries – as put by Bruno Latour, the tension between the modern sense of purity and the fact that in actuality 'we have never been modern'[41] since this purity has never been realized – gives birth to an existential anxiety. In Zygmunt Bauman's words:

No binary classification deployed in the construction of order can fully overlap with essentially non-discrete, continuous experience of reality. The opposition, born of the horror of ambiguity, becomes the main source of ambivalence. The enforcement of any classification means inevitably production of anomalies (that is, phenomena which are perceived as 'anomalous' only as far as they span the categories whose staying apart is the meaning of the order).[42]

It may be worth to note explicitly here what is often taken for granted in Israel: that the 'simple' acceptance of these 'strangers,' as they are, as part of the Israeli nation – or, rather, the nation of which Israel is the nation-state – is ideationally out of the picture. Needless to say, social life is more nuanced than such ideational binaries, and

[40] Goodman, 'Citizenship, modernity and belief in the nation-state,' 387.
[41] B. Latour, *We Have Never Been Modern* (Cambridge, MA: Harvard University Press, 1993).
[42] Bauman, *Modernity and Ambivalence*, 61.

Israeli political culture ultimately offers a practical venue for the inclusion of these non-Jews as part of the non-Arab majority. Moreover, as I shall discuss shortly, this inclusion-in-practice has been proactively promoted as a solution to the 'problem' of the former Soviet Union (FSU) non-Jewish immigrants.

Tellingly, such an outline (or reality) of a sociopolitical, or national – as in not-through-the-religious-rabbinical-gate – assimilation or inclusion of the non-Jewish immigrants from the FSU has been framed as a project, a mission even, of *'giyyur mamlakhti/le'umi.'* That is, a 'national' (or 'statist') conversion *into Judaism.* The Hebrew terminology used here is of importance: *Giyyur* is used specifically to denote someone's conversion into Judaism (in the sense of becoming a Jew, part of the Jewish people). The task (or sociopolitical reality) of inclusion and assimilation is seen not as *'hamara'* (the more generic Hebrew term for conversion), but rather as a *'giyyur'* that is nevertheless 'not wholly religious.' Advocates see this as an answer to 'the challenge of expanding the Jewish nation.'[43]

To understand this venue, and to see its limitations, we must first appreciate the degree to which Israeli culture is commonly taken to be, in essence, a *Jewish* culture. As one author rather triumphantly puts it, given that Israeli public, political culture is 'a culture that is (1) carried by Jews, (2) relates directly to their Jewishness and (3) to other Jewish cultures,' we must understand it as 'an independent Jewish culture.' Moreover, 'There are Jewish cultures that are not Israeli, but there is no mainstream Israeli culture that is not Jewish.'[44]

In light of this reality, a study of the social integration of non-Jewish citizens who have immigrated to Israel from the FSU and were awarded citizenship based on their familial relation to Jews depicts

---

[43] As put in the Hebrew subtitle of A. Cohen, *Non-Jewish Jews in Israel* (Jerusalem: Keter Publishing House, 2006). It is also important to note the nation-statist connotations of the term *'mamlakhti.'* See: N. Kedar, 'Ben-Gurion's mamlakhtiyut : Etymology and theoretical roots,' *Israel Studies*, 7/3 (2002), 117–33; N. Kedar, *Mamlachtiyut: Ben-Gurion's Civilian Conception* (Beersheba, Israel: Ben-Gurion University Press, 2009); D. Ohana, *Messianism and Mamlachtiyut: Ben Gurion and the Intellectuals between Political Vision and Political Theory* (Beersheba, Israel: Ben-Gurion University Press, 2003). See also my discussion on the secularist and nationalist connotations of the *mamlakhti* educational stream below.

[44] H. Shoham, *Let's Celebrate! Festivals and Civic Culture in Israel* (Jerusalem: The Israel Democracy Institute, 2014), 9, 10.

many of them as having gone through a 'social conversion' (again, the Hebrew term used is *giyyur*, not *hamara*). While never bothering to go through a rabbinically ordained conversion into Judaism, these immigrants' immersion in Israeli culture amounts, according to the author of the study at hand, to their '*giyyur*.' The story he tells is about the FSU individuals' *conversion into Judaism* by way of becoming Israelis. So much so that he labels them 'Non-Jewish Jews.'[45]

It may sound redundant, but the reader must remember that Israeli political culture does not offer Palestinian-Arab citizens of Israel a similar path of 'social conversion' into the Israeli in-group. For them, such a conversion would amount to an erasure or negation of their personal and collective identity, especially since so much of this Israeliness is built on the Jew–Arab dichotomy.

In any event, the dominant presence of the 'blood-centered' notion of Jewish identity in Israel proves to be stronger and more enduring than such 'social *giyyur*.' Ultimately, this non-rabbinical assimilation into Israeli/Jewish culture is not accepted as having solved the problematic stance of the FSU-non-Jewish citizen as the stranger who remains outside of the friend–enemy binary. One tragic expression of this is the problematic, heavily charged status of non-Jewish fallen soldiers of the Israeli military. While alive, these non-Jewish citizens are drafted to the army and sent to war for the sake of the state, fighting alongside their Jewish comrades (unlike some segments of the Palestinian-Arab population, they are not exempt from military service). As dead bodies, however, they are relegated (according to Jewish, 'religious' law) to a separate section of the military cemetery. This obviously raises misgivings, and at least once caused a public uproar when the Chief of Staff of the Israeli military was seen as passing over one of these non-Jewish fallen soldiers and preferring to commemorate a Jewish one during an official commemoration ceremony.[46]

Either an 'anomaly' or a 'time bomb,' the presence of a large minority of 'strangers' – that is, non-Jewish non-Arab citizens – in Israel has been the focus of public debate and has encouraged many to offer 'solutions' to what is clearly seen as a problem of national proportions.

---

[45] Cohen, *Non-Jewish Jews in Israel*.

[46] G. Cohen, 'Outcry prompts army to change its policy. IDF Backtracks: Last fallen soldier will be honored in ceremony, regardless of Jewish status,' *Haaretz*, April 11, 2013.

Critically, it is largely dealt with as an issue pertaining to (*religious*) conversion, or *giyyur*. This point must be stressed, for it is not 'obvious' that a matter of immigration and social integration or cohesion in the modern nation-state, even the one identified as the Jews' state, shall be framed in the context of a debate on *giyyur*/conversion. This may be further highlighted if we compare this debate to the public discourse on non-Jewish labor migrants and (mostly African) asylum seekers. While there is obviously much concern, at times panic even, surrounding their growing presence in Israel,[47] assimilation, and especially *giyyur* are not seen as relevant to the public debate on the issue, which tends to follow the Western European discourse on migration. Moreover, the state has been imposing severe restrictions on the ability of such other groups of non-Jews to convert to Judaism, introducing special bureaucratic hurdles characterized by 'an organisational culture, led by secular bureaucrats, of suspicion'[48] directed at members of such groups who wish to convert.

'Solving' the Problem by Reiterating the Racial Frame of Reference

Two documents purporting to offer a solution to the perceived problem of the presence of a large minority of non-Jewish citizens, migrants from the FSU, exemplify the Israeli fixation on *giyyur* – and, deductively at least, on blood or race – as the gateway for inclusion in Israeli, Zionist nationhood. Both documents tackle the issue legalistically – one from the point of view of a civil ('secular') law, the other from the perspective of Jewish ('religious') rabbinic law. While supposedly relating to two different, sometimes opposing notions of law – i.e., traditional/religious vs. modern/secular law – the two documents share the same fundamental (*Zionist*) concerns, and ultimately offer a similar solution, which preserves the symbolic infrastructure, by which inclusion and exclusion are viewed as matters of racial belonging.[49]

---

[47] M. G. Jaradat, *The Unchosen: The Lives of Israel's New Others* (London: Pluto Press, 2017); G. Sabar and E. Tsurkov, *Israel's Policies toward Asylum-seekers: 2002–2014* (Rome: Istituto Affari Internazionali, 2015).

[48] Kravel-Tovi, *When the State Winks*, 80.

[49] Needless to say, the Israeli public sphere has been teeming with various additional ideas attempting to neutralize this perceived existential danger. One of the most 'innovative' (in lack of a better term) in this regard has been Rabbi

One document at hand is a proposed parliamentary bill, drafted in one of Israel's leading 'think tanks,' the Israel Democracy Institute.[50] The other is a legal-rabbinical tract on the status of FSU non-Jews in Israel, written by Rabbi Ḥayim Amsellem, who at the time of publication of the tract was a member of the Orthodox Sephardi party, Shas.[51] For one thing, it is fascinating to see how these two documents, supposedly nourishing on two differing, if not outright conflicting political philosophies (liberal democracy, in the case of the Israel Democracy Institute (IDI) and religious Jewish particularism in the case of Amsellem) put forward what are at root very similar programs of reforming or 'tweaking' the rabbinical procedure of *giyyur* so as to allow an easier absorption of a large minority of FSU non-Jews in the Jewish collective. In other words, the two documents share the nationalist, Zionist concern as their guiding, determining ideology, and they both suggest solving it via the religious venue of *giyyur*.

In the context of the current discussion, the proposed bill drafted under the auspice of the IDI is more interesting, for it reveals the degree to which a liberal-Zionist understanding of Jewish national identity is

Yoel Bin-Nun's scheme of the mass baptizing of FSU immigrants in the waters of the Mediterranean. See Michal Kravel-Tovi's illuminating discussion of it: Kravel-Tovi, *When the State Winks*, 2–8, 107–9.

[50] Y. Z. Stern, S. Farber, and E. Caplan, *Proposal for a State Conversion Law* (Jerusalem: Israel Democracy Institute and ITIM, 2014). It should be noted that while this document is a part of a leger project of religion and state at the IDI, the proposed bill is sponsored – and published – with the cooperation of ITIM, a nongovernmental organization (NGO) which 'helps people navigate the religious authorities' bureaucracy in Israel.' The organization, which was founded by an American-born rabbi, aims

> to oppose the alienation that many Israelis feel at what are supposed to be the most significant moments of their lives as Jews: birth, marriage, divorce, burial, and conversion. The encounter with the religious establishment at these moments is often accompanied by fear, lack of knowledge, disgust, frustration, and anger.
>
> To contribute to positive and significant encounters with Jewish life, ITIM helps people navigate the depths of the religious authorities' bureaucracy in Israel, providing information, mediating, representing them, and working to simplify the process and solutions to complex problems.
>
> Over the years, we have helped tens of thousands of people, who have found a sympathetic ear in our outstretched helping hand. ITIM, 'About Us' (www .itim.org.il/en).

[51] Ḥayim Amsellem, *Zera' Yisrael* (Jerusalem: Mekhon Meqabeṣ Nidḥe Yisrael, 5770/2010); see also: Ḥayim Amsellem, *Meqor Yisrael* (Jerusalem: Mekhon Meqabeṣ Nidḥe Yisrael, 5770/2010).

nevertheless based on a 'blood-centered' notion of national belonging and otherness. Needless to say, the apparent interest in and engagement with the issue of *giyyur* are not unique to liberal-Zionists; but in the context of the Israeli, Zionist political culture, one would be forgiven if assuming that this is the least likely party to obsess over the intricacies of this supposedly religious matter. After all, liberal ideas almost by definition negate the relevance of one's religious denomination or racial identification for the application of human and civil rights.

An acknowledgment of the fundamental reliance of Israeli, Zionist nationhood on a 'blood-centered,' racial logic of inclusion and exclusion may indeed be just too devastating to a secularist, liberal mindset. A blunt (and admittedly provocative) exemplification of this could be found in the reaction of one critic, writing in the liberal, secularist newspaper *Haaretz*, to a television show, which was produced by the Israeli government's Ministry of Diaspora Affairs (headed at the time by Naftali Bennett, head of the religious-Zionist party). The show was designed to warn against what the producers depicted as the imminent danger of intermarriage between Jews and non-Jews.[52] This message, it must be stressed, was put in a wholly 'nonreligious' context; the matter at hand has to do, so the show claimed, with Jewish nationhood or peoplehood, not with Jewish religion. In this, the show was echoing a prevalent sense in the Jewish word (in Israel and abroad), by which intermarriage between Jews and non-Jews, merely by virtue of the difference in 'blood lines' of the married couples, entails a breaking of the Jewish generational chain. For the liberal, secularist critic, this entails, quite simply, an abhorrent racist view. As he writes of the show's presenter, a certain Y. Limore:

Limore is, of course, a racist. Exactly as is [Naftali] Bennett. And vastly different but like Hitler. Hitler almost killed the grandma just because of her being Jewish, and Limore is rejecting the [non-Jewish bride of a European Jew] just because of her being Christian. The only difference between Limore and Hitler is that Hitler was also a mass murderer, probably the worst known to the world . . . and Limore is just an inured journalist . . . But racism is racism.[53]

---

[52] *Na'alamim*, TV film, presented by Y. Limore. Keshet, Channel 2, 2016.
[53] R. Alpher, 'Hitler, hayehudim hitkavṣu,' *Haaretz*, December 21, 2016.

By this logic, one can indeed expect other, 'less-liberal,' segments of Israeli society to be more clearly committed to what is, at base, an ethnonationalist or racial discriminatory scheme of application of civil, if not human, rights; in which case, it may be seen simply as an Israeli manifestation of right-wing European nationalism. From this point of view, it is not surprising to learn, as a recent ethnography clearly shows, that the religious-Zionist mainstream is dramatically preoccupied with the matter of conversions, fully identifying with the statist view of the issue.[54]

Yet I would argue that the liberal-Zionist insistence on preserving the framework of *giyyur* as the *only* gate for national inclusion betrays the degree to which liberal-Zionism itself (the above-quoted critic's admitted provocation notwithstanding) understands the notion of Jewish national identity as essentially having to do with 'blood.' This is clearly manifested in the liberal-Zionist insistence on preserving the foundational distinction between a majority of Jews, identified primarily by descent as a matter of their 'ethnic' origins, and a non-Jewish minority of Palestinian-Arabs as the core of Zionist, Israeli nation-statehood.[55]

The work produced by the Israel Democracy Institute is a rather straightforward explication of the degree to which liberal, allegedly secular, Zionism is invested in the matter. The institute, which describes itself as a "think and do tank' dedicated to strengthening the foundations of Israeli democracy,'[56] has focused much of its own attention and resources on the wider issue of 'Religion and State,' aiming to 'develop identity and solidarity in a multifaceted society and to reduce tensions between religion and state.'[57] A 'reforming of the *giyyur* system in Israel, so as to make halakhic *giyyur* more accessible'[58] is stated as a primary means by which the IDI seeks to achieve this goal. Clearly, *halakhic, religious* conversion – *giyyur* – is taken to

---

[54] Kravel-Tovi, *When the State Winks*, ch. 2.

[55] In Israeli Hebrew, Palestinian-Arabs are commonly referred to in official parlance as *benei mi'outim* – literally, members of minorities. The two are indeed synonymous: to be a Palestinian-Arab in Israel is to be a minority

[56] Israel Democracy Institute, 'IDI - Israel's Leading Think Tank, 'Do Tank,' and Policy Institute, IDI's website, goo.gl/o25tkN.'

[57] Israel Democracy Institute, 'Religion and state in Israel.'

[58] Israel Democracy Institute, 'Religion and state in Israel.'

be a matter pertaining to the strength of Israeli democracy (and national cohesiveness).

The main aim of the proposed bill is to chart a 'middle way' between two competing 'extreme' views regarding whom the State of Israel should recognize as Jewish: One extreme position, which is also the instituted practice in Israel, gives the Chief Rabbinate the sole authority to issue a certificate of *giyyur*. The second 'extreme' stance demands a 'privatization' of conversion, so as to allow every rabbinical court to issue such certificates. The bill at hand seeks to allow for a 'halakhic multivocality' that is nevertheless contained in and controlled under a statist framework. This, the authors propose, will guarantee 'unity and not uniformity' among the Jews. Crucially, the bill views *giyyur* as a 'national issue, which Israeli society must address seriously and responsibly. This is our obligation to the generations to come.'[59]

The document leaves little doubt that in the liberal-Zionist hyphenation, the national, Zionist considerations take precedent. And it is quite apparent that this ideational supremacy dictates the limited nature of the application of foundational liberal ideas. Crucially, the bill never challenges the 'blood-centered' notion of national inclusion and exclusion. This can be learned from the very choice to devote so much attention to *giyyur* in order to solve, among other things, matters of personal, legal status and civil rights. Let me explain.

One critical matter entailed in the migration of hundreds of thousands of FSU non-Jews to Israel, and their almost immediate naturalization as citizens under the expansive application of the Law of Return, is that since most of them are not religiously affiliated (the state registers them as '*ḥasrei dat*,' literally 'lacking a religion'), they are left, in matters of personal status, in a kind of limbo. This is the case since, as mentioned earlier, the Israeli, *civil* law, endows religious courts with the authority to conduct these matters (primarily marriage and divorce; among other things, this legal practice greatly discourages the possibility of intermarriage between Israeli-Jews and non-Jews). Put simply, these people have no institutional framework through which to conduct these matters; they cannot legally marry in Israel.

The proposed bill clearly addresses this predicament, but it does so primarily in a nationally Jewish, Zionist context, not in a personal-civil one. The bill seeks to solve the predicament of the non-Jewish

---

[59] Stern, Farber, and Caplan, *Proposal for a State Conversion Law*, 6.

migrants' inability to conduct their personal matters in their state not by changing the civil framework so as to allow non-Jewish citizen to live normally, but rather by making them Jewish. It does not purport to offer, for example, a quintessentially liberal notion of civil, nonreligious framework for conducting these matters; this option is clearly outside the bounds of the bill's national frame of reference. Tellingly, the bill suggests that the main problem at hand is not the non-Jewish FSU citizens' inability to marry in general, but rather their inability to marry *Jews* in Israel.[60]

In any event, for the bill's authors, a purely liberal, civil solution to this predicament is not a viable option. They note that 'although this reality [i.e., the predicament of not being able to legally conduct their personal matters in Israel] could be changed by civil legislation, this would not amount to a solution for a large part of the Israeli population, who is interested in preserving the religious systems.'[61] (In other words, the 'religious' opposition is to blame; we will get back to this in a moment.) Nevertheless, it is rather clear that when the authors write that 'only joining the Jewish people by way of *giyyur* can bring about the [non-Jewish citizens'] full integration inside the Jewish society in Israel, on its various factions,'[62] their primary frame of reference is not the personal/civil aspect of the issue, but rather the national one. Moreover, they frame the latter as 'the damage to the unity of the nation.' Clearly, it is this national, Zionist, not civil-personal level that dictates the logic by which 'the completion of [these non-Jewish migrants'] joining the Jewish People' must be thought of and solved 'by way of *giyyur*.'

Again, the onus of responsibility is placed on the 'religious' (accompanied by traditional Jews, in this case): Although Israeli FSU non-Jews (designated here as 'members of the young generation of the group of those 'lacking a religion'') take an active part in Israeli life (they 'speak Hebrew as their mother tongue, serve in the military, are educated in the Israeli statist educational system and are fully integrated in Israeli

---

[60] Stern, Farber, and Caplan, *Proposal for a State Conversion Law*, 10. Critically, the bill aims to be only a one-time solution to the 'problem' caused by the mass immigration of non-Jews from the FSU, and sets a term limit for itself: it is to expire in a ten-year timeframe; Stern, Farber, and Caplan, *Proposal for a State Conversion Law*, 17.

[61] Stern, Farber, and Caplan, *Proposal for a State Conversion Law*, 10.

[62] Stern, Farber, and Caplan, *Proposal for a State Conversion Law*, 10.

society'), 'many of Israel's citizens, religious and traditional, assign significance to their classification as 'non-Jews' by halakha, and are thus troubled by the idea of marrying them. For them, it is about assimilation.' That is to say: the problem is that religious and traditional Jews fail to see that a social integration in Israeli society should amount to a de facto 'Jewfication.' This, the authors of the bill warn, may eventually amount to a 'historical divide in the nation.'[63]

The authors also warn that a de facto recognition of these immigrants as Jews without them going through a process of *giyyur* would amount to a break with Jewish tradition as it has been established 'since the days of Ezra and Neḥemya [fifth century BCE], and this change would have far reaching implications on the future of the nation as a whole.'[64]

Having reaffirmed *giyyur* as the only viable way for inclusion among the Jewish-Israeli population, the bill goes on to explicitly blame the Orthodox rabbinical establishment for greatly discouraging a project of mass conversion. The Orthodox rabbis, it turns out, seem to either not share the authors' concerns, or, in the least, adhere to a different set of considerations that ultimately prioritize these matters differently. They insist, so it appears, to preserve the 'religious' dictates (as they interpret them, of course), which famously manifest an apprehensive approach to an expansion of the Jewish people through conversion. The rabbis thus set 'a tough, rigid halakhic measure, originating in a stringent Orthodox worldview,' that aims at transforming the non-Jew into an Orthodoxly observant Jew. Given that 'most non-Jewish immigrants are not interested in religious observance,' this obviously poses a problem for anyone interested in using *giyyur* as the gateway for Jewish-Israeli inclusion.[65]

Critically, the bill advocates the case for including these migrants as Jews by referring primarily to their 'biological' origin: 'It is important to say,' the bill notes,

that although they are not recognised as Jews, the vast majority of this group has a biological tie to Judaism, since their father or grandfather are Jewish. Halakhic tradition classifies them as those who are 'of the seed of Israel' [*mizera' yisrael*], and this carries various implications. Likewise, many of

---

[63] Stern, Farber, and Caplan, *Proposal for a State Conversion Law*, 10.
[64] Stern, Farber, and Caplan, *Proposal for a State Conversion Law*, 11.
[65] Stern, Farber, and Caplan, *Proposal for a State Conversion Law*, 12.

them observe tradition like most Jews in Israel, they live here willingly and by choice, identify with the national goals of the Jewish people, and willingly participate in the defence of the nation-state of the Jewish people.[66]

In other words, the fundamental biological trait – being of a Jewish 'seed' or having a 'biological tie to Judaism' – is complimented by the subjects' loyalty to the 'nation-state of the Jewish People,' (manifested, one is led to assume, in their draft to the Israeli military).[67] The state's self-identification as a state of Jews renders these loyal subjects of the state Jewish, but only to a certain, insufficient degree.

The bill's main impetus is, of course, in the alternative, 'national' framework for *giyyur* – a national conversion which is nevertheless religious in essence – that the authors seek to promote. This appears to be concerned primarily with the interests of the nation-state: '*Giyyur* is a crucial element of the state's immigration policy, and the state must regulate it and keep in its own hands the jurisdiction over the matter.'[68] The bill does so without disrupting the status quo, according to which Orthodox rabbis determine the yardstick for *giyyur*. The state's main role, it seems, is in further regulating and bureaucratically enabling a process of mass (religious) conversion.

'Zera῾ Israel': A Halakhic Commitment to Nation-Statist Concerns

It may seem 'reasonable' – especially if we follow the reason guiding some of the vehement anti-rabbinical discourse prevalent among secularist liberal-Zionists – that an explicit concern with the 'blood origin' of these non-Jews would be of a prime concern for Orthodox rabbis. But an exception to the Orthodox rabbinical rule may shed a somewhat different light on the matter. The exception at hand is the aforementioned halakhic deliberation on the matter of conversion, written by Rabbi Ḥayim Amsellem.[69] This treatise does, indeed, seem to be taking the matter of one's 'blood origin' as a primary concern in determining one's Jewishness, especially in the context of *giyyur*. However, the all-out condemnation it ultimately received from the

---

[66] Stern, Farber, and Caplan, *Proposal for a State Conversion Law*, 9.
[67] See also: Kravel-Tovi, *When the State Winks*, 86.
[68] Stern, Farber, and Caplan, *Proposal for a State Conversion Law*, 17.
[69] Amsellem, *Zera῾ Yisrael*.

Orthodox rabbinical establishment shows it to be a diversion from the established rabbinical view of the matter. This case, in other words, suggests that the Orthodox rabbinical establishment takes the stand that ultimately rejects (counterintuitive to liberal, secularist thought as it may sound) the notion of basing one's Jewish identity primarily on one's 'blood origin.'

The text at hand is written and presented, in all matters of content, style and intended audience, as an Orthodox rabbinical, jurisprudential exercise. Unlike the authors of the proposed parliamentary bill discusses above, Amsellem does not aim to curtail the authority of the rabbinical establishment by reframing the matter in a *'mamlakhti'* (statist) context. Rhetorically at least, his concerns are purely halakhic, that is: legal.

However, the sociopolitical context of the publication of the text is too apparent to be ignored, and it sheds a wholly different light on the aims and guiding logic of the text. As Amsellem himself has made sure to explain in various media appearances, just like the IDI proposed bill, he, too, is primarily concerned with those non-Jewish immigrants from the FSU who are 'from Israel's seed ... there is room for leniency in regard to them.' For Amsellem, these non-Jews' service in the Israeli military constitutes proof of their wish to be part of the Jewish people. (It may be relevant to remind the reader here, again, that they are conscripted by law, as all Israeli citizens formally are. Some segments of the Palestinian-Arab population are exempt in practice, by the state's own choice to do so. But the point to stress here is that these former FSU-immigrants, non-Jewish citizens do not proactively volunteer to serve; they simply obey the law.) In any event, for Amsellem, the FSU Israeli citizens' service in the army, what Amsellem depicts as 'the convert's expression of willingness to give his life for the defense of the sacredness of the People and the Land' amounts to a declaration of the convert's wish to join the Jewish people. This declaration is, as Amsellem notes, an integral part of the rabbinical conversion process.

In short, these non-Jews' service in the military of the state of the Jews must be part of their 'observance of mitzvoth'[70] (as converts). This point is crucial, since for Amsellem it must allow for some leniency in regard to the formal demand that the convert shall maintain

---

[70] Amsellem, quoted in Y. Golan, 'Hasbarat shiṭat harav Ḥayim Amsellem benose hagiyur,' Shoresh.org.Il (blog), September 23, 2009.

an Orthodoxly observant Jewish lifestyle post-conversion. In short, Amsellem argues that since these non-Jewish decedents of Jews ('from the seed of Israel') serve in the military of the Jews' state, they may be allowed to convert even if they do not proclaim to observe Jewish law in an Orthodox manner.

The main motive behind this leniency is the same fear of intermarriage, expressed in the IDI proposed bill. According to Amsellem, those hardliners who refuse to allow leniency in the *giyyur* process of the FSU immigrants are wrong to think they are defending the Jewish people: 'on the long run, they do harm, and lead us all to intermarriage [of Jews and non-Jews] and to civil marriage in Israel'[71] – i.e., to a breaking of the rabbinical monopoly over marriages in Israel, since rabbinical courts do not allow for intermarriage between Jews and non-Jews.

As Amsellem himself repeatedly clarifies (in bold letters), the fact that these immigrants are 'from the seed of Israel' is the fundamental matter at hand. It means that they do not count as 'absolute Gentiles' (*goy gammur*). Hence the room for leniency:

I've never argued for changing a single thing about the [halakhicly Orthodox] *giyyur* process. *Giyyur* must be done only according to halakha … I only determined that part of the process and part of the [convert's] expression of willingness to convert and join the Jewish people is his wish to serve in the IDF [the Israeli military], and in this regard there is room for leniency with those who are from the seed of Israel.[72]

As mentioned earlier, the practical meaning of this proposed leniency has to do with the convert's lifestyle post-conversion. The Orthodox rabbinical courts overseeing *giyyur* demand that the converts observe an Orthodox lifestyle (as a matter of learning by practice before the act of conversion, and as a matter of obeying the Jewish legal code once they convert). This commitment, all sides involved seem to agree, is a tasking demand that most converts would rather forego. Why should they observe a lifestyle that most Israeli-Jews do not bother to even learn about, let alone observe in practice? Rabbi Amsellem, too, is keenly aware of the social fact mentioned earlier, that people who identify as Orthodox, and are (at least formally)

---

[71] Golan, 'hasbarat shiṭat harav Ḥayim Amsellem benose hagiyur.'
[72] Golan, 'hasbarat shiṭat harav Ḥayim Amsellem benose hagiyur.'

committed to observing a lifestyle dictated by the Orthodox interpretation of Jewish law account for only a minority among Israeli-Jews.
The vast majority of Jews in Israel identify either as '*ḥiloni*' (a problematic – both linguistically and practically – translation of 'secular'[73])
or '*masorti*' ('traditionist,' usually denoting a self-conscious disruption
of the secular-religious dichotomy, that is usually manifested in a
'partial' and 'selective' observance of the Orthodox interpretation of
Jewish law[74]). Why, then, would the non-Jewish immigrants be
demanded to become *Orthodox* Jews? Can't they just be Israeli-Jews,
like most other non-Orthodox Jews in Israel?

Amsellem, who is clearly sympathetic to this argument, thus suggests
that the 'biological' fact – these non-Jews' remote, partial Jewish
lineage – should account for the 'discount' given to them in terms of
their commitment to observe an Orthodox way of life. As he notes, for
his critics (on this see below), anything below the uppermost level of
Orthodox observance is insufficient: 'some argue against me that in
practice most of the converts are in actuality only partially converted,
and do not observe [after the conversion process has been completed]
all of the commandment of Judaism, but are more like *masortim*.' To
which he replies:

Well, since the matter at hand has to do with the seed of Israel [*zera' Israel*],
and with people who wish to become Jewish and sacrifice their souls for the
Jewish people, then if this person wishes to accept the commandments at the
time of the conversion this should be enough for the time being, and we hope
that at the first, immediate stage he shall observe some of the commandments, and we shall hope that with God's help, with time he shall become
more observant and will fully observe the commandments.[75]

'Blood origin,' then, can account – according to the logic proposed
by Amsellem – for the leniency in terms of observing (an Orthodoxly
defined) Jewish way of life.

The rather vehement condemnation of Amsellem by Orthodox
rabbis that followed the publication of his halakhic treatise highlights

---

[73] Y. Yadgar, *Beyond Secularization: Traditionists and the Critique of Israeli
      Secularism* (Jerusalem: The Van-Leer Institute/Hakibutz Hameuchad Publishing
      House, 2012), ch. 3.
[74] Yadgar, 'Traditionism'; Y. Yadgar, *Secularism and Religion in Jewish-Israeli
      Politics: Traditionists and Modernity* (New York: Routledge, 2011).
[75] Golan, 'hasbarat shiṭat harav Ḥayim Amsellem benose hagiyur.'

the degree to which the current interpretation of Jewish Orthodoxy shifts its attention *away* from one's biological origin as an element in determining one's Jewishness (the 'Jewish mother' criterion notwithstanding, of course[76]). As put in one public letter (among many of a similar kind):

Regarding the validity of a conversion of a person who intends to observe the commandment partially or like a *masorti*: We are hereby to clarify that there is nothing in halakha to certify such a conversion and *he is an absolute gentile* [*goy gammur*] for all matters concerned, and it does not make a difference whether his father and mother are gentiles or only his mother is gentile.[77]

This may be the place to remind the reader that the halakhic notion of a 'Jewish mother' – i.e., a matrilineal principal for determining Jewish identity – is *not* a 'genetic' principle. To begin with, as I discussed earlier in the Introduction, the very argument that Jewish tradition has been preoccupied with such matters is anachronistic, confusing as the current use of 'the seed of Israel' may be in this context. And in any event, the current Orthodox interpretation of Jewish law remains largely indifferent to genetic heredity, highlighting that the matrilineal principal has to do more with parenting than with mere conception. Thus, for example, with the advent of *in vitro* fertilization, Orthodox rabbinical rulings have determined that it is the woman carrying the embryo, and not the origin of the sperm and/or egg, that determines the Jewish identity of the new-born child. This means that 'if the gestating womb is Jewish,' then 'non-Jewish donor sperm and ova can be used in assisted conception clinics to produce babies that are legally Jewish,' while 'a child could have Jewish genetic material [i.e., to be conceived from a sperm and an egg taken from Jewish man and woman], but without a Jewish mother would not be considered Jewish.'[78]

---

[76] See also my notes on the matter in the Introduction.

[77] Rabbis Yosef Shalom Eliashiv, Shmuel Wosner and Nissim Karelitz, quoted in Ḥanan Greenwood, 'ḥasifa: mikhtav bekhirey harabanim neged hasefer zera' yisrael shel harav amsellem,' Kipa.co.il: June 21, 2015. The same news item also carries letters by other rabbis to the same effect.

[78] I. V. McGonigle and L. W. Herman, 'Genetic citizenship: DNA testing and the Israeli Law of Return,' *Journal of Law and the Biosciences*, 2/2 (2015), 475. On the study of genetics in the context of Jewish identity, see: N. A. El-Haj, *The Genealogical Science: The Search for Jewish Origins and the Politics of*

In any event, while the (mostly non-Zionist) Orthodox and Ultra-Orthodox leadership has rather unanimously condemned Amsellem, his supporters seem to have come largely from the religious-Zionist camp, which tends to consider the national, statist interest

Epistemology (Chicago: University of Chicago Press, 2014). For a legal discussion of some relevant issues of genetic testing, Jewish identity and citizenship in the Israeli case, see: McGonigle and Herman, 'Genetic citizenship: DNA testing and the Israeli Law of Return'; I. V. McGonigle, "Jewish Genetics' and the 'Nature' of Israeli Citizenship,' *Transversal*, 13/2 (2015), 90–102. I must note that the basic premise of these two articles, by which 'The Israeli State recently announced that it may begin to use genetic tests to determine whether potential immigrants are Jewish or not' (McGonigle and Herman, 'Genetic citizenship: DNA testing and the Israeli Law of Return,' 469) is misleading. As the original (Hebrew) journalistic report (referred to by the English publication cited by the authors of these two articles as their main source for the story) explicitly notes, the Israeli government's announcement regarding the viability of genetic testing has to do *not* with determining one's Jewish identity, but with determining biological paternity or maternity of certain children applying for citizenship by the application of the Law of Return. As the official statement notes: 'This has to do not with a [genetic] testing of Jewishness, but with testing a familial relation to a person eligible for *Aliya* [i.e., eligibility for almost immediate citizenship by the application of the Law of Return].' Y. Eli, 'Hamedina moda: Bedikot DNA hokhiku yahadut,' nrg.co.il, July 29, 2013. More recent reports, informed by the advocacy of the ITIM organization (see Note 50), repeat the argument that the 'Israeli Chief Rabbinate [uses] DNA testing to prove Jewishness'; J. Maltz, 'Israeli Rabbinate accused of using DNA testing to prove Jewishness,' *Haaretz*, February 14, 2019. It was also reported that Chief Rabbi David Lau has confirmed that in certain cases, where claims to Jewish identity are not verifiable by existing documentation, DNA testing might be offered as additional evidence to clarify the matter. This suggests that the tests are mainly aimed at proving paternity and maternity (the cases cited in the media reports suggest the same). Importantly, Lau insisted that 'a DNA test is not used to determine Jewish status in accordance with Jewish law and only to assist in the clarification [process].' J. Sharon, 'Chief Rabbinate admits using DNA tests to help determine Jewish status, *Jerusalem Post*, March 6, 2019. This was an especially important clarification, given that, as the same report notes, 'The admission is likely to generate outrage among mainstream religious-Zionist and Modern Orthodox groups, given that Jewish law does not recognize the validity of DNA testing to prove Jewishness.' In any event, these reports do suggest that the Israeli state, via the Chief Rabbinate, tends toward the use of DNA testing to verify claims of Jewish ancestry, regardless of the traditional and halakhic view of these matters. See also: O. Schwartz, 'What does it mean to be genetically Jewish?' *The Guardian*, June 13, 2019.

A more detailed report (the latest to be published before this book went into press) confirmed that 'Last year Israeli rabbinical courts began accepting the results of mitochondrial DNA testing as proof of Jewish heritage.' The report identifies one Rabbi Yisroel Barenbaum, a rabbinical judge in Moscow, as the person who have found a way to use this test to determine Jewish roots. The (i.e., preserving a Jewish majority as a prerequisite for the preservation of the nation-state of Jews as such) as preceding the Orthodox considerations regarding the prerequisite of the convert's Orthodox observance of halakha.[79] Not surprisingly, the leading rabbis in the campaign calling for leniency toward FSU converts have all come from the ranks of the religious-Zionist camp.[80]

Conclusion: 'A State of Jews' and the Politics of 'Blood'

The political debate over 'religious' conversion emanates from and is sustained by the political-Zionist (and, following the cue of Zionist ideology, the dominant Israeli) sense that as long as a majority of the nation-state's population are Jewish, the state can be seen as adhering to its *raison d'être*. This is manifested in an insistence on viewing Israel as the 'Jews' state' as opposed to a 'Jewish state.' This insistence has in effect been a dominant tenet of liberal-Zionism, which, adhering to a secularist agenda at its core, tends to view governmental attempts at 'bolstering' Israel's Jewish identity (or, more accurately, to propagate

report clarifies that 'the test is only considered supportive evidence for someone wishing to ascertain his Jewishness in a rabbinical court, as an addition to documentation.' The report also credits the Simanim Institute, established by Rabbi Ze'ev Litke, with the successful introduction of this change to the legal procedure. The institute is said to have invested 'huge resources in research and increasing the database.' The rabbinical court itself commented that 'their rulings are made according to Jewish law ... 'DNA testing is suggested only when an applicant cannot prove his Jewish origins. This is not compulsory.'' A. Rabinowitz, 'Israel's rabbinical courts begin to recognize DNA tests, potentially opening gateway to proving Jewishness,' *Haaretz*, August 30, 2019. A *Haaretz* editorial warned that this development is 'Spine chilling,' stating that 'No door should be opened for Israel to become a country where entry and citizenship will someday depend on a genetic test. This is a slippery slope, at the bottom of which Israel is liable to define itself not only as the nation-state of the Jewish people, but as the state of the Jewish race.' *Haaretz* Editorial, 'DNA testing to 'prove' Jewishness is spine-chilling,' *Haaretz*, September 1, 2019.

[79] Indeed, in the 2013 general election campaign to the Knesset, Amsellem departed from the Orthodox Shas party, and ran in a newly formed party, that positioned itself mostly inside the religious-Zionist field. Having failed to pass the electoral threshold, he eventually (after a short stint as a newly joined member of the non-Orthodox, right-wing Likud party, followed by membership in the religious-Zionist party, Habayit Hayehudi), ran in the 2019 elections campaign with the right-wing Zionist and libertarian party, Zehut.

[80] Kravel-Tovi, *When the State Winks*, ch. 2.

certain beliefs, practices, and views as having to do with the 'essence' of Israelis' Jewishness; more on this in the next chapter) as amounting to 'religious coercion.'

This stance, as I suggested earlier, has its roots in the rebellious anti-rabbinical (what some would call 'secular'; I would refrain from using this confusing term[81]) Zionist ideology. This fundamental ideological tenet amounts to a revolution in the historical understanding of Jewish identity, shifting the focus away from law, practice, and belief toward 'blood' and race. Having negated the authority of the rabbinical, traditional understanding of Jewish identity – of what makes a person Jewish – mainstream Zionist ideology tended to focus on one's 'biological' Jewish origin – one's race, one's 'blood' – to determine one's belonging to the 'nation.' This amounts to a claim that the biological fact of heredity determines not only who is a Jew but also what Judaism is (the latter being all that the former happens to do; see my discussion in the Introduction).

Put into the political-practical terms of the mechanisms of a state that proclaims to be the nation-state of the Jews, in the presence of a sizable constituency of Palestinian-Arabs who challenge the very founding premises of the state, this racial notion of Jewish political belonging has been translated into a rather crude arithmetical consideration: The preservation of a majority of Jews has become an existential feature of the very meaning of state sovereignty. As aptly put by one ethnographer of the performance of Jewish conversion in Israel, 'under the rubric of national mission, Jewish conversion has come to constitute a morally loaded Zionist biopolitical reality – an institutional channel for population policy through which the Jewish state strives to produce and reproduce the Israeli nation as Jewish.'[82]

Israel, in its current self-understanding, can proclaim to be the state of Jews *only* as long as Jews compose a majority among its citizens. It is thus required to actively preserve this demographic balance. In the words of a member of the (secularist, Leftist) Israeli Labor party:

It is a national interest to convert as many as possible … [*Giyyur*] serves the collective desire of all – religious and secular, Orthodox and non-Orthodox – to preserve and strengthen the Jewish majority in the State of Israel … Ultimately, the rationale of this state is to be a Jewish and democratic state,

---

[81] I elaborate this argument in Yadgar, *Sovereign Jews*.
[82] Kravel-Tovi, *When the State Winks*, 53.

and it is our most legitimate right to try and preserve Jewish hegemony and the Jewish majority in this State.[83]

This logic has, of course, dominated political thought since before 1948. It lies at the very basis of the notion of a partition of the land between a 'Jewish state' and an 'Arab state' (as outlined in the 1947 UN resolution), it strongly motivates the 'two states' scheme for solving the Israeli-Palestinian conflict, and it lies at the core of a widespread rejection of the 'one state' solution, arguing that this would amount to the annihilation of the State of Israel.

Yet, critically, Zionist ideology, followed by the State of Israel, had not developed a self-sufficient, independent notion of what constitutes one's Jewish 'race' or 'blood.' In other words, while making this issue the most critical aspect of its sovereignty, as well as the founding determinant of the friend–enemy binary, the state has failed (or simply neglected) to offer viable criteria for determining 'who is a Jew.' Instead, it has relied on the Orthodox rabbis, self-proclaimed guardians of Jewish 'religion,' to function as its national gatekeepers. Unfortunate as it may be to the Israeli state, this Orthodox and Ultra-Orthodox rabbinical elite does not subscribe to Zionist ideology, and has largely remained staunchly, conservatively committed to the notion that ethnicity/blood alone – or, in the case of converts, mere 'wish' or 'willingness' to symbolically join in this ethnos/race/nation – cannot positively, meaningfully be sufficient for one's identification as Jewish. The rabbis, in other words, have remained committed to the notion that it is Judaism that makes one Jewish, not the other way around. The rabbis' understanding of the meaning of this Judaism is a rather strict notion of a Jewish way of life to which, indeed, most people identified as Jews around the world do not subscribe.

This, then, is a story of one, critical implication of the Zionist 'exchange of the legal, covenantal, and communal basis of Jewish existence for the racial, the ethnic, and the national, a rupture whose further implications and deeper marks are only beginning to surface.'[84] It tells of the shortcomings of an understanding of Jewish polity and sovereignty as determined by the (numerically majoritarian) racial makeup of those wielding power. Clearly – and this can be seen

---

[83] MK Ofir Pines (Ha'avoda), quoted in Kravel-Tovi, *When the State Winks*, 78.
[84] A. Alcalay, *After Jews And Arabs: Remaking Levantine Culture* (Minneapolis: University of Minnesota Press, 1992), 52.

practically in all fields of Israeli sociopolitics – this is a manifestly shallow and dangerously narrow understanding of Jewish nation-statehood. The Israeli political field – or rather the mainstream Zionist parties and representatives dominating this field – have at least implicitly acknowledged this shortcoming, attempting as it were to somewhat belatedly anchor Israel's 'Jewish identity' in a semi-constitutional manner. This I shall discuss in the next chapter.

2 | *Israel as the Nation-State of the Jewish People?*

One of the 'core issues,' a fundamental disagreement which has reportedly inhibited the 'peace process' between the State of Israel and the Palestinian leadership, is Israel's demand that the Palestinians recognize Israel as a 'Jewish state.' The Israeli Prime Minister Benjamin Netanyahu has made such recognition a pillar of his negotiations with the Palestinians, calling it 'the real key to peace,' 'the minimal requirement,' and 'an essential condition.'[1] Netanyahu has also phrased the same stance as demanding that the Palestinians recognize Israel as 'the nation-state [*medinat haleom* in the original Hebrew]' of the Jewish people.[2] The prime minister's pronouncements make it clear that the two phrasings (i.e., a recognition of Israel as a 'Jewish state' and as 'the nation-state of the Jewish people') are identical. Thus, for example, one English report (which prefers to translate the latter phrase – *medinat leom* – as 'national homeland') quotes Netanyahu as alerting his fellow party members to the fact that 'The Palestinian Authority President was quoted as saying he is unwilling to recognize a Jewish state, when he knows that there won't be an agreement without recognition of a national homeland.'[3]

Now, while Netanyahu has presented this demand as so fundamental an issue as to be rather trivial, the history of Israel's negotiations with Arab states sheds a somewhat different light on the matter. As the president of the Palestinian Authority (PA), Mahmoud Abbas (who sees this demand as a red line that he will not cross[4]), was quick to

---

[1] J. Rudoren, 'Sticking point in peace talks: Recognition of a Jewish state,' *The New York Times*, January 1, 2014.

[2] For example: *Haaretz*, February 3, 2014.

[3] J. Lis, 'Netanyahu: Abbas' refusal to recognize Israel as Jewish state is 'absurd,'' *Haaretz*, February 3, 2014.

[4] A review of the Palestinian stance on the matter claims that while the leadership of the Palestinian citizens of Israel has been vehemently opposed to this demand, the leadership of the Palestinian authority had originally expressed willingness to recognize Israel as a Jewish state. A. Rudnitzky, *The Arab Minority*

note, Israel did not present a similar demand to Egypt and Jordan when signing peace treaties with them.[5] This, I suspect, should be read not as alluding to an earlier Israeli tolerance of an Egyptian or Jordanian refusal to recognize Israel as the 'Jewish nation-state,' but rather as manifesting the controversy – which has intensified in recent years – surrounding this very basic 'datum' of Israel's 'identity' as a Jewish state.

Clearly, the political discourse on the matter of Israel's 'Jewish identity' has gained a unique character as a *debated*, controversial even (rather than trivial), premise that lies at the core of not only the negotiations between Israel and the PA, but also the very foundation of Israeli sociopolitics. It is, in other words, yet another example of how 'internal' issues pertaining to the meaning of the 'Jewishness' of Israeli sociopolitics reflect on 'external' matters of the wider Middle East.

This issue raises several questions. First, what is the meaning of referring to Israel as a (rather: the) 'Jewish' state? More specifically, what would be the ramifications of a Palestinian recognition of Israel as a Jewish state – beyond, that is, the demographic consideration outlined in the previous chapter, which is encapsulated in the notion of a *state of Jews*, as opposed to a *Jewish* state? In other words, what does it mean for Israel to be a Jewish state, beyond its active preservation and preference of a majority of sovereign Jews over a minority of non-Jewish Palestinian-Arabs, who do not share in the state's sovereignty?

On an 'abstract' or 'theoretical' level, we may also ask: Does it make any sense, in the first place, to talk about a state's identity? This, after all, is one critical aspect of the demand that Israel is recognized as a Jewish state – it would mean that the state has a Jewish character, or identity (which, in turn, demands protection). Yet it is not clear at all if and how we can assume that this human construction of power and bureaucracy – the state – would carry that which we usually refer to when we talk about individual and collective identities. This is further complicated by the fact that in and of itself, 'identity,' one of the foundational concepts of the modern social or human sciences, has

---

in *Israel and the 'Jewish State' Discourse* (Jerusalem: The Israel Democracy Institute, 2015), 35.

[5] J. Rudoren, 'Palestinian leader seeks NATO force in future state,' *The New York Times*, February 2, 2014.

not been without controversy. As one critical review of the literature puts it, "Identity' ... tends to mean too much (when understood in a strong sense), too little (when understood in a weak sense), or nothing at all (because of its sheer ambiguity).'[6]

The Israeli case presents us with a rather stark explication of this ambiguity, especially when the concept is applied not to individuals and social groups, but rather to the abstract notion of the state. Political discourse in Israel has been rife with references to the state's identity as Jewish, but there seems to be little, if any, agreement on it, or even clarity as to the actual meaning of this identity.

As the following review of the matter shows, the debate on the issue betrays the fact that Israeli political culture fails to positively and meaningfully understand or construct Israeli politics as *Jewish* politics – beyond, that is, the 'biological' (i.e., racial, 'blood'-centered) makeup of those who rule and conduct this politics. In this regard, contemporary political discourse in Israel proves to be echoing – or rather painfully experiencing – the fundamentally unresolved nature of Zionism's understanding or construction of its very own Jewishness. To put it bluntly, Israelis (and others) cannot easily, if ever, agree on the meaning of Israel's being 'Jewish,' since the Zionist mainstream itself has not been able to clearly understand, or resolve, its own claim to Jewish identity.

A Constitutional-Level 'Purpose Clause'

Regardless of the ambiguity of the very notion of a state's identity, one would be excused if expecting, as dictated by common political practice, that at least some basic features of this 'Jewish identity' of the state would be enshrined in the state's constitution. Yet, Israel does not have a full-fledged constitution. Certain 'basic laws,' the supposed building blocks of a hoped-for future constitution, and especially those laws passed since the early 1990s do explicitly state that their aim is to anchor the State of Israel's *values* as a 'Jewish and democratic state.' (The Israeli Supreme Court has interpreted these basic laws as ushering

---

[6] R. Brubaker and F. Cooper, 'Beyond 'identity,'' *Theory and Society*, 29/1 (2000), 1.

in a 'constitutional revolution'[7] and assigned them the status of a constitution.[8]) But the meaning of this declaratory pronouncement is left – quite probably intentionally so – abstract and ambiguous. What values would be considered Jewish? Jewish histories, traditions, practices, and horizons of meanings (and, ultimately, values) are far too diverse to offer a clear, unequivocal sense of what would be the threshold for being considered either a Jewish or an un-Jewish value. This is further complicated by the rebelling impetus of the Zionist movement itself, which has sought to revitalize what it viewed as a stagnant, diseased even, Jewish 'religious tradition' by reclaiming an allegedly 'more authentic' pre-rabbinic 'national' (as opposed to 'religious') Jewish history.[9] The rebellious project explicitly, knowingly, and defiantly promoted and exalted values that predominant Jewish traditions would take to be misguided, if not outright un-Jewish.[10] Any 'definition,' or understanding of the very (Zionist, modern) meaning of Israel's values as a Jewish state is bound to be a complicated issue, to say the least.

The fact that the very phrasing, 'the values of the State of Israel as a Jewish and democratic state,' is unclear, indeed: 'hazy' ['*amoum*, in the Hebrew original], has been acknowledged by a most influential interpreter of this clause, the former president (chief justice) of the Israeli Supreme Court, Aharon Barak.[11] His take on the meaning of this clause renders it primarily an expression of Zionist ideology:

A Jewish state is a state that expresses the Zionist vision. It is the world of Zionism; it is the vision of the [nation's decedents'] return to their land; it is the vision of Israel as a national homeland of every Jew ... A Jewish state in the Zionist perspective is a state whose primary language is Hebrew, whose culture is Jewish, and whose holidays reflect the national revival of the

[7] A. Barak, 'A constitutional revolution: Israel's basic laws,' *Constitutional Forum*, 4/3 (1993), 83–4.

[8] A. Barak, 'The constitutionalization of the Israeli legal system as a result of the basic laws and its effect on procedural and substantive criminal law,' *Israel Law Review*, 31/1–3 (1997), 3–23.

[9] Y. Zerubavel, *Recovered Roots: Collective Memory and the Making of Israeli National Tradition* (Chicago: University of Chicago Press, 1995).

[10] C. S. Liebman and E. Don-Yehiya, *Civil Religion in Israel: Traditional Judaism and Political Culture in the Jewish State* (Berkeley: University of California Press, 1983); Yadgar, *Sovereign Jews*, ch. 2.

[11] A. Barak, 'The values of the State of Israel as a Jewish and democratic state,' *Baacademia*, 24 (2012), 60.

Jewish People. A Jewish state in the Zionist perspective is a state that redeems [*goelet*] the land for Jewish settlement.[12]

Tellingly, Barak, who is generally viewed as a champion of a liberal, secularist (he seems to prefer the adjective 'enlightened'[13]) worldview, and who has often attracted criticism for his alleged preference of Israel's liberal-democratic values over its Jewish ones, also notes that the values of Israel as a Jewish state must include the 'traditional [*morashtiim*; could also be translated as 'hereditary'] values,' that is (his phrasing), the 'world of halakha,' i.e., 'religious' Jewish law, the meaning of which must be dictated by Judaism's 'inner world.'[14]

Barak himself leaves the task of constructing a comprehensive understanding of the meaning of Israel's values as a Jewish state for the Israeli society as a whole to carry. Yet, as the following discussion will show, the political attempt at explicating the meaning of Israel's 'identity' as a Jewish state (and not 'just' the values derived from this per se) has been an ongoing exemplification of the unresolved nature of Zionism's stance toward its Jewish traditions, or histories.

A Basic Law to Determine the State's Identity

The past couple of decades have witnessed an apparent heightening of the political tension surrounding Israel's 'Jewish identity.' This has culminated in a legislative initiative to formulate a constitutional anchoring of this identity through the passing of a basic law that would enshrine Israel's identity as *the* Jewish nation-state. I would argue that the contentious nature of the debate on the newly passed law, some-times referred to in Israeli Hebrew as 'the nation law' (*ḥoq haleom*), or, more elaborately: 'Basic Law: Israel the Nation-State of the Jewish People,' encapsulates a wider history, namely the (largely failing) attempt to tackle the meaning of Israel's 'Jewish identity' beyond the concern for the demographic balance between Jews and non-Jews. A careful consideration of the law will allow us, then, a clearer under-standing of both the 'taken-for-granted' infrastructure of meaning dominating Israeli – or more accurately: contemporary Zionist –

---

[12] Barak, 'The values of the State of Israel as a Jewish and democratic state,' 61.

[13] A. Barak, *The Judge in a Democracy* (Princeton, NJ: Princeton University Press, 2006), 40, 60, 102, 133.

[14] Barak, 'The values of the State of Israel as a Jewish and democratic state,' 61.

construction of the notion of *Jewish* politics, and of what may be seen as its somewhat surprising shortcomings.

The law, which has cleared the final legislative hurdles in late July 2018, started off almost a decade earlier as an extra-legislative initiative, and tended at first to embarrass the political leadership more than to appeal to it. It has since gradually become a cause célèbre of mainstream Israeli politics. More importantly, it has put Israel's (Jewish) identity crisis into sharp relief. After more than sixty turbulent years of statehood, Israelis were presented with the most politically-fundamental question: what does the state's identity as Jewish amount to? What does it mean for Israel to be 'the *Jewish* state'?

The debate over the bill has offered the Israeli political and public spheres a unique, rather unprecedented clear view of the essential tensions at the very roots of the Israeli polity; specifically, as I have alluded to earlier, it highlighted the tension between Zionism's rebellion against what it has viewed as Jewish 'religion' and its (Zionism's) foundational claim to a Jewish history and identity that are, by the Zionist own account, saturated with the same 'religious' elements. More critically, it has exposed the Zionist inability to construct a full-fledged independent-from-religion (i.e., in Zionism's own terminology, 'national' and 'secular') sense of Jewish identity. Such an ideological construction could (or even should) have been the source that would clearly identify Israel's values as a 'Jewish state,' hence, ultimately, the Israeli meaning of Jewish politics. Instead, the law directs much of its impetus toward a *negative* construction of Jewish-Zionist nationhood, by way of refuting the Palestinian claims to nationhood, and attempting to buttress the preference of Jews over non-Jews in Israel.

A quick review of the history of the law and its basic tenets is of necessity here, for it can at least offer a context for understanding the diverging assessments of the law, which I shall discuss below. The bill, which was first submitted to the Israeli parliament for consideration in August 2011,[15] was originally initiated by an extra-parliamentary

---

[15] A. Dichter et al., 'Basic Law proposal: Israel is the nation-state of the Jewish people,' The Knesset, Pub. L. No. P/18/3541 (2011). English translations of various formulations of the law can be found at: S. Rabinovitch, 'Defining Israel, Part II: Jewish and democratic according to the law,' *The Marginalia Review of Books* [forum], February 2, 2015. Simon Rabinovitch has been curating and editing a forum on the law, in which he offers both updated versions of the

organization, The Institute for Zionist Strategies (IZS) a couple of years earlier.[16] We shall return to this original initiative later on for it offers some clearer answers to the questions surrounding the legislative saga that later ensued. The bill was presented before the Israeli parliament by MK (Member of the Knesset) Avi Dichter, a former head of the Israeli internal security service (Shin Bet), who was at the time a member of the centrist (and, it may be relevant to note, 'secular,' Zionist) party, Kadima.[17] Dichter's original initiative was endorsed by MK Zeev Elkin of the Likud party, and the two garnered the supporting signatures of some 40 other MKs.

Critics were quick to denounce the bill. Members of Dichter's own party, including the head of Kadima at the time, Tzippi Livni, poured 'scathing criticism'[18] on the initiative, and demanded that Dichter shelve the bill. Livni eventually imposed a party discipline against the bill, which resulted in the effective freezing of the original proposal in the 18th Knesset.[19] Yet the initiative was far from dead; it has reemerged as a cornerstone of certain coalition agreements on which Israel's 33rd ruling government was put into power in March 2013 by the newly elected 19th Knesset. Livni, who held the position of justice minister in this short-lived government, appointed a prominent law professor to counsel the government on the matter, an endeavor which culminated in a document negating of the very need to constitutionally anchor the 'vision of the State.'[20]

relevant documents and an ongoing discussion on the bill: https://marginalia.lareviewofbooks.org/?p=6705

[16] D. Helman and A. Arbel, 'doresh ʿiggun,' Institute of Zionist Strategies, July 2009. The IZS also published an English abstract of the document: D. Helman and A. Arbel, 'Jewish National Home,' Institute of Zionist Strategies, December 30, 2015. I shall refer to the Hebrew original here, consulting with the official English translation where possible.

[17] Dichter later left Kadima for the Likud party. At the time of the law's approval by the Knesset he was holding the influential chairmanship of the parliamentary Standing Committee on Foreign and Security Affairs.

[18] S. Avineri, 'New 'Jewish identity' bill will cause chaos in Israel,' *Haaretz*, November 21, 2011.

[19] J. Lis, 'Dichter replaces 'Jewish identity' bill with equally contentious draft law,' *Haaretz*, November 15, 2011.

[20] R. Gavison, *A Constitutional Anchoring of the State's Vision: Recommendations to the Justice Minister* (Jerusalem: Metzilah, 2014); R. Gavison, 'Defining Israel, Part I: Constitutional anchoring of Israel's vision: recommendations submitted to the minister of justice – with an introduction by Simon Rabinovitch,' *Marginalia Review of Books* [forum], December 30, 2014.

The original proposal has gone through several further reformulations, offering varying degrees of 'softening' and 'hardening' of the more controversial elements of the original proposal. The bill reemerged once again after the 2015 elections to the 20th Knesset. Becoming something of a competitive arena between the Likud and the religious-Zionist party (then labeled Habayit Hayehudi), it has been promoted by all central figures of the Israeli government, from the prime minister, through his justice and education ministers, and down to the backbenchers of their parties, as a fundamental issue of unprecedented importance to the very vitality of contemporary Israeli nationhood. Yet the bill has encountered formidable obstacles. It was only after much deliberations and heated debates that the law – celebrated by the Israeli prime minister as the affirmation of Herzl's vision (some 122 years later!)[21] – was finally approved by the Knesset.[22] Moreover, this saga is clearly far from over, as the law is bound to be reviewed by the judiciary sooner or later.

Obvious and Radical

To understand the wider history and political meaning of the law we may first ask, as did practically all commentators (both those supporting the bill and its opponents), what is the (true) purpose of the law? Tellingly, the various answers, and even the explanation offered in the law itself, all point at the same time to two seemingly contradictory claims: First, that the law's main motivation is rather 'obvious,' if not, according to its critics, outright redundant, since what it proclaims and seeks to constitutionally enshrine is, by all measures, a foundational notion of the (Zionist) politics of the State of Israel. It is, in other words, a law that simply states the obvious. And, second, that the bill's passing into the law of the land (after some 70 years of statehood based on the premised Jewishness of the state) marks a historical watershed, a redeeming ideational liberation of sorts, according to the law's supporters, or an ominous breaking point in Israel's history as a

---

[21] A. Bender, 'berov shel 62 tomkhim mol 55 mitnagdim: ḥoq hlaeom ushar baknesset,' *Maariv*, July 19, 2018.

[22] The final version of the bill: A. Dichter, A. Neguise, T. Ploskov, M. Yogev, Y. Kish, N. Boker, B. Smotich, O. Levy-Abekasis, R. Ilatov, D. Amsalem, and D. Bitan, Basic Law proposal: Israel – the nation-state of the Jewish people, The Knesset, Pub. L. No. P/20/1989 (2018).

democracy, according to its detractors. The Basic Law is, in other words, both obvious and radical.

Judged by its contents alone, isolated from its political and historical context and read naïvely (ignoring, that is, some critical implicit ramifications of its tenets), the bill may indeed seem largely redundant, making the controversy surrounding it perplexing. The bill states what Israeli political culture has historically taken to be the political-Zionist taken for granted, the very foundation of Jewish nationhood in the State of Israel itself. Thus, its opening paragraph, echoing the state's Declaration of Independence,[23] declares: 'The State of Israel is the national home of the Jewish people, in which it realizes its aspiration to self-determination in accordance with its cultural and historical heritage.'

Furthermore, other parts of the law are merely repetitions of already established laws, such as those designating Israel's official symbols (including the anthem, flag, and emblem, as well as the civil/national holidays), setting the Hebrew calendar as the state's official calendar, determining Saturday and the Jewish holy days as official days of rest, and enshrining the Jewish 'right to return,' i.e., the right granted exclusively to Jewish immigrants to acquire Israeli citizenship almost automatically and immediately on arrival in the Jewish state. Other parts still are so vague as to render them lacking any coherent legal implications (such is, for example, a clause stating that 'the state shall strive [*tishqod*] to secure the safety of members of the Jewish people and its citizens who are in distress and captivity due to their Judaism or citizenship').[24] Other clauses, stating Israel's duty to actively preserve and cultivate Jewish tradition, amorphous as they are, shed a unique light (to say the least) on Zionism's purported secularism, but would seem hardly novel to anyone even only shallowly familiar with Israeli political culture.

Yet, as many critics were quick to note, such a naïve reading of the law misses much of its meaning and its main political implications. Two issues emerged almost instantaneously as the flash points

---

[23] I am using here the commonly used name of the document, which is a misnomer. The document's actual name is the 'Declaration of the Establishment of the State of Israel.'

[24] The original version of the bill suggests a different metaphor, declaring that 'The state shall extend a hand to members of the Jewish people in trouble or in captivity due to the fact of their Jewishness.'

attracting most commentators' attention: The implied preference of
Israel's Jewish identity over the polity's (liberal-)democratic principles
when the two are understood to be in conflict, and the assertion
of Jewish nationhood through the blunt negation of Palestinian
nationhood.

By way of example, consider these two similar yet divergent appre-
ciations of the bill. The first is by Moshe Arens, a former leader of the
Likud party, who also oversaw, among many senior political positions
he has held, the Ministry of Defence. For Arens, the bill, which has
been championed by the head of the Likud party, Prime Minister
Netanyahu, as constituting 'an overwhelming response to all those
who deny the deep connection between the Jewish people and its land,'
is both 'useless and harmful.'[25] Useless, since, as suggested above, it
only states the obvious:

Ignore the self-righteous explanations that it is no more than a statement . . .
Who needs this statement, anyway? . . . There is no need for a declaration to
affirm that in Israel the Jewish people are exercising their right to national
self-determination, and that Israel remains committed to providing a haven
for all Jews seeking such a haven. All of Israel's citizens, Jews and Arabs, as
well as the rest of the world, are fully aware of that. Any 'statement' on this
matter is superfluous.

And the bill is harmful, since it is inattentive to the sensitivities of
'our fellow Arab citizens,' further stressing their degraded status.[26]
Ultimately, for Arens, the bill 'alienates Israel's Arab citizens for
nothing.'[27]

In a similar fashion, another commentator, who is commonly affiliated with the Zionist Left, deemed the bill – in both its original and
various redrafted, 'softened' versions, in a span of almost seven years
of debate over the bill – as not only 'unnecessary,'[28] but also 'fundamentally contradictory to the principles of Zionism and to the achievements of the State of Israel as the nation-state of the Jewish people.'[29]
He deems the bill as dangerously harmful: It 'deepens tensions between

[25] M. Arens, 'Israel's Jewish nation-state bill is not just useless – it's harmful,'
Haaretz, May 14, 2017.
[26] Arens, 'Israel's Jewish nation-state bill is not just useless – it's harmful.'
[27] M. Arens, 'The Jewish nation-state bill alienates Israel's Arab citizens for
nothing,' *Haaretz*, July 16, 2018.
[28] Avineri, 'New 'Jewish identity' bill will cause chaos in Israel.'
[29] S. Avineri, 'Herzl veḥoq haleom,' *Haaretz*, September 19, 2017.

Jews and Arabs, as well as among various parts of the Jewish population,'[30] and 'impedes on Israel's ability to uphold a democratic regime
in difficult domestic and international conditions.'[31] The bottom line is
clear: the bill is 'flawed [*pasul*] not only normatively and democratic-
ally, but also Zionistically. Its very existence will undermine the sensitive social contract on which the State of Israel is established, it will
cause severe international damage to Israel, will play into the hands of
the most extreme elements in the Arab public,' and will make life much
harder for the more moderate elements among 'Israel's Arab citizens
who seek additional achievements in their just and uneasy struggle for
integration and equality.'[32] As such, the bill would 'give Israel a bad
name'; its 'only remedy' is to shelve it completely.[33]

This 'deepening of tensions' between 'Jews and Arabs,' the 'absence
of sensitivity'[34] to the latter (encapsulated, for Arens, in the bill's
demotion of Arabic from the status of an official language; see below)
was read by some liberal-Zionist opponents of the bill as an outright
racist drive that motivates, so they argued, the bill in its entirety.
Haaretz' editorial (an unsigned opinion piece that allegedly proclaims
the stance of the paper as a whole) had only the harshest of words for
denouncing the original bill, calling it 'an apartheid law' that would
label Israel as a 'Jewish and racist state' (as opposed, that is, to the
common phrasing: 'a Jewish and democratic state'). This stance, not
unrepresentative of the liberal-Zionist critique of the law, is so harsh
(in the current atmosphere, many of the terms it uses would be considered out of bounds if used by critics of Israel outside of the state)
that it merits a longer-than-usual quotation:

The exclusion of the Arab minority in Israel has until now lacked a vital basis
to its institutionalization. There is no law discriminating against Arabs,
limiting where they may settle, negating their language as an official language
or determining that they are challenging the state's Jewish identity.

Israel has been forced until now to rely on tricks, excuses, and winks to
prevent Arabs from working in so-called sensitive places of work, delay
building plans in their communities, limit how many of them reside in Jewish
communities, and not enforce the use of Arabic in official correspondences.

---

[30] Avineri, 'New 'Jewish identity' bill will cause chaos in Israel.'
[31] Avineri, 'Herzl veḥoq haleom.'   [32] Avineri, 'Herzl veḥoq haleom.'
[33] Avineri, 'New 'Jewish identity' bill will cause chaos in Israel.'
[34] Arens, 'Israel's Jewish nation-state bill is not just useless – it's harmful.'

Only in a few instances did the High Court of Justice intervene and the government had no choice but to obey the ruling.

Coalition chairman MK Yariv Levin decided to put an end to this murky reality and provide the unofficial apartheid policy a legal basis. Levin is proposing the Basic Law: State of the Nation, which is nothing short of an apartheid law. If it will be accepted, Israel will be able to proudly hold the title of a Jewish and racist state, a unique political creation, which will certainly astonish the family of nations.

Levin proposes, among other things, mandatory construction of Jewish communities, while building Arab communities will need authorization; abolishing Arabic as an official language and mandating the courts to give precedence in their rulings to Jewish identity in questions of democratic values and equal rights. That is to say, to give precedence to 'Jewish' over 'democratic' in defining the state.

Arabs will enjoy at best the status of a tolerated minority, with the option of turning them into a non-tolerated minority down the line, one which needs to be rid of because its presence spoils the state's Jewish purity.

[...]

Instead of purging elements of racism from within its ranks, it turns out that the present coalition is also promoting apartheid in the guise of 'new politics.'[35]

In this liberal-Zionist reading, then, the main motive behind the law is an attempt – which the critic clearly sees as racist – to firmly establish the collective inferiority of Palestinian-Arabs in the nation-state of Jews. In this reading, the internationally accepted rightful affirmation of the Jewish majority's determination of Israel's 'Jewish identity' masks a more sinister, less acceptable practice of 'apartheid,' in which this affirmation is built primarily on the negation of the national 'Other.'

It must be noted that such critical readings of the bill, according to which it contradicts the foundational, democratic principle of the Israeli polity also came from the ranks of the Israeli Right. One such vocal critic, for example, has been Binyamin Begin of the Likud party, who decried a more advanced version of the bill (then promoted by the government headed by his own party) as failing to assert the equal

---

[35] *Haaretz* Editorial, 'Basic Law: Apartheid in Israel,' *Haaretz*, May 30, 2013.

rights of minorities, arguing that 'There cannot be any conflict between nation-state, nationalism and equal rights.'[36]

Given the centrality of the alleged duality of Israel's self-image as 'Jewish and democratic,' the law, in its exposing of potential fundamental contradictions between the two organs of this duality, was also presented by critics as undermining the very Zionist vision, if not the Zionist project per se. No other than the Israeli president (a mostly ceremonial post, but one that supposedly symbolizes the state itself, surpassing ideological, partisan politics), has rhetorically asked:

Does promoting this law not in fact question the success of the Zionist enterprise in which we are fortunate to live? … Does this proposal, not in fact encourage us to seek contradiction between the Jewish and democratic characters of the state? Does this bill not in fact play into the hands of those who seek to slander us? Into the very hands of those who wish to show that even within us there are those who see contradiction between our being a free people in our land, and the freedoms of the non-Jewish communities amongst us?[37]

The Bill and the Palestinian Challenge to Zionist Nationalism

Regardless of these critics' variations in tone, it would be hard for anyone who reads the text of the law to deny that it does indeed affirmatively assert a view in which the determination of Jewish nationhood is established by the negation of Palestinian nationhood. It reasserts the various expressions of Jewish-Zionist nationhood – or, to use the nationalist discourse itself, the 'rights' of the Jewish nation – by explicitly determining the exclusivity of these rights to Jews; Palestinians, the law clarifies, cannot claim similar rights.

---

[36] M. Newman, 'Begin breaks ranks to oppose Jewish nation-state bill,' *The Times of Israel*, July 26, 2017.

[37] A. Magnezi, 'Rivlin: What is the point of the 'Nationality Law'?' *Ynetnews*, November 25, 2014. In what must be seen as a last-ditch effort to curtail the bill, the Israeli president also sent a letter to the parliamentary committee considering the bill, in which he warns that the bill may 'hurt the Jewish people, Jews throughout the world, and the State of Israel, and can even be used as a weapon in our enemies' hands.' He was specifically worried about a clause of the bill that would allow the designation of certain settlements as open to Jews only.
A. Bender, 'Rivlin shiger mikhtav ḥarig laknesset: ḥoq haleom 'alul lifgo'a ba'am hayehudi,' *Maariv*, July 10, 2018.

The centrality of the Palestinian challenge to political-Zionist nationhood is most clearly explicated in the aforementioned predecessor to the original 2011 legislative proposal, a white paper of sorts that was published by the Institute for Zionist Strategies in July 2009.[38] Claiming to be 'promot[ing] and strengthen[ing] Israel's Jewish character and its democratic nature,' the IZS seeks to be true to its mandate by publishing works that 'help set just and Zionist based legal policies,' the culmination of which, so it seems (as noted most prominently in the IZS's website), is the bill discussed here.[39] A study of this first draft of the bill can be illuminating, for this text as a whole foregoes much of the nuanced and more carefully crafted language that came to characterize the bill in its later stages.

The IZS's proposal, too, presents itself as somewhat of a paradox – a long overdue attempt at legislating what is otherwise obvious, and should be taken for granted. Using interchangeably the term 'a national home' and 'a Jewish state' (foregoing, that is, a non-nation-statist reading of the meaning of the former term), the authors explain the newly formed need to legislate what used to be so obvious as to be considered natural:

In the past, the state's status as national home for the Jewish people was never questioned: it was obvious to the public and to the authorities, including the judiciary. Practical manifestation of the Jewish status of the state can be seen in the very name of the state and from a multitude of laws which are obvious [*muvanim me'eleihem*].[40]

The list of these obvious manifestations includes not only the symbolic aspects (the flag, anthem, state emblem, civil holidays, etc.) but also state policies such as the initiation of programs and resource allocation 'for the welfare of the Jewish people' at large. These include 'promoting *aliya* to the Land of Israel, the outposts program ('the Judaization of the Galilee')[41] to bring Jews to the Galilee, assisting in

---

[38] Helman and Arbel, 'doresh 'iggun.'
[39] The Institute for Zionist Strategies, 'About us', ISS.org.il/about-3/.
[40] Helman and Arbel, 'doresh 'iggun,' 5.
[41] *Yehud ha-galil* in Hebrew, the more commonly used name of a governmental settlement program intended to increase the Jewish population in the Galilee, a region with a Palestinian majority. See: O. Yiftachel and D. Rumley, 'On the impact of Israel's Judaization policy in the Galilee,' *Political Geography Quarterly*, 10/3 (1991), 286–96; G. Falah, 'Israeli 'Judaization' policy in Galilee,' *Journal of Palestine Studies*, 20/4 (1991), 69–85.

the *'aliya* of Ethiopian Jewry, supporting Jewish Zionist education, commemorating the Holocaust, and others.'[42]

This, indeed, is a mainstream Zionist view of the meaning of Jewish politics. Yet, so the authors narrate, something has gone terribly wrong in Israel's recent political history, and what used to be taken for granted is no longer the case. This new situation demands, they argue, a rewriting of the Zionist view that would also entail a more robust 'anchoring' of the Zionist vision of Jewish politics:

In recent years, a back-peddling trend has developed, which weakens the position of the State of Israel as the national home of the Jewish People. The State of Israel, which was established as a Jewish state with a democratic form of government, would be turned into a liberal-democratic country with Jewish characteristics only to the extent that these characteristics do not contradict the principle of absolute equality among all groups.[43]

There is indeed an urgent sense of a looming danger that is explicitly stated as the primary motivation behind the law. This is also clearly evident in the actual bill presented to the Knesset by Dichter and Levin, where 'the necessity of the law' is stated as the ultimate answer to this looming danger: The need for this law, they explain, 'assumes greater validity at a time when there are those who seek to abolish the right of the Jewish people to a national home in its land and the recognition of the State of Israel as the nation-state of the Jewish people.'[44]

Dichter's bill does not explicate who 'those who seek to abolish' the political-national rights of the Jews are; Yet, it is not too hard to see that this threatening trend, which the IZS's document labels 'back peddling' (*hipoukh yoṣrot* in the original Hebrew; could also be translated as 'perversion') has primarily to do with the status of Israel's non-Jewish Palestinian-Arab citizens. If left unopposed, the authors warn, this trend would lead to the transformation of Israel into what is sometimes called 'a state of all of its citizens' (as opposed to 'a state of Jews'): a liberal-democratic state, where all citizens, regardless of their national(ist) belonging and aspirations, enjoy equal status not only in face of the law, but also in the allocation of material and symbolic resources. For the IZS authors, this amounts to an outright

---

[42] Helman and Arbel, 'doresh 'iggun,' 5.
[43] Helman and Arbel, 'doresh 'iggun,' 6.
[44] Dichter et al., 'Basic Law proposal: Israel is the nation-state of the Jewish people.'

negation of the Zionist vision of a Jewish state: 'This radical liberal interpretation,' the 'elevation of equality by the back-peddlers to an exclusive supreme value in Israel ... distorts the intention of the Founding Fathers of the State of Israel.' It 'denies the Jewish people its right to self-determination' and 'leads to the warped conclusion that all laws contributing to the Jewish character of Israel are undemocratic (except for now, the Law of Return) and must therefore be annulled.'[45]

As Dichter himself has triumphantly put it immediately after the Knesset finally approved it, the Basic Law is aimed at 'preventing even a shadow of a thought, not to mention an attempt, to transform Israel into a state of all of its citizens.'[46] This point was further reiterated during the (first) 2019 election campaign, as Prime Minister Benjamin Netanyahu reacted to comments made by an Israeli actress on social media, regarding the status of Palestinian-Arab citizens of Israel. Netanyahu had 'an important correction' to make: 'Israel is not a state of all its citizens,' he proclaimed.[47] While explicating that all citizens, 'including Arabs,'[48] have equal rights, and celebrating the fact that his government increased public spending on Arab municipalities, Netanyahu referred to the nation-state law in order to set the record straight: 'According to the nation-state law that we passed, Israel is the nation-state of the Jewish people – and its alone.'[49] The prime minster later further reiterated this point by stating that Israel is 'a 'Jewish, democratic state' with equal rights, but 'the nation-state not of all its citizens but only of the Jewish people.''[50] Importantly, this exchange took place in the context of a debate over the legitimacy of a government based on a coalition with parties representing the Palestinian-Arab minority. Netanyahu's reiteration of the implications of the nation-state law aimed to delegitimize such a coalition. As *Haaretz'* Editorial angrily clarified:

---

[45] Helman and Arbel, 'doresh 'iggun,' 6.

[46] MK Avi Dichter quoted in Bender, 'berov shel 62 tomkhim mol 55 mitnagdim: ḥoq hlaeom ushar baknesset.'

[47] *Haaretz*, ''Israel is the nation-state of Jews alone': Netanyahu responds to TV star who said Arabs are equal citizens,' *Haaretz*, March 11, 2019.

[48] Agence France Presse, 'Benjamin Netanyahu says Israel is 'not a state of all its citizens,'' March 10, 2019.

[49] *Haaretz*, 'Israel is the nation-state of Jews alone.'

[50] Agence France Presse, 'Benjamin Netanyahu says Israel is 'not a state of all its citizens.''

The ugly, naked truth has been exposed: The nation-state law was meant to make it clear to Israeli Arabs that the state views them as second-class citizens. Admittedly, they have 'equal rights just like the rest of us,' but they should know that the state doesn't belong to 'all its citizens.' Moreover, since Israel isn't a state of all its citizens, any government that includes the Arab parties 'would undermine the security of the state and its citizens.'[51]

In this framework of nationalist political philosophy, the 'Jewish character' of the nation-state must amount to an explicit preference of people who are Jews over those who are not, at least in collective terms. Granted, 'The State of Israel, as a democratic state, is required to endow its citizens with their full civil rights'; yet, 'the right to equality ... is not an exclusive supreme right,' nor is it absolute. There are 'decisive reasons' for which it is permissible, required even, 'to limit the right to equality, like any other right.' Hence, 'the State of Israel, as the State of Jews, can endow all Jews the world over with privileges and benefits [*zekhuyot yeter ve-haṭavot*]' to which non-Jews have no rightful claim.[52]

In any event, the distortion of the 'original intent' of the Zionist Founding Fathers (i.e., the insistence that privileging of Jews over non-Jews as the application of the nation-statist logic amounts to undemocratic discrimination) manifests, at least according to the English extract of this document, 'Jewish self-denial.'[53]

The history narrated by the IZS's draft bill marks another document as the culmination of this 'trend of distortion' of the founding Zionist vision for the State of Israel: a document drafted by The National Committee for the Heads of the Arab Local Authorities in Israel, in which leaders of the Palestinian-Arab citizens of Israel present their vision for the state.[54] Although at the time of writing it is hard to see if this Vision document had any substantial impact on Israel's policies (unlike the IZS draft bill, it has not materialized into a clear initiative,

---

[51] *Haaretz* Editorial, 'A state for some of its citizens,' *Haaretz*, March 11, 2019.
[52] Helman and Arbel, 'doresh 'iggun,' 9.
[53] Helman and Arbel, 'Jewish national home.'
[54] The National Committee for the Heads of the Arab Local Authorities in Israel, 'The future vision for the Palestinian Arabs in Israel' (2006). An English version of this document is available at https://goo.gl/DBqzW9. This translation tends to be somewhat cumbersome. I will use the Hebrew version as the primary source, consulting with the English translation.

legislative or otherwise), it merits careful attention.[55] For, as the IZS's draft bill does indeed make very clear, it is exactly the Palestinian-Arab critique, or challenge of the hitherto taken-for-granted Zionist-Israeli construction of the meaning of Israel's being a 'Jewish state' that has been motivating what eventually became various, sometime competing initiatives to explicate this understanding in a constitutional or at least legislative manner. This Vision document, which was presented to the Israeli Parliament in 2006, amounts, according to the IZS's draft bill, to a negation of the very foundations of the state. Clearly, for the IZS's authors, this Vision document is proof that the Jewish character of the State of Israel is in serious danger; and what eventually became the 'nation-state bill' is the ultimate answer to this danger.

The Vision document presents a brisk narration of a Palestinian, anti-colonialist view of the history of the State of Israel:

Israel is an outcome of a colonialist act initiated by the Jewish-Zionist elites in Europe and the West. It was established with the help of colonialist countries and was strengthened by the increase of Jewish immigration to Palestine in light of the outcome of World War II and the Holocaust. After its creation in 1948 Israel has continued to implement policies derived from its self-perception as a representative of the West in the Middle East and continued conflicting with its neighbors. Israel also continued executing internal colonial policies against its Palestinian-Arab citizens.[56]

The document also clearly explicates the reality of discrimination that is encapsulated in Israel's 'Jewish character,' noting that 'Defining the Israeli state as a Jewish state and exploiting democracy in the service of its Jewishness excludes us [i.e., Palestinian-Arab citizens of Israel], and creates tension between us and the nature and essence of the state.'[57] This amounts to a negation of basic democratic principles, suggesting that Israel cannot be labeled or defined as a democracy. Instead, claims the Vision document, Israel should be seen as an

---

[55] It should be stressed that I do not intend to offer a comprehensive review of the Palestinian-Arab stance on Israel's 'Jewish identity.' My aim here is solely to explicate the perceived looming 'threat' that is the motivation for the nation-state bill. For a review of the Palestinian-Arab stances on the matter, see: Rudnitzky, *The Arab Minority in Israel and the 'Jewish State' Discourse.*

[56] The National Committee for the Heads of the Arab Local Authorities in Israel, 'Future Vision,' 9.

[57] The National Committee for the Heads of the Arab Local Authorities in Israel, 'Future vision,' 5.

'ethnocracy' in which the Palestinian-Arab minority is endowed with only 'partial equality.' This minority cannot fully partake in politics, society, economy, the media, and so on, leaving it forever in a position of inferiority. This is compounded by 'a permanent and continued policy of control and censorship which guarantees the hegemony of the [Jewish] majority and marginalizing the minority.'[58]

The remedy suggested by the Vision statement is a "Consensual Democracy' which is a regime that supports the existence of two national groups, one Palestinian, the other Jewish, and guarantees real sharing of rule, resources, and decision making between the two national groups.'[59] It is interesting to note that the suggested 'power sharing'[60] scheme does not attempt to challenge the prevalent Zionist understanding of Jewish politics; the parties sharing the power are Palestinian-Arabs and Jews, suggesting that the authors of the document accept the basic Zionist premise that Judaism or Jewishness is essentially a matter of nationality. This, indeed, is only a marginal aspect of the Vision document, but it is informative in suggesting the prevalence of the nationalist discourse.

The Nation-State Law and the Meaning of Jewish Politics

How, then, does the 'nation-state' law reassert Israel's 'Jewish character'? What does it offer by way of reaffirming the Jews' right to a national home? Interestingly, the law's text is far from rendering this crucial matter clear. The law's attempt – or failure – to address the matter satisfactorily has indeed attracted much of the critics' ire. As discussed earlier, these critics see the law's reassertion of Israel's 'Jewish character' as both redundant and radical.

Some of the more controversial aspects of the law have to do with what has been widely interpreted as its redrawing of the balance between Israel's Jewish character (which should, according to the law's supporters, amount to a preference of Jews over non-Jews) and its commitment to democracy (which would delegitimize this preference).

---

[58] The National Committee for the Heads of the Arab Local Authorities in Israel, 'Future vision,' 9.

[59] The National Committee for the Heads of the Arab Local Authorities in Israel, 'Future vision,' 10.

[60] The National Committee for the Heads of the Arab Local Authorities in Israel, 'Future vision,' 14.

It aims to redraw, or reassert the 'original' Zionist framework, where nationalist considerations overcome democratic, universal principles of individual rights. As Israel's justice minister, Ayelet Shaked, put it in 2017, the law, like other legislative policies promoted by the government, asserts that 'Zionism should not continue . . . to bow down to the system of individual rights interpreted in a universal way that divorces them from the history of the Knesset and the history of legislation.'[61] As the justice minister's comments made clear, this redrawing of the balance, in which the supremacy of Zionist ideals is preserved, had to do primarily with 'demography' (i.e., the proactive preservation of a Jewish majority).[62]

Thus, while the purpose clauses of previously legislated basic laws assert a commitment to preserve Israel's character and values as a 'Jewish and Democratic' state, the nation-state law tends to establish a clear hierarchy: Jewish first, democratic second, if at all, as the final version of the bill approved by the Knesset drops all references to Israel's democratic regime. Put simply, the law aims to give a legal, constitutional green light for the (undemocratic) preference of one group (Jews) over another (Palestinian-Arabs) – or, to reverse the point of view, the discrimination against the latter in the name of preserving the 'national rights' of the former.

The first clause of the law[63] determines this by stating three 'basic principles': First, it identifies the Land of Israel as 'the historical birthplace of the Jewish people,' and the locus of the State of Israel. Second, echoing Israel's Declaration of Independence, it states that 'The State of Israel is the nation-state of the Jewish people, in which it realizes its natural, cultural, religious and historical right to self-determination.' And third, it determines that 'the right to exercise national self-determination in the State of Israel is uniquely that of the Jewish people.' Meaning, that Palestinian-Arabs cannot claim a similar national self-determination.

---

[61] R. Hovel, 'Justice minister slams Israel's top court, says it disregards Zionism and upholding Jewish majority,' *Haaretz*, August 29, 2017.

[62] As reported: '[Shaked] added that the [Supreme] court's rulings do not consider the matter of demography and the Jewish majority 'as values that should be taken into consideration.'' Hovel, 'Justice minister slams Israel's top court, says it disregards Zionism and upholding Jewish majority.'

[63] As I noted earlier, the bill has gone through several rewritings; I will refer here to both the original version, which opened the debate, and the final one, which was approved by the Knesset in July 2018.

It is telling that the original bill attempts to negotiate these basic principles (which it titles as 'A Jewish State' – *medina yehudit*) with Israel's commitment to democracy. It does so by charting a clear hierarchy: It first determines that the provisions of any other legislation shall be interpreted in light of what is determined in the 'Jewish State' clause. Meaning, that when Israel's 'character' as a Jewish state clashes with other principles, the former must gain precedence. Only after having established this does the draft bill's second clause, titled 'A Democratic State' (*medina democraṭit*), laconically states that 'The State of Israel has a democratic regime.' Clearly, as set by the first paragraph, the democratic principles of this regime are bound to the state's 'Jewish character.' Crucially, during the ensuing debate on the bill this clause was nevertheless seen as detrimental to the bill's declared aims, and the clause was dropped altogether. The Basic Law passed by the Knesset does not mention democracy at all.

Probably the most controversial clause of the law, derived directly from this newly charted hierarchy (Jewish first, democratic, if at all, second), has to do with the segregation of Jews from non-Jews in Israel, and the preference of the former over the latter. One paragraph in the original draft aims directly at legalizing a policy of segregation (of Jews and Palestinian-Arabs), namely the designation of certain settlements as reserved for Jews only, and the preference of Jews in the allocation of lands held by the state. This is a policy which had been practiced for years, but was ruled by the Supreme Court in 2000 to be illegal.[64] (Interestingly, the court's reasoning for prohibiting the establishment of settlements designated for Jews only has been that this practice contradicts the value of equality, to which the state is bound by its *Jewish* character.[65]) Under the headline of 'The Right to Heritage Preservation,' the clause states that 'The state may allow a community that includes followers of a single religion or members of a single nation to establish a separate communal settlement.' As mentioned before, this clause, which explicitly aims to subvert the Supreme Court's ruling, has attracted much of the critics' ire. It was ultimately, after much heated debate, rephrased to state (in the language of the bill

---

[64] *Aadel Ka'adan* v. *Israel Lands Administration*, HCJ 6698/95 (2000).

[65] G. Barzilai, 'Fantasies of liberalism and liberal jurisprudence: State law, politics, and the Israeli Arab-Palestinian community,' *Israel Law Review*, 34/3 (2000), 425–51; R. Gavison, 'Zionism in Israel: After the Ka'adan case,' *Law and Government*, 6 (2001), 25–51.

approved by the Knesset as law, under the title 'Jewish Settlement') what must be read as a Zionist taken-for-granted fact: 'The state sees the development of Jewish settlement as a national value, and shall act to encourage, promote, and strengthen it.'

In addition to territory, the same motivation is applied to language (thus covering two basic tenets of nationalist ideology that are only precariously tied to Judaism): A clause titled 'Language,' positively asserts that 'Hebrew is the official state language' and that 'The Arabic language has a special status,' leaving the details of this designation to future regulations. Put negatively, this amounts to the national demotion or exclusion of Arabic. While Israel had not previously passed a 'native' law specifying the state's official languages (the state has carried over the British mandatory law that identifies three official languages: English, Arabic, and Hebrew), Arabic has historically been put in a precarious position aptly described as 'official yet unrecognized.' Meaning that, while it did have the status as an official language, 'due to various considerations and procedures this status [did] not receive a wide-ranging articulation in the Israeli public sphere.'[66]

The law redraws a legal hierarchy in which Hebrew alone is an official language. This undermining-in-practice of Arabic – the language of not only the Palestinian-Arabs but also of a very large constituency of Jews from Arab-speaking countries; a language in which many of the foundational texts of the Jewish world were written[67] – is part of a continuing trend in which Arabic has come to be

---

[66] Y. Mendel, D. Yitzhaki, and M. Pinto, 'Official but not recognized: The precarious status of the Arabic language in Israel and the need to redress this,' *Giluy Da'at*, 10 (2016), 17–45; see also: Y. Mendel, *The Creation of Israeli Arabic: Security and Politics in Arabic Studies in Israel* (Basingstoke, UK: Palgrave Macmillan, 2014).

[67] One of the first appeals to the court against the basic law states that the law's demotion of Arabic renders it 'an anti-Jewish law, that seeks to give the history of the Jewish people a free-from-Arabness character. The degrading of the Arabic language ... emerges out of a creation of a wall separating the Jewish People from the Arab language and culture, in a manner that distorts reality and excludes the rabbinical, popular and contemporary Arab-Jewish culture and history of Jews who originate in Arab and Islamic countries.' 'Petition to the High Court of Justice: *S. Michael and Others* v. *The Knesset*,' (2019). By the time of publication of this book, the petition has yet to be considered (and given a cataloguing number for referencing purposes) by the court. The full text of the petition is available at: t.ly/rM9x9. For a detailed news report of the petitioning

seen 'in parts of the Jewish sector and the political establishment' as the enemy's language, hence 'as threatening the status of the State of Israel in general and of Hebrew in particular.'[68]

Other clauses in the law simply restate elements of already established laws in an obvious attempt to encourage a reading of these as having to do with Israel's 'Jewish identity.' Thus, for example, a paragraph titled 'The State's Symbols' determines once again (this has already been done by previous laws) the national anthem, flag, and emblem. Indeed, these symbols are widely identified as 'Jewish'; they clearly nourish on traditional Jewish imageries and objects, and they would surely be difficult for non-Jews to identify with. But they are novel, Zionist-statist creations. As Jewish objections to Zionism shows, one can be viewed (and view oneself) as 'wholly Jewish' and still fail to revere these symbols (or even actively desecrate them).[69] In other words, these symbols do not represent something that would (traditionally, at least) be viewed as 'essentially Jewish' – but they surely are of a Zionist essence.

Similarly, another clause repeats the determination of the 'Hebrew calendar' as the official state calendar (adding that the Christian calendar will be in use alongside it, leaving the practical meaning of the determination symbolic at best). The law also repeats the designation of Saturday and the Jewish holy days as official days of rest. Beyond merely restating already practiced laws, the basic law at hand offers very little, if any at all, by way of deciding the practical implications of these clauses – such as their influence on the conducting of commerce during the official days of rest, a matter that has been debated for decades.

The final version of the bill also states that Jerusalem 'whole and unified' is the capital city of Israel (the original draft failed to mention this). This is a mere repetition of the Basic Law: Jerusalem the Capital City of Israel (passed in 1980).

The law also seeks to assert the Jews' 'national rights' and values; yet these assertions are either redundant – as they simply restate existing laws – or so vague as to be practically meaningless. One paragraph, for example, originally titled 'Return' and later changed to 'Ingathering of

    see: O. Noy, 'Israel's nation-state law also discriminates against Mizrahi Jews,' *972 Magazine* (blog), January 2, 2019, 972mag.com/?p=139541

[68] Mendel, Yitzhaki, and Pinto, 'Official but not recognized,' 17.

[69] Rabkin, *A Threat from Within.*

Exiles,' would fall under the first category. It states that 'The state should be open to Jewish immigration and the ingathering of exiles.' This is obviously already determined by the Law of Return, a foundational element of Zionist-Israeli nationalism.[70]

The law also states that 'The state shall act in the diaspora to strengthen the affinity (*ziqa*) between the state and members of the Jewish people.' Regardless of the fact that Israel has been (successfully) positioning itself as a core element of modern Jewish identity outside of the state, it is hard to see what the legally binding practical implications of 'acting to strengthen' this relationship would be.

Similarly, one clause in the original draft states that 'Hebrew law' (i.e., Jewish law, *halakha*) 'shall serve as the source of inspiration for lawmakers.' Critical commentators were quick to suggest that this amounts to a preference of a patriarchal, undemocratic legal tradition over Western, liberal-democratic ideals,[71] (a critique that ultimately brought about the deletion of this clause from the final version of the bill). Yet the language of the bill is far too abstract to clarify what would be the practical meaning of designating 'Hebrew law' as a putative 'source of inspiration' for the judicial class. This is further emphasized by the original bill's undetermined dictate that 'Should the court encounter a legal question that demands a ruling and be unable to find an answer through the body of legislation, legal precedent, or clear analogy, it shall decide in light of the principles of freedom, justice, integrity, and peace associated with the heritage of Israel.' It is not hard to see that these principles – which may be equally described as universal, and not just 'Jewish' – can be easily interpreted so as to promote decisions that may explicitly collide with what many Jews would take to be traditional Jewish values. The definition is just too wide and the language too abstract to be meaningful. In any event, as mentioned before, this clause was dropped from the final version altogether, allowing for the aforementioned critique.

Other clauses in the bill tended at first to be more explicit in setting a 'more Jewish' tone. These rely on 'tradition,' 'heritage,' 'history,' and even 'religion.' A clause in the original draft thus determines that 'The state shall act to preserve the cultural and historical heritage [*moreshet*]

---

[70] Gavison, *The Law of Return*.
[71] *Haaretz* Editorial, 'Prescribing Jewish law in absence of legal precedent sacralizes Israel's judicial system,' *Haaretz*, September 18, 2017.

of the Jewish people and to cultivate it in Israel and the diaspora'; and that 'In all educational institutions serving the Jewish public in Israel, the history, heritage, and traditions of the Jewish people shall be taught.' These statements were apparently read as suggesting an opening for religious coercion and had attracted much criticism. They were cut off in practice from the *Israeli* context of the law. Yet the final version of the bill did not forego of these clauses altogether; instead, it aims the state's 'Judaizing' impetus toward non-Israeli Jews: the law passed by the Knesset omits the words 'in Israel' from the original clause, and adds 'religion' into the mix, now stating: 'The State shall act to preserve the cultural, historical and religious heritage of the Jewish people among diaspora Jews.' This phrasal maneuver reflects a wider reality in which Jewish religion or tradition is seen in Israel as suspicious when referring to Israeli Jews and as wholly legitimate when referring to non-Israeli Jews. I shall expand on this in the next chapter.

The Nation-State Law, Its Alternatives, and the Limits of Zionist Discourse

During almost a decade of debate the Israeli public sphere has seen several attempts at either 'fixing' Ditcher's original bill or to counter it altogether, before an amended version of it was finally passed by the Knesset.[72] The various proposed bills, and the debates over their details, offer a rather straightforward view of the basic outlines of Israeli political culture. They reveal both what is debated inside the perimeter of 'accepted' political discourse in contemporary Israel and what is considered to be out of bounds and as undermining the state's

---

[72] Dichter et al., 'Basic Law proposal: Israel is the nation-state of the Jewish people'; A. Eldad, 'Basic Law proposal: Israel – the nation-state of the Jewish people,' The Knesset, Pub. L. No. P/18/4096 (2012); R. Calderon, A. Mitzna, R. Frenkel, S. Solomon, E. Stern, R. Hoffman, D. Tzur, B. Toporovsky, and B. Ben-Eliezer, 'Basic Law proposal: The Israeli declaration of independence and the Jewish and democratic state,' The Knesset, Pub. L. No. P/19/1939 (2013); Z. Elkin, 'Basic Law proposal: Israel – the nation-state of the Jewish people,' The Knesset, Pub. L. No. P/19/2502 (2014); A. Shaked, Y. Levin, and R. Ilatov, 'Basic Law proposal: Israel – the nation-state of the Jewish people,' The Knesset, Pub. L. No. P/19/1550 (2013); E. Stern, M. Sheetrit, A. Mitzna, D. Tzur, and A. Peretz, 'Basic Law proposal: Israel – the nation-state of the Jewish people,' The Knesset, Pub. L. No. P/19/2883 (2014); M. Regev, 'Basic Law proposal: Israel is the nation-state of the Jewish people,' The Knesset, Pub. L. No. P/19/2530 (2014).

raison d'être. The various versions – dubbed in the Israeli press as 'harsher' or 'softer' – differ in the degree to which they reassert the preference of Jews over non-Jews. These may be described as oscillating along Israel's constitutive dilemma: The continuum stretched between a Zionist/Israeli understanding of Israel's 'Jewish identity' – i.e., the assertion of the sovereignty of the state as a nation-state of Jews at the expense of individual and minority rights – and the democratic principles of its regime, which would be more attentive to the need to preserve and protect these rights. Thus, the 'more centrist' proposals make a point of designating Israel a 'Jewish and democratic' state alongside constituting it as the 'nation-state of the Jewish people.'[73]

Yet all of these versions accept the Zionist axiom by which Israel's 'Jewish character' amounts to the preference of Jews over non-Jews. They also all fail to instill this 'Jewish identity' with substantial positive meaning that we may identify as 'Jewish' – beyond, that is, the abstract Zionist notion of reclaiming and 'secularizing' this identity. They all, in other words, accept the basic premise by which Israel's Jewish identity is a matter of demography – or, more basically, of the arithmetic of 'blood.' Basically, they all perpetuate the Zionist Jewish identity dilemma or crisis.

Two proposals that were presented to the Knesset to challenge the then proposed nation-state bill merit consideration, for they highlight the limits of the 'internal' Zionist-Israeli debate by either striving to reassert the 'classic' (i.e., the one prevalent prior to the ensuing of the debate over the nation-state bill) notion of 'Jewish and democratic' or to break out of these bounds altogether.

The first of these bills was presented to the Knesset at the end of 2016. Unlike its counterparts, this bill is short enough to be quoted in full:

1. The Essene of the State: Israel is the nation-state of the Jewish people, based on the principles of liberty, justice, and peace in light of the visions of the prophets of Israel, and upholds an equality of rights to all of its citizens.

---

[73] Stern, Sheetrit, Mitzna, Tzur, and Peretz, 'Basic Law proposal: Israel – the nation-state of the Jewish people.'

2. The Regime of the State of Israel: The State of Israel is a democracy.[74]

Rather confusingly, this bill, which was commonly considered in the Israeli public sphere as a 'leftist' challenge to the nation-state bill, was presented to the Knesset by Binyamin Begin, of the right-wing Likud party (Begin abstained in the final vote on the bill sponsored by his government in July 2018). In the context of the debate over the nation-state law, this proposal is eccentric in ignoring the very motives behind the various initiatives to constitutionally anchor Israel's Jewish identity. Or, in other words, it is eccentric in not referring to Israel as a (or the) *Jewish State*. Instead, it reasserts the Zionist notion that Israel is the State of Jews, or of 'the Jewish people.'

The second bill illuminates the outlines of the debate at hand by challenging the Zionist vision altogether, standing, as it were, 'outside' of the debate. This bill was presented to the Knesset by the members of Ḥadash (The Democratic Front for Peace and Equality), which draws largely (but surely not exclusively) on a constituency of non-Jewish Palestinian-Arab voters. (In the terms commonly used in Israeli political discourse, it is an 'Arab party.') The bill has five short clauses. These assert democratic principles of liberty and equality, denounce discrimination, and establish affirmative action to counter established practices of discrimination.[75] As the explanatory text adjoining the bill states, it aims to explicitly 'anchor' the democratic value of equality in Israel's regime:

At the core of this bill stands the principle of equality. This principle has been hitherto absent from the Israeli book of laws. The principle of equality is explicitly protected in the constitutions of democratic states, and the time has come, 66 years after the establishment of the state, to explicitly protect this principle in the Israeli book of laws, too.[76]

The bill is radical – in the sense of breaking out of the bounds of the debate of the nation-state bill – by completely foregoing any mention

---

[74] B. Begin, 'Law proposal: The essence of the State of Israel, 2016/5777,' The Knesset, Pub. L. No. P/20/3541 (2016).

[75] M. Barakeh, H. Sweid, D. Khenin, and A. Agbaria, 'Basic Law proposal: Israel – a democratic and egalitarian state,' The Knesset, Pub. L. No. P/19/2913 (2014).

[76] Barakeh, Sweid, Khenin, and Agbaria, 'Basic Law proposal: Israel – a democratic and egalitarian state.'

of a nationalist, Jewish or otherwise, agenda. In a sense, it plays into the 'Jewish and democratic' debate by implying (this is surely a matter of context and subtext, not of the text itself) that a definition of Israel as Jewish would necessarily amount to discrimination against non-Jews in Israel. In other words, the bill completely foregoes the attempt to challenge the Zionist or Israeli prevalent reading of the meaning of Israel's 'Jewishness' as amounting primarily to a preference of Jews over non-Jews.

The Jewish Opposition to the 'Jewish State'

The nation-state bill has been insistently opposed by two groups who are usually considered to be on the sidelines of mainstream Israeli sociopolitics: Palestinian-Arabs and Ultra-Orthodox Jews. As for the former, whose objection is encapsulated in both the Vision document and the Ḥadash-sponsored bill discussed above,[77] the reasons for rejecting the bill seem quite obvious: Palestinian-Arabs object to a political configuration of power that puts them in a precarious position of a minority who lacks equal protection of its rights. But why would the Ultra-Orthodox Jews object to it? Wouldn't a reaffirmation of Israel's 'Jewish identity' be something naturally favored by those who conservatively observe Jewish law?

As anyone even slightly familiar with the history and politics of Israel would surely see, this is a manifestly naïve question, that ignores a long history of Ultra-Orthodox Jewish opposition to and rejection of Zionism.[78] The Ultra-Orthodox objection is not directed at the purported 'strengthening' or 'reaffirmation' of Israel's Jewish identity, but rather at the very attempt by Zionism and Israel to appropriate the meaning of Jewishness (and of Jewish politics). Their objection, in other words, is directed at the state's very claim to a 'modern' or 'secular' *Jewish* identity.

Interestingly, the Ultra-Orthodox leaders, probably sensing the 'sensitive' nature of their position as opposing a bill that aims, at least

---

[77] The National Committee for the Heads of the Arab Local Authorities in Israel, 'Future vision'; Barakeh, Sweid, Khenin, and Agbaria, 'Basic Law proposal: Israel – a democratic and egalitarian state.'

[78] Rabkin, *A Threat from Within.*

rhetorically so, to strengthen the Jewish character of the Israeli polity, have largely avoided giving coherent or comprehensive accounts of the reasons for their objections to the nation-state bill.[79] Moreover, they were convinced to vote for the bill in the very last minute, after having secured a commitment by the governing Likud party that the bill will be amended in case it is found to hurt the status quo.[80]

Yet the wider Ultra-Orthodox discourse on the matter makes it clear that the opposition is not aimed at the bill per se, but rather at the overall epistemology from which it nourishes. Simply put, the Ultra-Orthodox view rejects the very notion that Israel is a 'Jewish' state, since in the Ultra-Orthodox view the Jewishness of the state must amount to more than the Zionist understanding of Jewish politics (i.e., mainly the calculation of the demographic composition of the state's population).

Two not uncharacteristic comments on a website catering for Ultra-Orthodox audience put this rather straightforwardly:

EISEN: The nation-bill, which defines Israel as a Jewish state, was
          approved today by the government. And I wonder what exactly
          makes us a Jewish state? Why is this important to them? Could it
          be primarily for the flag and official documents?

---

[79] The leaders of the Ultra-Orthodox parties have largely preferred to forego offering a coherent explanation for their objection. It has been reported that 'The Haredi parties expressed opposition to the bill on two fronts: opposition in principle to the Basic Laws as well to the bill's lack of distinction between Orthodox Jews and non-Orthodox Jews, treating them equally.' No direct sources are given to this assertion. J. Lis, 'Knesset set to give initial approval of bill allowing Jewish-only communities,' *Haaretz*, April 30, 2018. In the rather muted explanation given in 2014, Moshe Gafni, the Chairman of Degel Hatorah, protested the fact that the bill would transfer the authority to decide Israel's Jewish identity to the judicial branch. See: A. Shiff, 'Gafni: hasiʿot haharediyot yaṣbiʿu neged ḥoq haleom,' *Behadrei haredim*, November 21, 2014. In 2015 it was reported that the Ultra-Orthodox objection to the bill forces the Likud party to freeze it: Z. Qam, "al pi derishat heḥaredim: halikud yiqbor et ḥoq haleom,' nrg.co.il, April 9, 2015. Similarly, in 2017 in was reported that, again, Ultra-Orthodox objection would mean that the bill shall not pass. An anonymous source was laconically quoted as saying: 'regarding the nation bill, there are matters which are sensitive to us in term of values.' I. Klein, 'yahadut hatora monaʿat et qidomo shel ʿhoq haleom,' *Actuaclic*, May 23, 2017.

[80] Y. Cohen, 'Gam eichler: yahadut hatora titmokh beḥoq haleom' *Kikar Hashabat*, July 18, 2018.

They have ruined conversion.

They have ruined the registration of marriages [a data bank aimed at preventing marriages that are deemed illegal by Jewish law].

They've undermined the rabbinical Courts.

They've been ruining the right to study the Torah.

So, what makes us Jewish?

DAFTAR: Bibi [Prime Minister Binyamin Netanyahu] addressed [Justice Minister Tzippi] Livni and asked rhetorically: I do not understand how is it that there are people who are willing to recognize two states for two nations, meaning nation-states for the Palestinians and for the Jews, but when the matter amounts to an anchoring [of this principle] in law, they object ...

And I also am asking a naïve question: How is it that you demand the whole world to recognize this state as the state of Jews when there is no Judaism in it at all, and even the very little that was in it in the past, you have almost entirely erased during one term? Oh God! In what is this state a Jewish state?[81]

The challenge here is not against the intended 'strengthening' of Israel's 'Jewish character,' but against the Zionist understanding or construction of this 'character.' In this regard, the Ultra-Orthodox objection to the nation-state bill sheds light on the fact that the bill and the nation-state whose vision it seeks to constitutionally enshrine play a decisive role in the context of the normative or ideational world of Judaism, and in the wider context of world Jewry, that far exceeds the borders of the sovereign nation-state. Among other things, this means that Israel's aspired identification as the nation-state of the Jewish people or as the Jewish state necessarily sheds light on the complicated relation between the state and world Jewry.

To understand this, let me reiterate an argument presented earlier: A core element of the Zionist vision and the Israeli sociopolitical reality is the predominance of a national, political view of Jewish identity. In this view, the State of Israel embodies a culmination of a historical revolution, in which Jewish identity 'breaks free' from what the nationalist ideology would mark as 'religion,' and re-forms as a political,

---

[81] bhol.co.il, 'forum: beḥadrei ḥaredim – diyun be'iqvot ishur ḥoq hale'om,' Beḥadrei ḥaredim, November 23, 2014.

so-called secular entity. As I suggested earlier, this shift embodies a dramatic epistemological change: from 'Judaism' to 'Jews' (or to Jewishness).

Yet there is one critical caveat in the Zionist worldview, which sees non-Israeli Jewishness, as well as any other non-Zionist (or non-Israeli nation-statist) Jewish way of life essentially lacking. In this Zionist, *political* understating of Jewish identity, only Jews who partake in the politics of the Israeli nation-state (even if simply by virtue of being part of it, or more accurately being subjects of the sovereign state of Jews) can be regarded as 'whole,' as fully deserving of their humanity. Other Jews – diasporic in either a physical sense (i.e., those living outside of the nation-state of the Jews, beyond the limits of its sovereignty) or in a symbolic sense (i.e., those living in Israel, but oppose Zionist politics and refuse to fully partake in the life of the nation-state, in effect rejecting state sovereignty) are deemed 'partial' and 'lacking.' Their humanity is, so to speak, missing, for their detachment from the political framework of the sovereignty of the nation-state of Jews does not allow them to fully experience the meaning of their 'essence' as Jews.[82]

Combined with Israel's (admittedly abstract) view of itself as the State of the Jewish people (and not only of its citizens), this has given birth to a complicated relation between Israel and diaspora Jewry. This, obviously, is a long and complicated story that cannot be told here in full.[83] What I wish to stress here is how a debate over the meaning of Israel's Jewishness plays into the already charged history of Israel–diaspora Jewry relations, a matter with which I will open the next chapter.

---

[82] This is a quintessentially Ben-Gurionist view. In recent years, the author and essayist A. B. Yehoshua has been a vocal propagator of this view. See, for example: A. B. Yehoshua, American Jewish Committee, and Dorothy and Julius Koppelman Institute on American Jewish–Israeli Relations, *The A. B. Yehoshua Controversy: An Israel-Diaspora Dialogue on Jewishness, Israeliness, and Identity* (New York: American Jewish Committee, 2006). For a detailed analysis of the sense of statist Jewish identity instilled in this view, see Yadgar, *Sovereign Jews*, ch. 8.

[83] I. Z. Baron, *Obligation in Exile* (Edinburgh: Edinburgh University Press, 2014); E. Ben-Rafael (ed.), *Reconsidering Israel–Diaspora Relations* (Leiden, Netherlands: Brill, 2014); J. Habib, *Israel, Diaspora, and the Routes of National Belonging* (Toronto: University of Toronto Press, 2004).

Conclusion

At the time of writing, the debate over the nation-state law is far from over. The law is bound to remain controversial and debated.[84] Its approval by the Knesset has encouraged continuous protests, the most salient of which led by representatives of the Druze minority.[85] Having been historically treated by the state as separate from other Palestinians, explicitly noted for their 'loyalty' to the state (ultimately expressed in their service in the Israeli military),[86] Israeli Druze found themselves to be offensively marked out of the national picture by the nation-state law. The Druze campaign against the law seems to be a rather 'sectorial' reaction to the law, by which Druze leaders (the public faces of the protests being mostly former generals in the Israeli military) decry what many Israelis seem to agree is a specific case of inattentiveness to their 'unique' relation to the state of the Jews. As some positive reactions to these protests show, their ultimate aim is to 'fix' the nation-state law, without questioning its basic premises.[87]

As I suggested earlier, this bill – or, more precisely, the discourse from which it arises – captures 'the core essence'[88] of the Israeli polity.

---

[84] The first judicial petition to the Israeli High Courts of Justice against the law was filed in early August 2018 by Adalah – The Legal Centre for Arab Minority Rights in Israel: High Follow-Up Committee for Arab Citizens, the National Committee of Arab Mayors, and the Joint List Members of Knesset v. The Knesset 'Petition to the High Court of Justice,' HJC 5866/18 (2018); Adalah, 'Arab leadership takes action against Israel's new Jewish Nation-State Law,' Adalah, The Legal Center for Arab Minority Rights in Israel, August 7, 2018. https://adalah.org/en/content/view/9574. See also Note 67, about the Arab-Jewish petition against the law.

[85] M. Loveday, 'Deluge of opposition to Israel's nation-state law builds with new court petition' *The Washington Post*, August 7, 2018; B. Peleg, 'Druze protest nation-state law outside Israeli party leaders' homes; politicians vow to 'fix' legislation,' *Haaretz*, January 16, 2019.

[86] On the Druze in Israel, see: K. Firro, *The Druzes in the Jewish State: A Brief History* (Leiden, Netherlands: Brill, 1999); K. Firro, 'Reshaping Druze particularism in Israel,' *Journal of Palestine Studies*, 30/3 (2001), 40–53; J. Oppenheimer, 'The Druze in Israel as Arabs and non-Arabs: Manipulation of categories of identity in a non-civil state,' in A. Weingrod (ed.), *Studies in Israeli Ethnicity: After the Ingathering* (New York: Gordon and Breach, 1985), pp. 259–80; O. Yiftachel and M. D. Segal, 'Jews and Druze in Israel: State control and ethnic resistance,' *Ethnic and Racial Studies*, 21/3 (1998), 476–506.

[87] B. Peleg, 'In first public statement, Benny Gantz vows to 'fix' nation-state law' *Haaretz*, January 14, 2019.

[88] To borrow the phrase from Begin, 'Law proposal: The essence of the State of Israel', 2016/5777.

The debate over the bill is not a political argument per se; rather, it may be described as an 'epistemological' debate on how to approach the very constitutive notion of Israel's 'Jewish character.' The unresolved nature of the basic law at hand, the fact that it manages to be seen both and at the same time as 'obvious' or 'redundant' and as 'radical' or 'dangerous,' and its ultimate failure to positively instill this designation (i.e., 'Jewish state') with explicitly positive meaning all reflect some of the foundational tensions in the Zionist ideology and the Israeli nation-state. They all touch on the Zionist taken-for-granted claim for Jewish nation-statehood – that is, the reading of Jewish identity as pertaining to 'nationality,' in the ideological meaning of the term – and the just-as-obvious Zionist failure (or neglect) to construct a positive meaning of a 'secular' (as in not related to what Zionist ideology would see as 'religion') Jewish identity. Instead, Zionism and the Israeli polity have shifted the discourse from 'a Jewish state' to a 'Jews' state'; from asking 'what makes someone or something Jewish?' to constructing a polity based on a majority of 'Jews.'

The need to pass the bill – the initiative that propelled this debate from the very beginning – has nothing meaningful to do with the challenge to positively define or identify the meaning of the 'Jewishness' of Israel or of Jewish politics. Indeed, it does a manifestly muddled work in trying to assert Israel's claim to 'Jewish identity.' As my discussion of the bill's attempt to tackle these issues shows, the law seems to handle these matters rather offhandedly, leaving them mostly too abstract to be meaningful. Instead, the bill has been motivated by the sense that the Zionist taken-for-granted understanding of Jewish nation-statehood has been put in question, primarily due to its inconsistency with basic democratic principles of equality.

This, then, is among other things also a story of an attempt to overcome the narrow reading of Israel's Jewishness as pertaining primarily to 'demography' and to the preference of a majority of Jews over a minority of Palestinian-Arab non-Jews. Yet this attempt was motivated precisely by the need to preserve this configuration of power, and not necessarily by a wish to finally resolve Zionism's confused understanding of its own relation to Jewish tradition. This, in other words, is a discussion that some of its primary spokespeople never attempted to have; it was forced on them by their wish to preserve the political-Zionist taken-for-granted understanding of

Jewish nationhood. In this, the crippled debate that has ensued echoes a fundamental trait of the political-Zionist ideology, which, confronted with the dilemma of its own Jewish identity, preferred to forego the discussion and focus instead on establishing a configuration of power in which 'Jews' hold sovereignty.

3 | *Two Contemporary Debates on Zionism and Secularism*

This chapter traces two parallel contemporary debates over Jewish identity in Israel, which highlight some of the main features – and limits – of the Israeli, especially the liberal-Zionist, secularist, discourse on Zionism, Judaism, secularism, and Jewish politics. The first is a debate over the introduction of 'Jewish identity' programs in Israel. The second debate deals with the meaning, value, and future of Israeli secularism. I would argue that these public discussions attest to the problematic nature of Israel's very claim to Jewish identity, and derived from it (or, if we flip the image, driven by) the Israeli-Palestinian conflict.

'Strengthening' Jewish Identity in Israel and Abroad

Israel has played a determined hand in positioning itself as the center of Jewish life outside of the state. This has been a largely successful project, bringing one critic to note that

'Israelism' has replaced traditional Jewish identity, making it difficult for Jewish students to distinguish between divergent political views and attacks on their identities ... It is no secret that young Jews often find it difficult to separate Zionism from the Jewish identity as it has been taught to them. Their identity is often centered on political support for the State of Israel, and they see advocacy for Israel – a special course in the curriculum of many private Jewish schools [outside of Israel] – as a key part of being Jewish.[1]

This reality is a culmination of an extended, sustained effort by the state, which has involved a long and diverse list of policies and projects run by the state and its supporting agencies, which are aimed at strengthening non-Israeli Jewry's commitment to the State of Israel. Interestingly, many of these projects focus on the strengthening or

---

[1] Y. M. Rabkin, 'Conflating Zionism and Judaism leaves Jewish students exposed,' +972 *Magazine*, December 8, 2017.

maintenance of non-Israeli-Jews' *Jewishness*, or Jewish commitments and even religious observance. These programs are illuminating, for they betray the Zionist state's reliance on what Zionism would ultimately mark as 'religious tradition' for reaffirming the (supposedly secular) state's role as the center of (national, so-called secular) Jewish life.

Such is, to give but one example, the Jewish Agency for Israel's emissaries ('Shlichim'[2]) program. In one branch of this program the emissaries – people identified as 'idealistic and dedicated Israelis' – are sent to 'serve' in Jewish communities throughout the world. They relocate to these communities for extended periods of stay, and partner with their host communities to engage community members 'in a range of Jewish cultural, educational, and social activities.' Note: these are *Jewish* activities, in a rather traditional and religio-cultural sense; they are not explicitly political and/or Zionist – or even Israeli, for that matter. The emissaries' goal is to 'plant the seeds of a secure Jewish future.' Tellingly, when it comes to non-Israeli Jewry, matters of the 'Jewish blood' (fighting intermarriage between Jews on non-Jews, for example) are only secondary to more culturally and traditionally meaningful aspects of Jewish life for 'securing' the Jewish future. Moreover, in this framework, the political, support-for-Israel aspect of the program seems to take second stage, being almost a trivial matter. The Jewish Agency, in its own words, hopes to secure the future of the Jewish people by 'implementing programs that are designed to increase Jewish awareness, knowledge, and pride; and to promote an understanding of Israel and its ideals.'[3] Note how 'Jewish awareness' and 'an understanding of Israel and its ideals' are tied together into one whole logic for the missionary program.

Similarly, we may consider what is probably the most famous of the various projects currently being run in this context, the Taglit-Birthright tours project, in which young non-Israeli-Jews are brought to visit Israel.[4] These tours tie Zionist ideology with various matters of

---

[2] The Jewish Agency, 'Community Shlichim,' The Jewish Agency's website, www.jewishagency.org/shlichim-israeli-emissaries/program/287.
[3] The Jewish Agency, 'Community Shlichim.'
[4] S. Kelner, *Tours That Bind: Diaspora, Pilgrimage, and Israeli Birthright Tourism* (New York: New York University Press, 2012); T. Sasson, M. Shain, S. Hecht, G. Wright, and L. Saxe, 'Does Taglit-Birthright Israel foster long-distance nationalism?,' *Nationalism and Ethnic Politics*, 20/4 (2014), 438–54;

Jewish identity, aiming to position Israel as the center of meaning for the young non-Israeli-Jews through a reaffirmed commitment to their Jewishness. The proclaimed aim of the project is quite substantial: 'Birthright Israel seeks to ensure the future of the Jewish people.' A two weeks tour of Israel is supposed to achieve this by 'strengthening Jewish identity, Jewish communities, and connection with Israel.' The trips are supposed to motivate the young non-Israeli-Jews to 'explore their Jewish identity and support for Israel and maintain long-lasting connections with the Israelis they meet on their trip.'[5]

I do not aim to offer here a critique of these projects; for the purposes of the current discussion, what is probably most striking about these various initiatives, in which Israel positions itself as the center of non-Israeli Jewish life via the 'strengthening' (or emphasizing) of what would commonly be seen as pertaining to cultural-traditional *Jewish* identity, is the degree to which similar programs are controversial and raise fierce objections in the intra-Jewish-Israeli context itself. Opposition to such similar projects in Israel has indeed become a rallying cry for the secularist, liberal-Zionists in Israel.

As a backdrop to this we may recall that debates over the degree of knowledge, awareness, or ignorance of Israelis on matters of Jewishness, Judaism, or Jewish identity have been a staple of public discourse in Israel.[6] Already in 1956, a mere 8 years after the establishment of the state, Israel's Ministry of Education initiated a program for 'fostering Jewish consciousness' (*hanḥalat toda'a yehudit*) among students of the national school system. This was motivated by a strong sense that the Israeli ('nonreligious') youth are alienated from their Jewish history. Israel's minister of education at the time, Zalman Aran, identified three missing 'bridges' in this regard: 'the bridge between the youth in the country and the historical past of the nation,' the one connecting 'the Israeli youth and religious and traditional Judaism of contemporary diaspora,' and 'the bridge between the Israeli youth and

---

Y. Abramson, 'Making a homeland, constructing a diaspora: The case of Taglit-Birthright Israel,' *Political Geography*, 58 (2017), 14–23.

[5] Birthright Israel's website, 'About us,' www.birthrightisrael.com/about_us.

[6] These concerns have predated the establishment of the state. See Note 39 in the Introduction.

the religious and traditional [population] inside the State of Israel.'[7] This seems to have set the tone for an ongoing concern for the level and viability of the Israelis' 'Jewish consciousness,' which concerned parties see as both essential for the survival of the state and critically weak.

Such discussions on the 'diminution of the uniquely Jewish in Israeli life'[8] and the way it encourages the apparent alienation of the Jewish-Israeli youth from Judaism usually carry a sense of a looming danger that Israelis (especially Israeli youth) would lose their ties to their Jewish identity, in the Jewish state of all places. Commentators often express their fear that Israelis have been losing their meaningful sense of Jewishness, and are growing alienated from both non-Israeli Jewry and the very core of Zionist nationalism.[9] These commentaries are illuminating in shedding light not only on the degree to which the 'strengthening' of Jewish identity is taken to be an essential *political*, Zionist necessity (following the same line of the missionary programs abroad), but also, as I noted earlier, on the vehement objections that they encounter. These objections and the debate they have encouraged regarding the very meaning of Israeli secularism, in turn, tell quite a lot about the contours of a secularist, liberal-Zionist understanding of Jewishness, Judaism, and Jewish politics. Specifically, they highlight the limits of what most commentators consider to be 'secular' (national) definitions of Jewishness.

By way of example, let us consider one of the latest endeavors in the context of the 'strengthening' of Israelis' Jewish identity: the establishment in 2013 of a governmental administrative unit (*'minhelet'*) for Jewish identity, located inside the Ministry of Religious Services. The unit's mandate is to 'increase respect, love and [mutual] identification among the various elements of the population by incorporating the

---

[7] Quoted in Y. Greenberg, 'Mi sheroṣe liḥyut beshalom 'im hadatiyim ṣarikh lehakhriaḥ otam, ṣarikh lishbor otam,' *Haaretz*, November 29, 2017.

[8] D. Zisenwine, 'Jewish education in the Jewish state,' *Israel Affairs*, 4/3–4 (1998), 146–55.

[9] One of the earlier and more perceptive of these commentaries was offered by Baruch Kurzweil, who also noted the degree to which the anti-Jewish Hebrew nationalist movement of the Young Hebrews was able to capitalize on the Israeli youth's sense of alienation from Judaism; B. Kurzweil, 'The new Canaanites in Israel,' *Judaism*, 2 (1953), 3–15; B. Kurzweil, *Our New Literature: Continuation of Revolution?* (Tel Aviv: Schocken, 1971), 270–300. See also: Zisenwine, 'Jewish education in the Jewish state'; A. Shapira, 'Spiritual rootlessness and circumscription to the 'here and now' in the Sabra world view,' *Israel Affairs*, 4/3–4 (1998), 103–31.

basic elements of the historical identity and the national heritage of the Jewish people – 'to bring the soul back to the State of Israel.'[10] (Needless to say, the lack of adjective to designate which 'population' this governmental program is aimed at – Jews? Israelis? – is not coincidental; by definition, this is a matter of Jewish unity, in which non-Jewish Israelis cannot partake.)

As the person appointed to oversee this Jewish Identity Administration explained, apparently trying to ease concerns that the unit will end up proselytizing, 'The goal is not *haḥzara bitshuvah* but strengthening the Jewish identity in the State of Israel.' His outlook for the Administration's public outreach is based on the same dismal appreciation of the degree of Jewish knowledge and commitment among Israeli-Jews: 'The idea is to strengthen the Jewish identity, which is in bad shape in the country.' Most importantly, as he explained, the administration's aim is not cultural or religious, but primarily political, in a specifically Zionist reading of Jewish politics; it is about the Zionist lingering sense of the looming dangerous political implications of Jewish detachment, in face of an Israeli-Palestinian conflict:

This is not folklore, this is not [about] Jewish knowledge ... This is [meant] to strengthen the connection of the people not to the land, but to itself, its heritage. This is in my eyes a matter of survival. A person who does not know the Bible will, in moments of crisis, not last here. Today Jewish identity is very weak.[11]

In other words, it is the conflict, that which makes Jews 'last[ing] here [in Israel]' a precarious matter, that demands the upholding of Israelis' Jewish identity. One is tempted to conclude by this logic that were it not for the conflict, Israelis may be allowed to forego their Jewish identity altogether.

This, indeed, is the same basic motivating logic of the Jewish Agency's outreach programs discussed earlier: A strengthening of one's commitment to the State of Israel and to Zionism via a reconfirmation (or, in some cases, outright creation) of one's ties to 'Jewish identity.' The similarities between the programs also extend to matters of form:

---

[10] Ministry of Religious Services, 'Jewish Identity Administration.' www.dat.gov.il/About/Units/Pages/JewishIdentity.aspx.

[11] Y. Ettinger, Ex-IDF chief rabbi takes over Israel's new Jewish Identity Administration,' *Haaretz*, May 21, 2013.

one of the first initiatives of the Jewish Identity Administration has been the appointment of what might be termed 'Jewish community organizers' (*rakazey yahadut* in the original Hebrew phrasing, which may be clumsily translated as 'Judaism facilitators'). According to a critical report on the program, these agents are tasked with 'strengthening religious values among [Jewish] seculars' in Israel. In the administration's own terminology, these organizers – the almost exact equivalent of the Jewish Agency's emissaries discussed earlier – would 'propel a process of renewal of the communal texture.' This project is meant to respond to 'the ongoing decline in the status of the values of Jewish identity and the general lack of knowledge regarding Jewish heritage. This decline and lack of knowledge bring about ignorance, unequal share in burden, loss of national identity, a sense of not-belonging to the Jewish people, and social alienation.'[12]

There is, then, an obvious sense of a looming danger, by which Israeli-Jews' indifference to matters of what would usually be termed 'Jewish tradition' might bring about a national, political (as defined in the Zionist outlook) disintegration. This may indeed be seen as yet another instance of the 'confusion' or lack of separation between 'religion and politics' or even of 'the religious' and 'the secular' – specifically when viewed through a Zionist prism. The program thus echoes the fears that motivate the State of Israel's various initiatives among world Jewry: in both cases, the malaise is fundamentally 'political,' as it has to do with the state's role in the lives of Jews (in the case of non-Israeli-Jews), and with the very preservation of the statist configuration of power (in the case of Israeli-Jews); and in both cases the remedy is fundamentally the same: a 'strengthening' of Jews' Jewish identity, in what eventually entails a reliance on matters of (religious) 'tradition.'

As I mentioned earlier, unlike in the case of the Jewish Agency's programs to 'strengthen' the Jewish identity of non-Israelis, which do not attract much opposition in Israel, the institution of a similar program inside Israel encountered vehement opposition. In the intra-Israeli case, such endeavors to 'strengthen' Jewish identity, at least when they are read through a liberal-Zionist, secularist lens, amount to religious coercion. These objections show that the matter at hand

---

[12] O. Kashti, "'Judaism facilitators' will strengthen religious values among seculars across the country,' *Haaretz*, March 2, 2014.

touches directly on the most sensitive nerves of the Israeli polity, namely the contested nature of Israel's Jewish identity. *Haaretz* editorial's reaction to the establishment of the new Jewish Identity Administration, for example, claims that Israel should not aim to be Jewish at all. Calling the newly established Jewish Identity Administration a 'Jewish Coercion Administration,' the editorial proclaims:

> Zionism dreamed of a state for the Jews, not a Jewish state: a refuge for members of the Jewish people, not a state with an official religion like Muslim Saudi Arabia. The Balfour Declaration promised a national home, not a religious one. On Israeli identity cards, 'Jewish' describes a nationality [that is, *not* a religion].[13]

In other words, what is presented by the Israeli authorities as a project of 'strengthening' Israeli-Jews' Jewish and Zionist commitments is read in the liberal-Zionist frame as a matter of an ongoing *Kulturkampf* between secular and religious Israelis. Indeed, the editorial finds it important to insist that 'Israelis don't have an identity crisis.' Rather, they are facing a growing trend of religious coercion:

> In recent years, a worrying trend has taken root in the education system and the IDF, in which encounters with religious content are being forced on secular youth. But not, of course, the reverse: Boys and girls from Bnei Brak and Mea She'arim [urban areas with large concentration of Ultra-Orthodox communities] aren't being systematically bused to north Tel Aviv and to kibbutzim.[14]

This, then, is a zero-sum game of sorts, where what was previously discussed by Zionist, secularist leaders as 'fostering Jewish consciousness,' ultimately amounts to a secular submission to religious coercion.

Zionist Identity, Secularism, and 'Religionization'

The secularist suspicion that what is presented as national, Zionist (Jewish) education ultimately amounts to religious coercion has won a stark expression in a campaign run by the Secular Forum, an Israeli

---

[13] *Haaretz* Editorial, 'The Jewish Coercion Administration,' *Haaretz*, May 22, 2013.

[14] *Haaretz* Editorial, 'The Jewish Coercion Administration.'

social union, against what it calls an encroaching process of 'religionization' (*hadata* in the original Hebrew) or 'religious radicalization.'[15] While it is hard to estimate the size and influence of this organization, there can be no doubt that its campaign has touched a rather sensitive nerve in the liberal-Zionist body politic. It surely won the attention of the Israeli media, who have amplified the forum's claims of a disturbing encroachment of 'the religious' in Israel and of the sinister 'penetration' of religious messages, values, and worldview into the otherwise 'nonreligious' public (statist, or *'mamlakhti'*) educational system, harming, as it is, the most vulnerable children.[16] Hence, while the argument may indeed be made that this is a numerically minor movement, I would argue that it distills and broadcasts rather clearly and forcefully a (problematic, un-self-aware) liberal-Zionist, secularist working-out of the Jewish identity crisis that lies at the very heart of the Zionist ideology and the State of Israel. I will suggest, then, that the claims made by the forum merit attention, as they illuminate a certain, rather influential, understating of the meaning of Jewish politics in contemporary Israel.[17]

The Secular Forum defines *'hadata,'* its rallying cry, as 'transforming [something or someone] to religious; the opposite of *'hilun'* [secularization].' Or, more concretely, 'the religious-orthodox taking over of

---

[15] The Secular Forum's website offers both Hebrew and English pages. These are not identical. Interestingly, the English pages do not use the term 'religionization' (as a translation of *hadata*) and instead use 'religious radicalization.' I am referring here to the Hebrew pages, consulting in my translation with the English pages. For an academic presentation of the argument on religionization see Y. Peled and H. Herman Peled, *The Religionization of Israeli Society* (London: Routledge, 2018).

[16] The Secular Forum's website curates the reports of its activity in the Israeli media. Between the forum's first media appearances in late 2015 and the time of writing (late 2017), the website references more than 65 such items in the Israeli media. The Secular Forum, 'Min hatiqshoret – haforum haḥiloni.' goo.gl/ q1RGkG.

[17] This is clearly manifested by an inflation of references to *'hadata'* in the Israeli media. Yehouda Shenhav found that since the term was first coined (by himself, in 2003 alluding to the projection of 'religion' on colonial subjects: Y. Shenhav, *The Arab Jews: Nationalism, Religion and Ethnicity* (Tel Aviv: Am Oved, 2003), 76, 119, and then recognised (in 2006) by the Academy for the Hebrew Language, 'Hadata,' hebrew-academy.org.il/?p=22525) there has been a steady growth in the use of the term, with the number of references to it quadrupling between 2016 and 2017. Y. Shenhav, 'Angel-less skies: The debate on religionisation under the canopy of the Protestant ethic,' *Israeli Sociology*, 19/2 (2018), 8–30.

the public sphere, while disturbing the proper balance between Jewish
and democratic, and between particular and universal, and the dim-
ming down [*im'um*] of Judaism's varying and diverse appearances.'[18]
The forum's diagnosis of Israeli political culture echoes the sense of an
ominous triumph of the dark forces of 'religion' in the alleged secular-
religious *Kulturkampf*. Under the headline 'Fighting against religionization,' the union depicts a stark image before calling for a fight for the
very survival of the (nonreligious) mainstream of Israeli society:

> The bad news: In the last decade, the forces in the State of Israel that try to
> turn it into a more religious and nationalist and less democratic and liberal
> state have gained strength. We have been witnessing the rise of religious and
> nationalistic elements within the State of Israel. These elements operate
> vigorously in the public education system, which is currently undergoing
> an aggressive religious radicalization to the detriment of our democratic
> society. One of the arenas where these forces are forcefully active is the
> *mamlakhti* education system,[19] that is going through an aggressive process
> of religionization … We have been working in all arenas to expand the
> secular consciousness and to allow our children a secularist and humanist,
> pluralistic and Zionist education.[20]

The forum's campaign has been focused primarily on textbooks and
educational programs approved by the state. It has 'researched' and
'exposed' the 'penetration' or 'permeation' (*ḥilḥul* in the original
Hebrew news report,[21] a word suggesting an encroaching infection)
of 'religious content' in the *mamlakhti* (i.e., the supposedly 'nonreligious') textbooks – culminating in 'religious indoctrination.'[22]
The problem identified by The Secular Forum appears to be one of
an improper use of 'Jewish' or 'religious' sources 'without due explanations' in these textbooks. But before tracing this argument further,

---

[18] The Secular Forum, 'Hamadrikh lahoreh haḥiloni,' www.hiloni.org.il/?p=1025.
[19] The English pages of the forum's website use the term 'the education system that
     represents the secular public.' While this may be a generally accepted usage of
     '*mamlakhti*,' in the context of education, it completely ignores – or rather
     assumes as obvious, as does the movement's overall campaign – the heavily
     Zionist, statist meaning of this term.
[20] The Secular Forum, 'haforum haḥiloni.' www.hiloni.org.il.
[21] O. Kashti, 'behemot tehorot vesiyur bebeit hamiqdash,' *Haaretz*, April 20, 2017.
[22] O. Kashti, "'Jews' advantages to non-Jews': Religious indoctrination seeping into
     Israeli textbooks,' *Haaretz* (English edition), April 22, 2017.

allow me to digress for a moment and note how the 'problem' of translation offers us, in this case and others, a fascinating glimpse into the very confused nature of the Israeli, Zionist discourse on the 'problem' or 'danger' of religion and religionization (as opposed to what the forum celebrates as the enlightenment of the 'secularist and humanist, pluralistic and Zionist'[23] worldview): The original Hebrew report on the forum's campaign in *Haaretz*,[24] addressing Hebrew speaking Israelis, warns against the '*ḥilḥul*'/permeation of '*dati*'/religious sources into otherwise *mamlakhti* textbooks. The English version of the same newspaper,[25] catering mostly to English speaking Jews in Israel and abroad, refers to the permeation not of religious but of *Jewish* sources. This minor slippage – from '*dati*,' that is 'religious,' in the Hebrew original to 'Jewish' in the article's English official translation, attests to the contested matter of the issue at hand: the very Jewishness of the text is taken to be anathema to the statist nature of the national, allegedly secular education offered by the Jewish state. Its very 'Jewishness' renders it 'religious.'

In any event, the very exercise on which the 'findings' of The Secular Forum's report and subsequent campaign are based is in itself an illuminating manifestation of the Zionist-Jewish identity crisis: Assuming a fundamental distinction between the 'religious' (i.e., 'Jewish') and 'secular' (i.e., 'Israeli,' and '*mamlakhti*') realms, the forum's representatives conducting the review 'were asked to find content from Jewish sources or religious contexts' in the state-approved textbooks. These religious references include, according to the forum's guidelines, such matters as 'the dress code of boys and girls, head covering, separation of genders,' the use of 'language of belief' ['*safa emunit*'], and whether a distinction between 'beliefs and customs' and 'facts and dictates' is made. The basic premise of this exercise has been that 'the secular person is sovereign,' and that this individual sovereignty should be expressed 'with the question mark – the courage to ask; the courage to cast doubt; the courage to choose.'[26]

---

[23] The Secular Forum, 'haforum haḥiloni.'
[24] Kashti, 'behemot tehorot vesiyur bebeit hamiqdash.'
[25] Kashti, 'Jews' advantages to non-Jews.'
[26] Kashti, 'behemot tehorot vesiyur bebeit hamiqdash'; The Secular Forum, 'hamadrikh lahoreh haḥiloni.'

Utilizing the secular-religious prism to study certain textbooks,[27] the review found, as was widely reported in the Israeli media, that the 'textbooks include frequent references to Shabbat and Jewish holidays, and that 'there is often a massive penetration of religious sources: quotes from the Bible and the Jewish sages, some presenting myths and beliefs as facts.'[28]

A closer look at the contested matter at hand – those 'religious' or 'Jewish' sources that have managed to infect the otherwise healthy body of secular national textbooks – might leave the uninitiated observer quite confused. For, the transgressions identified by The Secular Forum's review would quite commonly be included in any proper list of basic culturally, *nationally* Jewish matters. In other words, what The Secular Forum, and the Israeli media following it, highlight as an encroaching religionization could just as easily – when viewed outside of the Israeli, Zionist rendition of the prism of a secular-religious *Kulturkampf* – be conceived of as pertaining primarily to 'secular' matters of Jewish history, culture, and language. Moreover, even when focusing on the Israeli context, one can safely claim that what the various reports have identified as 'religious' matters have to do with Zionist-Israeli, national identity at least as much as they do with 'religion.'[29]

Let us, by way of example, consider one such textbook review, which has figured prominently in the media coverage of The Secular Forum's report. The book at hand, a basic-level Hebrew reading textbook, was found to be so saturated with elements of '*hadata*' that the reviewer marked it as 'not fit for use.' Her experience of reviewing the book has been rather gloom. She reports that reading the book left her 'shocked … I did not think the situation is so bad.'[30]

The elements of the text found by the reviewer to be 'irrelevant' – that is, as amounting to a 'pushing' of religious matters which have

---

[27] The forum offers a growing body of such review on its website: The Secular Forum, 'hadata besifrei halimud.' goo.gl/UFpr1d.

[28] Kashti, 'Jews' advantages to non-Jews.'

[29] This is echoed in a comment made by the person who initiated and oversaw the review, according to which, at bottom, these 'religious' contents are not unacceptable to a secular Israeli mind-set: 'These can be still used, simply by skipping the aspects of belief (*hebetim emuniyim*).' Quoted by Kashti, 'behemot tehorot vesiyur bebeit hamiqdash.'

[30] D. Snir, 'Review of Hebrew language reading textbook,' The Secular Forum. https://goo.gl/bkkA1K.

nothing to do with the ('secular') topic of study (Hebrew reading, in this case) – are illuminating in themselves. For example, she critically notes: 'Shabbat, Shabbat, and more Shabbat ... various texts on the subject of Shabbat.' She supports this judgment by textual and imagery examples, that have all to do with the notion of Shabbat being a family focused day of rest. The reviewer goes on to identify a poem by Lea Goldberg (*Zemer Leshabbat*) as 'an explicitly religious song,' and notes the appearance of traditional symbols of Shabbat ('a Shabbat dinner table, candles, challah bread, table cloth, a bottle of wine') as expressions of religiosity. It is quite apparent that in the case of this reviewer, Shabbat is by definition a matter of 'religion,' and any mention of the uniqueness of the day is an expression of religiosity – and an act of religionization.

Other matters of religion the reviewer has highlighted have to do with Yom Kippur (depicted in the textbook as a day of mutual asking for forgiveness) and the holiday of Sukkot. The reviewer protests against images of kippah-wearing children, and critically notes 'another quote from the sources ... – *vesamaḥta beḥagekha* [And you shall rejoice in thy feast].' She is further critical of references to the Hebrew calendar, and 'A quote from the sources: ''Honor your mother and your father'' followed by an exercise in which the students are asked to discuss the idea of respecting one's parents is also presented as an irrelevant and improper introduction of religious material into the curriculum.

As examples of 'language of belief' the reviewer offers the following quotations from the textbook: '*shabbat hamalkah* [the Sabbath queen], *goy veyehudi* [gentile and Jew], *se'udat shabbat* [Sabbath meal], *piyyutim* [hymns], *hayamim hanora'im* [days of owe].' She also protests the distinction made in the text between Jews and non-Jews, 'stories about the advantage of Jews and Judaism over the horrible gentiles.'[31]

This ultimately constitutes a disturbing pattern: 'The amount of Jewish contents, from the sources and otherwise, ramming of quotations from the Bible in irrelevant places, followed by questions on the role of religion in the life of the child.' For the reviewer at hand, this

---

[31] Snir, 'Review of Hebrew language reading textbook'; This last quote is the source of the headline in *Haaretz*'s (English) report of the findings; Kashti, 'Jews' Advantages to non-Jews.'

amounts to brainwash: 'I see this as a one-sided discussion, which is aimed at instilling attitudes of religion in the minds of children.'[32]

It should be stressed that The Secular Forum is not, by any measure, anti-Zionist, as was the case with other anti-Jewish or antireligious Israeli movements such as the Young Hebrews, nor is it anti-statist, as is the case with universalist secularists in the country. On the contrary, The Secular Forum's is a fight to 'save the *mamlakhti* education ... we have acted in all arenas to expand secular consciousness and to allow our children a secularist and humanist, pluralist and Zionist education.'[33]

Israeli Secularism's Menacing Defeat?

Following the exposition of the endemic 'religionization' in the statist educational system, The Secular Forum has organized 'an emergency conference [*kinus ḥerum*],' in which they demanded that the state recognizes a new, secular educational stream. This stream, they suggested, should be able 'to defend itself against the trend of the religionization of the educational system.' This demand has a manifestly defeatist tone to it, as it broadcasts a sense of a lost battle against religionization at large. As the head to The Secular Forum was quoted saying: 'The secular public should understand that it is a minority, and that in the State of Israel minorities have more power than the silent majority. We in The Secular Forum have accepted the burden of leading this minority.'[34]

A similar sentiment is evident in the wider liberal-Zionist discourse, for example, in numerous reports, debates, and op-ed pieces in *Haaretz* (and see my discussion below). Thus, for example, in an opinion piece by a resident columnist in the newspaper that caters primarily to the Israeli liberal-Zionist elite:

I belong to a repressed minority group in Israel ... As a matter of fact, this is the only distinct repressed minority to which I have ever belonged in my life. It took me a while to understand this, and it seems to me that this is also the case with many of my friends. Hence, our minority consciousness is still in its

---

[32] Snir, 'Review of Hebrew language reading textbook.'
[33] The Secular Forum, 'haforum haḥiloni.'
[34] A. Somfalvi and S. Ḥai, "ein ḥinukh ḥiloni beyisrael': hahorim haḥilonim yotz'im lemaavaq,' *Ynet*, May 12, 2016.

infancy, even though we are a large and important minority ... It took time [to realize this], like those frogs who are slowly boiled in a pot. But today there is no longer room for debate ... I find it funny to call this 'religious coercion' ... In fact, this is tyranny. A violent tyranny of the state. I am refraining from using the word 'terror' only for the sake of not derailing the discussion.[35]

Granted, this is largely a rhetorical maneuver; at the end, The Secular Forum and the liberal-Zionist elite at large insist that secular Israelis are the silent majority, who used to be 'hegemonic,'[36] and they clearly seek the reinstallation of this hegemony. The notion of referring to themselves as a minority aims to protests this majority's inability to uphold its status and adjoining values, echoing a familiar complaint of 'religious coercion,' or 'religious terror.'[37] Yet this sentiment is not insignificant, for it has encouraged a debate among this elite on the reasons for its failure to spread the message of secularist, liberal, leftist Zionism to the wider Israeli public. 'The sense is that there is no one to talk to, no one to listen. Politically and publicly, it [i.e., the secularist resentment against religious coercion] is almost a taboo. The mainstream is growing distanced from us.'[38]

Maybe even more significant in this regard is the opposition to this secularist initiative, and the minority outlook it broadcasts, as attested by the head of The Secular Forum, Ram Fruman. As he notes, secular Israeli-Jews commonly reject his initiative because of their adherence to a mainstream Zionist-statist outlook.[39] He also testifies to being astonished by the fact that 'other sectors in the state – Ultra-Orthodox, Arabs, *masrotiyim*, and even religious Zionists, who are not taken by their leaders' megalomania' express sympathy to his cause. It is 'those sectors from which I allegedly wish to separate myself' who are more attentive to Fruman's arguments.

In other words, the hegemonic secular public refuses to harm the configuration of power in which it is the hegemon, while the various minorities inhabiting the lower strata of this configuration are open to new ideas. As Fruman aptly notes: 'the secular desire for statism [*mamalkhtiyut*]' is only a cover for hegemonic thinking. 'The nice

---

[35] U. Misgav, 'kefiya datit? teror dati,' *Haaretz*, December 4, 2015.

[36] O. Kashti, 'Group seeks to counter religious 'coercion' in Israeli public schools,' *Haaretz*, January 5, 2016.

[37] Misgav, 'kefiya datit? teror dati.'   [38] Misgav, 'kefiya datit? teror dati.'

[39] R. Fruman, 'ḥilonim, matai tavinu eifu atem ḥayim?' *Haaretz*, July 4, 2016.

words' of coexistence and mutual respect sounded by his secular audience are nothing but rhetoric that 'hides a wish to regain control over the other sectors' of Israeli society. 'It is not the wish to live together as equals' that guides them, but 'the wish to live together while enforcing their attitudes on the other groups.'[40]

The debate among secularist Israelis, in this reading, is a debate on the proper way to confront a new emerging configuration of power, in which the (secular, statist, Zionist) hegemon is no longer able to freely exert control over other groups in Israeli society. 'The secular-democratic-liberal public has lost the hegemony in 1977 [the year in which the Likud party took over the governing coalition, ending decades of Labor rule over the Zionist movement and the State of Israel], and the demographic trends won't enable it to regain control.' Israeli society is no longer unified (as was supposedly the case in the first decades of statehood); it has become 'tribal and sectorial. My tribe [i.e., secularist Israelis] is indeed the largest, but it is nevertheless a minority, and does not have a super-status [*ma'mad 'al*]; it is one tribe among many.' The secular public's 'refusal' to acknowledge this reality is, in this reading, 'the gravest danger for the existence of the secular society.' The 'hegemonic-statist fantasy' prevents the secular sector from readapting to this new configuration of power and amassing political power; 'The statist consciousness prevents the seculars from forming a sectorial consciousness,' and this leaves them at an 'enormous disadvantage' vis-à-vis other sectors, culminating in 'the onslaught of religionization we currently experience.'[41]

In sum, the debate on secular education, religionization, religious coercion – or even 'religious terror'[42] – and so many other adjoining matters, has to do with a realignment of the *political* map in Israel. 'Religion' or 'religionization' are here codenames of an emerging

---

[40] Fruman, 'ḥilonim, matai tavinu eifu atem ḥayim?'

[41] Fruman, 'ḥilonim, matai tavinu eifu atem ḥayim?'; Ram Fruman and The Secular Forum also instigated the founding of a 'Secular Lobby' in the Israeli parliament. Tellingly, one of the speakers at the inaugural event of this lobby, sociologist Eva Ilouz, is reported to have criticized the focus put on the limitations on commerce during the Sabbath, insisting: 'Secularism is found in many political camps. It is oftentimes seen as a struggle for consumer rights [i.e., as the right to shop during the Sabbath]. This is not enough. Secularism has to be a different religion.' J. Lis, 'beoulam male uvli yesh 'atid: hushka hashedula haḥilonit baknesset,' *Haaretz*, January 17, 2018.

[42] Misgav, 'kefiya datit? teror dati.'

competing reading of the meaning of political Zionism, which threatens the status of the 'secular-democratic-liberal public.' The diagnosis is rather gloom: This sector, the 'us' in this discourse, those who used to be the hegemon, are both 'hated and lack political power.'[43]

Zionism, Socialism, and the Future of Israeli Secularism

That this sense is shared by many others in the Israeli secularist Left is evident in, among other things, a debate that ignited on the pages of *Haaretz* in late 2016 and early 2017, in which various writers debated what they all agreed is a general trend toward religion – or religionization, a process in which 'nationalism and Jewish orthodoxy are taking over Israel' – and that something 'has gone wrong with secularism.'[44]

This general sense that Israeli secularism has been on the losing side and facing some formidable challenges seems to have simmered for years. The assassination of Prime Minister Yitzhak Rabin in 1995 – to note but one milestone in this regard – was read by many as a watershed in the religious-secular *Kulturkampf* and has in hindsight played a major role in the narrative of the decline of the liberal-Zionist, secularist Left. More immediately, the continuous inability of this secularist Left to challenge the coalition of the Israeli Right was read by many as attesting to not just a political or party-ideological deficiency, but rather to a more ominous ideological, epistemological even, crisis, in which the Israeli mainstream fails to adopt the secularist worldview.

The debate at hand manages to encapsulate both the sense of crisis and the reassertion of the secularist, liberal-Zionist worldview (as well as its shortcomings, quite clearly emanating from what I propose we see as the over-arching Jewish identity crisis at hand) and can thus be used as an illuminating illustration of the wider picture of contemporary Jewish-Israeli secularism. I do not intend to claim, as it seems to be done (even if implicitly) by many of the writers involved, that a debate over the pages of *Haaretz* necessarily amounts to a national debate in which 'everyone' is involved. Indeed, it is hard to assess how

---

[43] Fruman, 'ḥilonim, matai tavinu eifu atem ḥayim?'

[44] C. Strenger, 'Why nationalist and Jewish orthodoxy are [sic] taking over Israel,' *Haaretz*, January 12, 2017.

widespread are the ideas expressed in it. Yet this debate does offer a clear view of the nature of the discourse at large, and it would be helpful to carefully trace some of its main moves.

An opening shot of sorts of the debate has been a piece by Rogel Alpher, a columnist who writes almost daily in *Haaretz*, and is known for his provocations.[45] Alpher seems to have run a similar exercise to those encouraged by The Secular Forum and scanned a primary school textbook for traces of 'religionization.' He was apparently scandalized by his findings, claiming to have traced 'a direct line' connecting 'extreme, religious and racist nationalism and the reading anthology for learning Hebrew in second grade.' This textbook, he asserts, amounts to 'spitting in the face of the nonreligious.' Summarizing the narrative plot of one story (a Jewish 'legend'), he concludes that

The entire new Israeli fascism is rolled up in this legend. There is a clear connection between the figure of the righteous and victimized Jew, who God rewards for his righteousness [a plot which Alpher had found to be depicted in the book], and the apartheid steps that [Education Minister Naftali] Bennett is leading in Amona [an illegal settlement outpost that has been the focus of much contention at the time].[46]

This leads Alpher to consider the wider reality of encroaching religionization in Israel. In his enraged reading, the very mention of the Jewish Sabbath as a special (not to say 'holy') day amounts to religious indoctrination. He thus protests, in the same breadth, both a promotion by the Ministry of Education of a series of music performances (by artists from the mainstream, nonreligious Israeli pop scene) under the title of 'Shabbat Shalom,' and a publicity campaign, 'Shishi Yisre'eli' (Israeli Friday), ran privately by Israeli business people aiming to encourage Israelis (Jews) to hold Friday night Kiddush ceremonies

---

[45] These have reached the status of international celebrity curse fight when Roseanne Barr sparred with Alpher over Twitter, following his call to the Jews of France (in the wake of a terror attack) that 'Fleeing to Israel is to escape from the arms of Muslim fascism into the arms of Jewish fascism.' See: R. Blum, 'In wake of Paris attacks, Roseanne Barr blasts *Haaretz* writer for bashing Israel,' *Algemeiner.Com*, November 23, 2015, www.algemeiner.com/?p=298294.

[46] R. Alpher, 'The reading list for learning fascism in second grade,' *Haaretz*, December 11, 2016.

and meals,[47] as amounting to the same trend of a religious spitting in the face of the secular.

Interestingly, Alpher himself does not explicitly voice the same defeatist tone, by which this religious spitting in the face amounts to a failure of secular Israeliness, who should now adopt the tactics of a minority (as was argued by Fruman and Misgav; see above). But he was apparently read to be saying so, and hence the ensuing debate over the pages of *Haaretz* on the reasons for this alleged defeat.

It may be worth to highlight here that in this and other similar writings, the secularist stance is conflated with what is usually viewed as a leftist political stance. While the debate on the nation-state bill (discussed in Chapter 2) has clearly shown that liberal-democratic concerns were shared – at least rhetorically so – by people from the Right who oppose the bill, the general tendency over the pages of *Haaretz* has been to assume that secularism is a staple of leftist liberal-Zionism, and vice versa. Correspondingly (and here lies the onus of this identification), xenophobic nationalism (or 'fascism' and 'apartheid' in Alpher's terminology) is taken to be 'religious' by definition; and the rejection of these is understood to be the domain of the secular – ignoring, as it were, the whole infrastructure of the theopolitics of the modern, liberal, 'secular' nation-state, where a conflation of territory, sovereignty, and identity has been a motivating force behind pervasive xenophobia and continuous bloodshed.

All commentators involved seem to assume as given the identification between the secularist worldview and a leftist, liberal-Zionist political stance, and they all agreed that the failure of one front brings about the failing of the other. As put by another *Haaretz* regular contributor, Rami Livni, Alpher's rage should not be addressed against the Minister of Education Naftali Bennett (of the religious-Zionist party), since he, Bennett, only does what is logical or 'natural' for him to do:

---

[47] The campaign's manager describes it as aiming to encourage mutual respect and unity in Israeli society. She identifies the social union who initiated the campaign and funds it as composed of 'secular business people.' They see the traditional Friday night meal – and the ritual of Kiddush – as a 'quintessentially Israeli tradition,' presenting the campaign as completely unrelated to religious matters. See: Shishi Yisre'eli, 'kidush – masoret shel shishi yisre'eli,' Dvar Hamefarsem's website, goo.gl/yUhyME; The campaign's Facebook page offers a wider view of it: Shishi Yisre'eli, 'shishi yisre'eli – home,' Facebook.com, bit.ly/2AOE7ux.

Bennett isn't the address, just as there is no point blaming a cat for its healthy instincts when it licks the cream left in a dish. Settlers have a built-in political interest in weakening not only the left but also Israeli secularism as an ideological, existential and cultural option – because it is clear to them that a potential threat to their enterprise can only blossom in a secular setting.[48]

For this commentator, the failure of Israeli secularism is self-inflicted: 'Israeli secularism is committing suicide'; It is 'Secular Israelis ... and only the secular' who are to blame for a failure that seems to be primarily one of inability to oppose the (religious) enemy and defend oneself. Critically, in this reading, this incompetence is nourished by the secularist commitment to, or at least respect for, matters of Jewish identity. Livni detects a slippage from the confused secularist respect for Jewish identity to a 'natural' coercion of illiberal religious values. Hence, 'What used to irritate, inflame, and drive them ['secular Israelis'] to revolt two decades or even a decade ago, they now greet with a nonchalant shrug, forgivingly, all in the name of openness, tolerance, and, of course, 'Jewish identity."

Livni offers several reasons for 'the decline of secularism.' These have to do primarily with a weakening of the secularist Left's ideological, *Zionist* commitments and the resulting inability of the liberal-Zionist Left to promote or impose its secularism on the Israeli public at large. Echoing other commentators' lamentation that the liberal commitment to identity politics with its ever-growing sensitivity to the Other's worldview has prevented the Left from assertively promoting its worldview,[49] Livni argues that secularism has been 'privatized,' and transformed from 'a Zionist, national issue into a sectorial, class one.' The liberal-Zionist balance, i.e., the balance between the liberal values of the Left and its national, Zionist (Jewish) commitments has been disturbed, and as a result 'left-wing voters have lost interest in the character of their country in recent years. After all, it's not very liberal to tie yourself in knots in order to shape a society in accordance with your own values.'

Identity politics and the preoccupation with the individual's right to choose have, in Livni's reading, 'sucked the energy out of secularism,

---

[48] R. Livni, 'Three reasons Israelis stopped being secular,' *Haaretz*, January 2, 2017.

[49] M. Lilla, *The Once and Future Liberal: After Identity Politics* (New York: Harper, 2017).

leaving the central arena – the constant tug of war between religion and secularism – to the presence of only one side.' The image here is a decisively dichotomous picture of secularism and religion fighting in a zero-sum game over the very soul of the Jewish-Israeli mainstream, which, Livni acknowledges, is nevertheless 'traditional but not very observant.'

In this binary image, Jewish matters are almost by definition marked as belonging to the religious side. Hence, in Livni's account, another reason for the decline of secularism is precisely its attempt to re-appropriate historical or traditional Jewish culture and text. 'Jewish identity has become an obsession,' and 'the phenomenon of Jewish Renewal, which has morphed from being a harmless hobby into a dangerous problem' is nothing less than 'a Trojan horse of religion and the Right.' Israeli secularists' endeavors to reacquaint themselves with foundational texts of the wider historical Jewish world and 'their pursuit of Jewish identity' are but expressions of the fatal secularist 'internalization' of the insulting canard that 'the secular wagon is empty, and the religious wagon is full.'[50]

Livni's is, at bottom, a manifestly conservative, reactionary even, Zionist stance. He decries 'secular Israelis'' adoption of 'the kitschy and false argument that the fathers of Zionism – who strove to establish a modern model of national Judaism without religion – robbed them of something immeasurably precious,' and ultimately sees this 'modern model of national Judaism' as the remedy to the decline of secularism. This is a manifestly theological – or rather theopolitical – remedy, by which the (allegedly secular) values of the 'miraculous' project of political-Zionism are reasserted against the encroaching reemergence of their enemy, religious Judaism.

Livni thus wishes for a return to the allegedly secular 'Israeli-Hebrew culture that was miraculously created here.' The fruits of this miracu-lous culture (a list of which includes, in Livni's reading, ironically, the poet Lea Goldberg, whose poem for Shabbat was marked by The

---

[50] Livni has more systematically articulated his argument in a recently published book, where he decries the failure of a *secular* Jewish nationalism (what he terms as 'Hebrewness'). Reviving (and mourning the death of) the basic Zionist notions of a 'New Jew' and the negation of exile, Livni blames the rise of a hawkish, right-wing version of Jewish ethnonationalism on the failure of the Left in buttressing secular Jewish nationalism. R. Livni, *The End of Hebrewness* (Jerusalem: Carmel, 2018).

Secular Forum's aforementioned commissioned review as amounting to 'religionization'[51]) should have been, beyond their cultural value, 'the flak jacket that protected secularism from religion, the conclusive proof of its overflowing knapsack and attractiveness for the muddled middle and those on the margins.' Yet, Israeli seculars, 'on a suicidal impulse, instead of guarding it like a precious treasure and ensuring that it would always be fresh and attractive,' have

turned their backs on their baggage, on their identity pack, and failed to replenish it. Or they abandoned it in favor of ethnic folklore, Yiddishkeit and piyyutim (liturgical poems) or, alternatively, cosmopolitan pretentiousness – which doesn't work anywhere and certainly not in the Middle East, where religion is a constant challenge.[52]

Ultimately, then, this has to do with the Zionist enterprise's sense of itself as (in Herzl's phrasing) 'form[ing] a portion of a rampart of Europe against Asia, an outpost of civilization as opposed to barbarism.'[53] Or, in the more concise phrasing of Ehud Barak, a (secular) 'villa in the Jungle.'[54] Israel is here conceived of as an outpost of (secularist) European enlightenment in the culturally arid Middle East, which is – by this colonialist definition – ravaged by benighted religiosity. The matter at hand, then, is not 'just' the meaning of secularism, but a Zionist reading of the term, in which the configuration of power of the modern nation-state – that nevertheless self-identifies as a nation-state of *Jews* – rules over a stretch of land in the Middle East, and over large minorities of Middle Easterners.

This was echoed in an otherwise positive reaction to Livni's analysis, in which the writer – the veteran journalist, activist and sometime politician, Uri Avneri – stressed the role of an initially strong and gradually weakening commitment to political-Zionist ideology in the initial triumph and eventual decline of Zionist (and then Israeli) secularism.

For Avneri, the 'decisive' cause for 'the taking over of the state by religion' is that 'Israeli secularism has become void of ideational

---

[51] Snir, 'Review of Hebrew language reading textbook.'
[52] Livni, 'Three reasons Israelis stopped being secular.'
[53] T. Herzl, *The Jewish State*, trans. Louis Lipsky (New York: Dover Publications, 2008), 96.
[54] E. Bar-Yosef, *A Villa in the Jungle: Africa in Israeli Culture* (Jerusalem: Van Leer Institute, 2013).

content.' To prove this, he narrates a history in which the founding, triumphantly secular moment has been one of unparalleled commitment to Zionist ideology: The 'revolutionary idea' that fueled the Zionist 'revolutionary act' has been "pioneering', socialist, national-secularist.' Ben-Gurion, who embodies this idea, 'was a radical antireligious' person, who 'refused' to cover his head, as is the Jewish custom, 'even in funerals.' In the same dichotomous worldview, where religion and nonreligion (here, then, identified with the values of socialist, political-Zionism) are locked in a zero-sum type of relationship, this triumphant moment also had to relegate religion to the decaying realm of 'the old men and women' who were looked down on 'with mercy' by Avneri and his fellow (young) ideologues; a defeated, anachronistic idea, that could not stand the onslaught of youthful secularist Zionism.[55]

The next chapter in this history, which marks the decline of the secular is, then, an episode of Zionist ideological decline. Post 1967, the 'secular public ... has sunk into the comfortable life.'

It despised ideologies. Pioneering has expired. The kibbutzim, the backbone of Israeli secularism, have given up on their values. The new Hebrew culture, which is essentially secular, loosened, and almost dissipated. Religion penetrated every corner, in the guise of 'Judaism.'

Note how the dichotomous image of a zero-sum framework demands that the triumph of the religious side is the result of the decline of secularism; religion seems to be 'penetrating' and polluting national, secular life by osmosis: once secularism declines, religion must rise.

Avneri is also attentive to the limits of the secularist impulse in a Zionist, nationally *Jewish*, framework. He notes with apparent approval the 'various attempts at creating a new secular ideology' that would be completely independent from (if not outright opposed to) Jewishness. Yet, these attempts, culminating with the movement of the Young Hebrews, who 'preached a total detachment from the Jewish people and Jewish religion,' fell prey to their own radicalism. Thus, in an apparent move of pragmatic shrewdness, a new movement established by Avneri and his comrades (under the name *Bamaavaq*), 'also

---

[55] U. Avneri, 'Yair Lapid hu dugma lahitrapsut haḥilonit,' *Haaretz*, December 27, 2016.

claimed that we compose a new 'Hebrew' nation in the country,' but unlike the Young Hebrews also claimed that 'this nation belongs to the Jewish people.' Yet, in Avneri's telling, this too seemed to push the limits of Zionist secularism to extremes, which were soundly rejected by his fellow (secular, Zionist, but not non-Jewish or anti-Jewish) ideologues.[56]

In Shlomo Avineri's reaction to Avneri and Livni,[57] the centrality of nationalist, Zionist ideology for the very viability of Israeli secularism is so fundamental as to render the very notion of secularism independently meaningless: "Secularism' is by nature a concept which lacks any content in for itself.' It is an empty vessel, since it is primarily a negation, 'an antithesis to religion, to the belief in a creator, to observance.' As such, 'secularity' cannot be truly used as an adjective. Going back to the role model of Ben-Gurion, Avineri notes that while the leader was indeed 'secular' ['ḥiloni'] – a 'militant' one, at that – it will nevertheless be wrong to identify him as such. 'If asked, he would have identified himself as Jewish, as Zionist, as socialist. As much as we can call Ben-Gurion and his generation 'secular', this is no more than mere factual description – secularism in for itself has never been their self-identity.'

For Avineri, secularity or secularism are but a fact of the very essence of Zionism. (Needless to say, as I have expanded elsewhere,[58] this renders religious-Zionism an anomaly by definition). That all political factions of Zionism, from the leftist socialist to the rightist revisionists were 'secular' is a 'fact,' which 'has not amounted to a common denominator' among these factions: 'One cannot imagine' members of the leftist Palmaḥ and the rightist Etzel paramilitary organizations saying 'we are both secular' since such an utterance 'has no meaning.' Moreover, the very idea of 'secular Judaism [or Jewishness]' is also meaningless: 'There is no such thing, just as there is no secular Christianity; there is Zionism, there is socialism.'

Ultimately, Avineri and Avneri agree that the contemporary malaise of Israeli secularism is its lack of ideological commitment – whether 'Zionist,' 'national,' 'socialist,' or otherwise, but surely not 'secularist.' For both of them, the decline of Jewish, Israeli, Zionist secularism has

---

[56] Avneri, 'Yair Lapid hu dugma lahitrapsut haḥilonit.'
[57] S. Avineri, 'neged ḥiloniyut ḥalula,' *Haaretz*, January 5, 2017.
[58] Yadgar, *Sovereign Jews*, 73.

nothing to do with the very concept of this secularism; rather, it has to do with the decline of the Zionist Left. (Needless to say, this stance ignores secularist streams in the Zionist Right. In this view, only the Left can be meaningfully secular.) Hence, in Avineri's formulation, the only way to 'return Zionist secularism to its glory' is to 'fill it with positive ideational contents – of social justice, of equality, of solidarity.' For him, liberal-Zionism's only chance to win the battle against the 'religious Right,' who, given its high (nationalist) ideological commitment has been able to appropriate the notion of Jewishness and Jewish nationalism, is to reassert the Left's reading of this same nationalism: 'Only a Zionist Left that is proud of its Zionism and Jewish nationalism – which obviously recognizes the nationalism of the Palestinian people, but does not identify with it – can be an alternative to the current outlook of our society.'[59]

This last sentence in Avineri's piece leaves no room for doubt that the backdrop for this discussion is, again, the Israeli-Palestinian conflict. He suggests that the Left's ideological failure has to do exactly with a distortion of the liberal-Zionist balance, in which the Left tilts away from Zionism and toward the liberal values, that would ultimately render the preference of one nationalism (Jewish, Zionist) over the other (Palestinian) illegitimate. Avineri is adamant to note that a liberal-Zionist 'recognition' of the 'nationalism' (i.e., political aspirations) of the Palestinians should not amount to an 'identification' with the Palestinian side. Ultimately, then, the gist of the Zionist secularist impulse is toward national particularism, which is, by its own self-definition, Jewish; It is Jewish nationalism that should justify the lack of identification with Palestinian nationalism. Yet Avineri is far from giving any positively meaningful sense of what this Jewishness of the Zionist infrastructure should amount to.

Secular Zionists versus Israelis

Avineri's judgment of secularism as ultimately an empty concept was vehemently rejected by other advocates of secularism and has propelled a renewed debate that stretched over months and included

---

[59] Avineri, 'neged ḥiloniyut ḥalula.'

various writers.[60] This debate tended to focus on the role of Zionist ideological commitments in the preservation of secularism. At bottom, it has revolved around a matter that is of fundamental importance to liberal, secularist Zionism: the balance, and co-dependence, between, on the one hand, the Zionist rebellious, secularist impulse which propels it away from what it, Zionism, views as 'religion,' and, on the other hand, the Zionist claim for *Jewish* nationhood. As the debate has shown, the differing readings of this balance ultimately decide the very nature of the modern Israeli polity.

Contrary to Avineri's (and, in this regard, Avneri's, too) 'more nationalist' or even 'more (nationally, Zionistically) *Jewish*' understanding of the viability of secularism, other advocates of secularism stressed its independent value, promoting a sense of secularism that is largely indifferent to the idea of *Jewish* nationalism. (They will read the term 'Jewish' as essentially religious, preferring to refer to their nationality as *Israeli*, not Jewish.) These writers, in other words, presented what we may call a 'post-Jewish' or simply 'non-Jewish' secularist stance.

One such vocal spokesman was Ram Fruman, who heads The Secular Forum (the organization whose initiative to expose the 'religionization' of the Israeli textbooks was discussed earlier). In Fruman's reading, the historical connection between secularism and Zionist-Jewish nationalism (in its socialist rendition, which is celebrated by all writers as the historical carrier of Zionist secularism) is a bygone matter of history. Judged by contemporary criteria, he argues, Avineri's solution of 'going back to the values of Mapai's Socialist-Zionism,' in which a commitment to Jewish nationalism figures prominently, 'belongs to the past, both in its definition of Zionism and in its preference of this Zionism over Israeliness, and in the type of socialism it held. We mustn't return to the past.'[61]

---

[60] R. Fruman, 'ḥiloniyut ḥadasha veatraqtivit,' *Haaretz*, August 1, 2017; Y. Eilam, 'emuna datit he beriḥa meaḥrayut,' *Haaretz*, January 23, 2017; S. Avineri, 'neged ḥiloniyut ḥalula (2),' *Haaretz*, February 2, 2017; R. Fruman, 'hapitaron ho qodem kol yisre'eli,' *Haaretz*, February 9, 2017; S. Avineri, 'neged ḥiloniyut ḥalula (3),' *Haaretz*, February 23, 2017; Strenger, 'Why nationalist and Jewish orthodoxy are [sic] taking over Israel'; R. Fruman, 'ma ʿim haḥerut le'ekhol ḥameṣ bepesaḥ?' *Haaretz*, April 9, 2017; S. Avineri, 'neged ḥiloniyut ḥalula (4),' *Haaretz*, April 14, 2017; S. Sand, 'How Israel went from atheist Zionism to Jewish state,' *Haaretz*, January 21, 2017.

[61] Fruman, 'ḥiloniyut ḥadasha veatraqtivit.'

A similar reaction to Avineri, by Yigal Eilam, a historian of Zionism whose work finds a fundamental, essential disjunction between Zionism and 'historical Judaism,' is a fiery defense of universalist secularism, largely detached from nationalist concerns – Jewish or otherwise. In this reaction, Avineri's negative assessment of secularism, by which it is only defined as nonreligion, is seen as 'baseless … It is not the secular who is created by the negation of the religious, but just the opposite – the religious is the one who is created by the negation of the secular.'[62] It would seem that for Eilam, who advocates an Israeli identity that is detached from Zionist (read: Jewish) considerations, the tie between Zionist ideology and the viability of secularism is simply meaningless. Secularism stands for itself, and the demise of Zionist ideological commitment mourned by others is irrelevant to the persistence (or demise) of Israeli secularism.

Fruman's and Eilam's are, then, a manifestation of the 'radical' solution to the Israeli Jewish identity crisis by way of severing the tie between Israeli (secular) nationalism and Judaism. As we shall see in the next chapter, this is far from being a fully devised alternative, and it encounters a resolute rejection by advocates of liberal-Zionism. In the context of the current debate, it functions as an outlier of sorts, by not sharing the concern for a meaningful rendition of Jewish or Zionist nationalism, which characterizes practically all other contributions to the debate at hand.

On his part, Avineri (whose role as a regular contributor to *Haaretz*'s opinion pages put him as the center of the debate at hand) is doubtless attentive to the fact that 'the term 'Jewish' is completely absent' from Fruman's critique. He sees this as attesting to the fact that 'the secularism he [Fruman] is proposing is in the end hollow.' Avineri identifies in Fruman a 'recoiling' from any reference to Jewish matters, which is, he argues, symptomatic to a larger secular public who tend to 'identify the concept 'Jewish' with a religious worldview.' This is unfortunate, for it 'plays into the hands of the religious public, who seeks to exert monopolistic control over everything that has to do with the term [Jewish].'[63]

As we already saw above, for Avineri a commitment to Jewish-nationalist ideology is a precondition of Zionist secularism; the latter

---

[62] Eilam, 'emuna datit he beriḥa meaḥrayut.'
[63] Avineri, 'neged ḥiloniyut ḥalula (2).'

(i.e., the antireligious, or more precisely anti-rabbinical rebellious impulse of Zionist ideology and the movement it has propelled) cannot stand by itself. To prove this point, Avineri revisits (as do his interlocutors, each trying to prove his point by reference to a founding moment in European Jewish history) the *haskala*, or 'Jewish Enlightenment' movement. In his narration of this history, Avineri puts the emphasis squarely on the 'Jewish' adjective of the movement. A general understanding of the *haskala* movement as universalist and rationalist, he asserts, is accurate, but missing: it fails to see the Jewish essence of the movement. The *haskala*'s 'opening to the world was not abstract. Rather, it was anchored by a deep connection to the Jewish history and cultural heritage.' In Avineri's reading, *maskilim*, the prototypical European, modern, secular Jews were at bottom national, cultural (as in not 'religious') *Jews*: They 'did not deny their Jewish identity but strove to reshape it as a modern national and cultural identity. They correctly understood that one cannot be a 'human' without being rooted in a specific national culture.'[64]

As long as Israeli secularism lacks a coherent, meaningful Jewish (read in national terms, whatever these may be) content, Avineri warns, it shall 'remain hollow,' and its association with the *haskala* movement will be verging on deceit. Furthermore, it will fail to reach wider audiences. If secularism orients itself, as suggested by Fruman, toward, 'globalism, individualism, and even modern capitalism,'[65] it is bound to fail to appeal to Israelis. 'After all, these can also be achieved in Berlin and New York.'[66]

Faced with this critique, Fruman is, rhetorically at least, reluctant to fully dispense with a claim to Jewish identity (this is more evident when Fruman's is judged against the yardstick of essays by other advocates of non-Jewish Israeliness, who did not take part in the debate at hand; see Chapter 4). In this, he rather clearly manifests the Israeli secularist 'Jewish problem,' which is fed by a commitment to a nationalist worldview. Given that the nationalism at hand is largely understood to be Jewish (however abstract this may be), not Israeli, and that Judaism is read to be essentially 'religious,' the secularist impulse seems to be unable to run away from its carriers' Jewishness.

---

[64] Avineri, 'neged ḥiloniyut ḥalula (2).'
[65] Fruman, 'ḥiloniyut ḥadasha veatraqtivit.'
[66] Avineri, 'neged ḥiloniyut ḥalula (2).'

Fruman suggests a 'realignment' that would reassert the supremacy of Israeli identity over Jewishness, but he is clearly reluctant to completely forego the latter. Clarifying that he has never advocated a 'cosmopolitan identity that lacks any national context' he clarifies: 'What I object to is the transformation of Jewish identity into the central identity in the ensemble of identities that compose the image of the secular Israeli nowadays.'[67] He describes his identity as a complex composition of various elements: 'Israeli and Zionist and Western and Middle Eastern and secular and liberal-democrat, and cosmopolitan, and more.' His Jewish identity is indeed part of this composition, 'but it is only a part of the whole. If I had to choose one leading identity from this list, I would choose Israeli identity, and not Jewish.'[68] Indebted to the nationalist worldview as he is, Fruman views the claim that what he presents is a universalist stance as an insult: his, he makes a point at clarifying, is a *national* stance. He would thus 'surely' not choose the cosmopolitan element as the primary part of his composite identity.

The problem, Fruman notes, is that following a continuous process, 'which gained momentum in recent years, especially inside the educational system,' the balance between the various elements of this multi-layered identity has been disrupted, and many Israelis prefer their Jewish identity over the Israeli one. The remedy Fruman offers would necessarily reflect negatively on the central Zionist idea of a worldwide Jewish (national) unity, as it in effect marks a clear distinction between Israelis and (non-Israeli) Jews. 'Most of us, when we think of this, will agree that what unites us with other Israelis is more substantial than what unites us with other Jews.' His explication of this idea echoes – positively so – what critics of Israeli secularism have presented as a danger of a rift between Israelis and Jews:

Most of us shall admit that what unites us with the young man or woman who passed with us through the press of the Israeli educational system, and have grown with us here, in Israel, and in Hebrew, whether they are from an Arab, Asian, or African descent, are closer to us than that American Jew, who has never been here, and does not speak Hebrew.[69]

---

[67] Fruman, 'hapitaron ho qodem kol yisre'eli.'
[68] Fruman, 'hapitaron ho qodem kol yisre'eli.'
[69] Fruman, 'hapitaron ho qodem kol yisre'eli.'

This is the framework in which Jewish identity is seen as a threat, no less, to Israeli identity. Fruman identifies a 'trend' of 'undermining' Israeli identity 'both vis-à-vis Jewish identity and in other ways. I feel that the apparent effort to impose on me Jewishness as a basis for my identity is an attack on my complex identity.' The solution to the decline of secularism must, then, be 'first and foremost Israeli and [only] afterward Jewish.'[70]

In Avineri's Zionist worldview, this idea is incomprehensible. 'I do not know what precedes what' he writes in reaction to Fruman. 'But I do know that I am Israeli because I am Jewish.' Avineri does not see any merit in the argument that Israeliness is a self-sufficient identity construct: 'Israeliness does not emanate from itself.' Rather, it is a 'political' or 'nation-statist' [*medini* in the original Hebrew] matter of 'the Jewish people's right to self-determination. Without this root – which is national and not necessarily religious – the State of Israel would not have been established.' Once again, he addresses the matter of the Zionist nomenclature to assert Jewish nationalism as the core element of Israeli secularism, minimizing the importance of the Zionist ideologues' preference of the adjective 'Hebrew' over 'Jewish':

> Israel ... was created by the gathering of people who came here because they viewed themselves as Jewish, and they sought to create here a framework for their Jewish identity. In order to distinguish themselves from the Jewish existence in exile [*gola* in the original Hebrew] they preferred sometimes to use the term 'Hebrew' ... but this was [just] a nuance in their Jewish identity.

The notion of detaching Israeliness from its Jewish sources, is, then, 'simply wrong.'[71]

In the same vein, Avineri sees Fruman's assertion that Israeliness is both more inclusive (in encompassing non-Jewish Israelis) and stronger than Jewish nationhood as 'completely detached from reality.'[72] He corrects Fruman and notes that 'when he says 'Israeli' ... he actually means Jewish-Israeli.' This correction necessitates a reassertion of the exclusiveness of Jewish-Israeli nationalism: While emphasizing the need to fight for civil equality for 'Israel's Arab citizens' and against 'racist trends of some parts of the Right,' Avineri nevertheless notes that 'it is hard to ignore the cultural difference between Jews and Arabs

---

[70] Fruman, 'hapitaron ho qodem kol yisre'eli.'
[71] Avineri, 'neged ḥiloniyut ḥalula (3).'   [72] Avineri, 'neged ḥiloniyut ḥalula (3).'

in Israel . . . Jews in Israel nevertheless celebrate different holidays than those celebrated by the Muslim and Christian Arabs.'[73] Interestingly, Avineri reads Fruman's notion of the inclusivity of Israeliness as suggesting that Israelis must identify with the religious celebrations of Christian and Muslim Palestinian-Arabs. As he warns: 'this must not be blurred: I must respect the Ramadan and Christmas of the non-Jewish citizens in Israel, but they are not part of my identity . . . I have no problem with aesthetically enjoying a midnight Christmas mass . . . but to identify [with it]?'[74]

Ultimately, Avineri offers a reassertion of Jewish-nationalist ideology, especially (but not exclusively) in its socialist-Zionist rendition. He reminds his readers that Marxist predictions of a universalist (proletarian) overcoming of the nation-state have ultimately failed and commends Ḥayim Arlosoroff's early understanding that the international workers' movement has failed 'because it had adhered to abstract universalism and ignored the fact that the worker, too, has an affinity to the national culture of his people.' This understanding guaranteed the victory of socialist-Zionism, which was wise enough 'to weave Jewish historical memory and identification into a vision of communal responsibility and solidarity.'[75]

Another way to summarize this debate, then, would be to see it as stretching between two poles: *Jewish* secularism (defined nationally, Zionistically, and understood primarily through a 'leftist' lens) vs. non-Jewish (call it 'Israeli' or 'universalist') secularism. As already noted, from Avineri's Jewish-nationalist, Zionist, point of view, universal or non-Jewish secularism either simply does not make sense, or is hollow, to a degree that it is not self-sustaining. He does not see the notion of an Israeli, non-Jewish national identity as viable, and judges the values of liberalism and social democracy to which he adheres to be ultimately dependent on a national anchoring. Those like him, who wish to 'fight the religious-nationalist attempts at taking over the public sphere' in Israel 'must be aware of the need to anchor their secularity in an awareness of Jewish history and concrete [read: national] social solidarity.'[76]

---

[73] Avineri, 'neged ḥiloniyut ḥalula (3).'
[74] Avineri, 'neged ḥiloniyut ḥalula (3).'
[75] Avineri, 'neged ḥiloniyut ḥalula (3).'
[76] Avineri, 'neged ḥiloniyut ḥalula (3).'

Avineri's interlocutors, as we have already seen, wish for an Israeli identity construct that is largely liberated from 'Jewish' – which they read as 'religious' – constraints. Some of them obviously seem to be unable to completely forego a claim to Jewishness, but they all see this as a problem, as this Jewishness (in their reading, of course) necessarily inhibits secularism. As I will discuss in the following chapter, their horizon is indeed one of an Israeli identity that is fully detached from Jewish nationalism. Interestingly enough, as we have seen with Fruman, they do not necessarily see this as a breaking with Zionism. Rather, like their predecessors in the Young Hebrews movement, they see this as a rational development of the rebellious impulse (which Zionism shares) against the 'old,' 'exilic,' 'religious' Jewishness.

This stance was more methodically presented by Shlomo Sand, an Israeli historian who, following his publicized critique of Zionism, announced that he 'stopped being a Jew.'[77] Sand finds the 'secular melancholy' echoed in the public debate at hand to be obstructing. In order to clear the view of reality, he proposes to restate the affinity – and difference – between secularism and atheism. '[T]here is a profound connection between the terms secularism and atheism, but they are by no means congruent or identical ... Secularism is – not only, but mainly – a political viewpoint, whereas atheism is firstly a philosophical viewpoint.'[78] Sand sees this distinction as critical for understanding the Zionist predicament, for it highlights the trajectory of Zionism and of Israeli political culture *not* from secularism to religiosity, as claimed by most other writers, but rather from 'atheist Zionism to Jewish state.'

In Sand's narration, a pure, atheistic Zionist impulse which has propelled the movement from the beginning was originally successful at reclaiming main elements of *Jewish* (i.e., theistic, in this reading) nationalism without being hampered by them. Sand sees the (mostly socialist) Zionist reinterpretation, nationalization and appropriation of Jewish tradition[79] as a political act of the secularization of Judaism,

---

[77] S. Sand, *How I Stopped Being a Jew*, trans. D. Fernbach (New York: Verso, 2014); S. Sand, *The Invention of the Jewish People*, trans. Y. Lotan (New York: Verso, 2010); S. Sand, *The Invention of the Land of Israel: From Holy Land to Homeland*, trans. G. Forman (New York: Verso, 2014).

[78] Sand, 'How Israel went from atheist Zionism to Jewish state.'

[79] Shimoni, *The Zionist Ideology*, 269–332; Liebman and Don-Yehiya, *Civil Religion in Israel*, 25–58; E. Don-Yehiya and C. S. Liebman, 'The symbol system

which, in his reading, could nevertheless remain loyal to the atheist philosophical stance. What ultimately brought the demise of atheist Zionism has been its inability to offer an alternative, nonreligious, understanding of Jewish identity: 'The problematic nature of defining the 'Jew' according to secular criteria – cultural, linguistic, political or 'biological' (despite all efforts, it's still impossible to determine who is a Jew by means of DNA) – was what eliminated the option of a secularized identity.'[80]

This lack of an alternative, secular (or 'atheist') definition of Jewish identity, combined with the 'fear of assimilation [which] was the nightmare shared by Judaism and Zionism,' meant in effect the demise of the distinction between the two (Judaism on the one hand and Zionism on the other). 'Within a short time, the principle of the religious definition was accepted in identity politics,' and the potential opening for a secular definition of Zionist nationhood was sealed: 'Since there is no secular Jewish culture, it's impossible to join by secular means something that doesn't exist.'

In Sand's history of the demise of Zionist atheism and the triumph of Judaism, which he seems to identify with non-liberal nationalism, 1967 marked a watershed. Following the war, two complementing developments took place: 'The State of Israel expanded significantly, but at the same time a large non-Jewish population was also brought together under the country's muscular Jewish wing.' It is this historical moment – and not the very creation of Israel as the nation-state of the Jewish people some 20 years earlier – that marks for Sand the (re-) definition of Israeli politics as Jewish politics, at the expense of Zionism: 'From now on, more than ever, the emphasis had to be on the heading 'Jewish' – in other words, the state belonging to those who were born to a Jewish mother or converted according to Jewish law and, God forbid, not the country of all its citizens.'

The implied argument, that the Zionist state was 'originally' meant to be 'a state of all its citizens' can only make sense in a framework where Zionism is completely separated from Judaism, and the latter, identified in turn with 'religion,' bears the guilt for all non-liberal manifestations of nationalism. Similarly, the settlements project in the

---

of Zionist-socialism: An aspect of Israeli civil religion,' *Modern Judaism*, 1/2 (1981), 121–48; Yadgar, *Sovereign Jews*, 119–50.

[80] Sand, 'How Israel went from atheist Zionism to Jewish state.'

territories occupied in June 1967 is blamed not on ('atheist' and secular) Zionism, but on Judaism: 'The justifications for the appetite for renewed settlement also relied less on the Zionist demand for independent sovereignty and far more on the biblical idea of the Promised Land. That's why it is no coincidence that the clerical establishment became increasingly inflated at the same time.'[81]

Ultimately, for Sand any notion of Jewishness must amount to an impeding of an initially pure national, secular, atheist impulse. Against a contemporary background of identity politics, which gives rise to 'ethno-religious' and 'ethno-biological' nationalism he sees the defeat of the 'synthesis of Zionism and socialism' in face of 'a winning symbiosis of religion and strong ethno-nationalism' as inevitable. The only way out, it would appear, is a reassertion of the distinction between atheist Zionism and the notion of the 'Jewish state.' The latter cannot, in this reading, by any stretch of imagination, be truly secular.

Other regular contributors to *Haaretz* offered alternative reasons for the failure of Israeli secularism and reached different conclusions regarding the viability of a liberal-Zionist secularism. For the psychologist Carlo Strenger, the main cause for this failure is one of identity and meaning, or rather lack thereof. Agreeing in principle with Livni's abovementioned celebration of the 'miraculous Israeli secular culture from Lea Goldberg to Arik Einstein,' Strenger nevertheless insists that this culture ultimately fails, since 'for most Israelis this is not enough to sustain their identity and need for meaning.' Citing empirical research as evidence, Strenger sees secularism's weakness as emanating from its failure to answer the human fear of mortality: 'humans have a tremendous need to connect their identity to cultural and religious traditions that have historical depth. We all fear death, and we all want to belong to something larger than ourselves that promises immortality. This is religion's enormous strength.'[82]

Yet this universal psychological truism is further amplified by the violent politics of the Middle East:

The need for the promise of immortality increases even more when humans feel threatened in their survival and reminded of their mortality. Unfortunately, Israel is located in one of the globe's most unstable and violent regions, and Israelis constantly feel under threat. As a consequence, the

[81] Sand, 'How Israel went from atheist Zionism to Jewish state.'
[82] Strenger, 'Why nationalist and Jewish orthodoxy are [sic] taking over Israel.'

young Israeli-Hebrew culture does not provide enough psychological protection and Judaism becomes ever more attractive for Israelis.

This unfortunate reality of (political) violence explains Israelis' purported turn to religion: 'Israelis are embracing religion because ... Israelis feel deeply insecure, and because they have doubts about the Zionist project succeeding in the long run.'

Once again, then, the Zionist (secularist) void is filled by religion, only this time the cause for this osmosis is a combination of psychological nature and political 'unfortunate' reality. This is further amplified by liberalism's suspicion of nationalist particularism. 'Western liberal secularism is indeed a powerful value system,' yet 'it is generally antinationalist and has always been universalist and cosmopolitan.' As such, 'liberal secularism can therefore not be specifically Israeli.'

Strenger's ultimate judgment is that for liberal secularism to triumph, it must forego Zionist national particularism. Since this secularism cannot offer 'solace' to the masses who, in fear of death 'want to connect to 3,000 years of Jewish history and the biblical promise that Abraham's offspring will live forever – that the Messiah will come and the world will recognize the Jews as the Chosen People,' it must remain limited to the realm of an elite minority: 'Israel's secular liberals must realize that we are a minority, that our cosmopolitan enlightenment ideals do not satisfy the needs of most Israelis, and that we are unlikely to shape Israel's dominant culture and political identity in the foreseeable future.' The only choice left for this minority is 'to carve out a space where we can live according to our own ideals and values,' accepting defeat and realizing 'that liberal Zionism has lost the battle for Israel's soul against religious-Zionist ideology.'[83]

The continuous debate between Avineri and his interlocutors gained a more concrete character around the time of the Pesaḥ (Passover) holiday of 5777 (2017). For Fruman, advocating the non-Jewish or Israeli secular stance, the various restrictions imposed by state ('secular') law on the presentation and selling of leavened foods during the week of the Jewish holiday amounts to a severe infringement of individual rights. In a rather rambling opinion piece, he decries these restrictions (they 'drive him crazy'), criticizes the notion of *kashrut*

---

[83] Strenger, 'Why nationalist and Jewish orthodoxy are [sic] taking over Israel.'

generally (it was originally meant to 'separate Jews from gentiles in the exile,' and now it 'protects the Jews in the State of Israel ... from the seculars'), protests against the specific *kashrut* laws pertaining to wine, decries the 'Shishi Yisre'eli' campaign (see above; Fruman insists that the organizers of this campaign are religious Jews), and more. His ultimate claim seems to be aimed against the notion of national unity, which is used to justify, he argues, the coercion of secular Israelis by (religious) Jews. And this brings him to the most determined call to (secular, Israeli) battle:

We have become a minority in Israel, and our values are under attack. The only way to fight for our place here is to stop being ingratiating and flattering in face of the religious leadership. We must understand that we are a large public, but we are no longer rulers of this state. We must understand that we do not currently have political representation, and so we do not have any power in the Israeli arena. We must rebuild our secular pride, unite, reform, and create real political power.[84]

Avineri's reaction, which has been a closing of sorts of this specific debate (parallel ones have of course emerged; the matter is surely far from begin concluded), sees Fruman's stance as 'simply pathetic,' for it understands its secularism strictly in terms of Jewish religion. Fruman's focusing on *kashrut* to reassert his secular position proves that 'he is still completely snarled by the shackles of religion. For him, secularity is to do exactly the opposite from what religion orders.' In place of this 'pathetic' notion of secularism, Avineri offers the Zionist appropriation of Jewish tradition as an ingenious act of liberation, conducted from a position of individual and communal (secular, socialist-Zionist) sovereignty: 'One of the achievements of Zionism – a political and secular movement at its core – has been its ability to put modern, humanist and liberating contents in religious traditions and concepts.' He gives by way of example the rewriting of the rituals and ultimately meaning of Passover, which transformed a theologically focused holiday into 'an example and role model of national liberation.'[85] Indeed, the fact acknowledged by Fruman, that 'many seculars celebrate the

---

[84] Fruman, 'ma 'im haherut le'ekhol ḥameṣ bepesaḥ?'
[85] Avineri, 'neged ḥiloniyut ḥalula (4).'

seder, and some even observe the *kashrut* of the holiday,'[86] is seen by Avineri as a Zionist triumph:

The fact that most of the Jewish families in Israel celebrate the Passover in one way or another point to one of the achievements of the Zionist revolution – how to put new content in old vessels: Not only to renew our old glory, but to find a contemporary expression to Jewish identity on its historical roots.[87]

By Way of Conclusion

As I have been suggesting throughout this discussion, the debates reviewed above may all be seen as manifestations of an inevitable pushing of the Zionist-Jewish identity crisis to its limits. The Zionist negation of 'religion' and exile, which are identified as 'Jewish,' combined with its insistence on a configuration of power that is Jewish (i.e., of Jews) yet 'secular' has never formed into a self-sufficient construct of modern, national identity. At root, it had remained committed to an incoherent sense of Jewish 'blood,' and chained to an Orthodox rabbinical mechanism for its 'ethnic' self-preservation.

In this regard, the debates outlined above can be understood as the outcome of the Zionist internal contradictions being pushed to their limits. This brought about an implosion of sorts, from which two main threads have emerged. While all speakers remain, at root, committed to a nation-statist configuration of power, they nevertheless differ on the degree to which it must remain 'Jewish.'

What these debates (along with the deeper motivations that have propelled them) ultimately amount to is a sense that Israeli identity, or what we may call 'nonreligious' Zionist-Israeli nationalism, views itself as having in effect separated from what it views as traditional (religious) Judaism; yet it fails to account for its (still enduring, for most writers) claim for Jewishness. Moreover, as the texts reviewed make clear, this debate is being conducted under the looming shadow of a violent conflict that is seen at root as one between Jews and non-Jews.

---

[86] Fruman, 'ma 'im haherut le'ekhol hames bepesah?'
[87] Avineri, 'neged hiloniyut halula (4).'

All of this may indeed be simply seen as the endurance, or resurrection, of the Zionist negation of exile, in which Hebrew (and later Israeli) 'new Jewishness' has been contrasted with the allegedly diseased, exilic 'old Judaism.' This sense is surely apparent in The Secular Forum's drive to 'extract' lingering traces of 'religion' from 'Israeli' textbooks, as well in the writings of the essayists who profess a non-Jewish-Israeli identity. In this regard, this is an old story that has been already told and retold, debated, and reaffirmed.[88] Yet the historical perspective available to us at this point of time clearly emphasizes the limits of this negation, and its ultimate implosion, in what brings about the downfall of Zionist-Jewish secularism. (This, I must stress, seems to be an assessment on which all writers agree.)

A rather gloomy and frustrated reaction from another regular *Haaretz* columnist, Uri Misgav, to a controversy surrounding the 'Jewish' nature of some comments made by a politician from the Israeli Left (see Chapter 4) brings this trajectory into a sharp relief. For this columnist, the very fact that Israelis are preoccupied with matters of Jewishness and Judaism is indicative of a national disease. Note how this is tied back directly to the Israeli-Palestinian conflict, and to the Israeli demand that the Palestinians recognize Israel as Jewish:

This Jewish mumbo-jumbo has to stop. It's an obsession. Israel has become an intolerable place for a Jew to live in ... We're dealing with a national mental illness. From right and left, from top to bottom, the preoccupation of Jews with their Jewishness is simply obsessive. And all this is taking place, paradoxically, after they received a state of their own and have long ensured its thriving existence. They're demanding that even the Arabs recognize its Jewishness.[89]

---

[88] Raz-Krakotzkin, 'Exile, history and the nationalization of Jewish memory'; A. Shapira, 'Whatever became of 'negating exile'?' in A. Shapira (ed.), *Israeli Identity in Transition* (London: Praeger, 2004), pp. 69–108; E. Don-Yehiya, 'The negation of Galut in religious Zionism,' *Modern Judaism*, 12 (1992), 129–55; A. Raz-Krakotzkin, 'Exile within sovereignty: Toward a critique of the 'negation of exile' in Israeli culture, Part 1,' *Theory and criticism*, 4 (1993), 23–55.

[89] U. Misgav, 'For God's sake, enough with this obsession over Judaism,' *Haaretz*, November 16, 2017.

For Misgav, then, nationalism should have solved what is an exilic, Jewish preoccupation with (and fear for) the viability of Jewish life.[90] The very fact that Israelis are still preoccupied with their Jewish identity is proof of nothing else than the failure of the Zionist project:

> The sad conclusion is that the Israeli project has failed. The Declaration of Independence's statement of intentions has gone bankrupt. Instead of a modern state with a solid, confident sense of citizenship, we've returned to the ghetto. A shtetl with nuclear submarines and a national cyber headquarters. The agents of this ethno-Christian obsession aren't only politicians but all the Dov Alboims and Sivan Rahav-Meirs [media personalities who deal with Jewish matters in their shows] throughout the generations, with the endless harping on the week's Torah portion. It's a clever move: Any attempt to deny the holiness of this folklore is portrayed as 'condescension.'

To counter this failure, the Zionist remedy must go back to the core nationalist notion of Jewish identity as superseding the old, historical understanding of Judaism or 'Jewish religion':

> [I]t's necessary to remind everyone: Judaism germinated as a religion but developed into a people. A Jew is a person whose mother is Jewish or has chosen to join the Jewish people. He can be Ultra-Orthodox, religious, observant, a believer, secular, atheist. Zionist or not, leftist or not, it doesn't matter. As long as he's a human being. For God's sake, so to speak, leave us alone.[91]

A point that must be noted here is the degree to which the spirit of these discussions is detached from what most studies and reviews of Jewish-Israeli identity tell us regarding the mainstream Jewish-Israeli understanding of the conflation of Judaism, Jewishness and Israeliness. It may be safely stated that for the vast majority of Israelis the distinction between the adjectives Israeli and Jewish is artificial. Most Israeli-Jews would use the two interchangeably. This is also true in terms of their practice: they would observe 'religious' Jewish practices as an assertion of their Israeli nationalism, and vice versa (i.e., they would view their advocacy of and loyalty to Israeli, Zionist nationalism as expressing their Judaism). This has to do, of course, with the way in which the State of Israel has been using elements of religious tradition

---

[90] This is forcefully echoed in A. B. Yehoshua's recurring complaint against the exilic obsession with Judaism, which ultimately permeates and corrupts Zionist, Israeli nationalism. See Yadgar, *Sovereign Jews*, ch. 8.

[91] Misgav, 'For God's sake, enough with this obsession over Judaism.'

and Jewish law to maintain the configuration of power of a sovereign state of Jews. Without belaboring the point,[92] suffice it to note the degree to which the elitist discourse reviewed above is detached from the predominant understanding of Jewishness, Israeliness, and Judaism broadcast by the state and practiced by its subjects.

[92] I have expanded my discussion of the matter in my previous work: Yadgar, *Sovereign Jews*.

4 | Non-Jewish Israeli Nationalism and the Limits of Israeliness

While the previous chapters outline an unresolved debate over the meaning of Israel's Jewish identity, the reader may wonder: why bother with this matter of Jewishness in the first place? Regardless of Zionist ideology's claim to Jewish identity, shouldn't Israelis simply forego this confusing identity discourse and instead focus on Israeli nation-statehood? In other words, isn't a discourse on Israeli – as opposed to Jewish – nationalism the logical way out of the entanglement discussed here? Why should we insist on confusing Israeliness with Jewishness? Wouldn't the designation 'Israeli' be more inclusive, by incorporating the non-Jewish Palestinian-Arab minority (indeed, as the common parlance in Israel dubs them, '*Israeli* Arabs')? Wouldn't it also be clearer, by demarcating the line distinguishing the Israeli nation-state and its citizens from Jews who are citizens of other nation-states? Isn't Israeliness, then, the remedy to the Zionist Jewish identity predicament?

This, as we saw above, is indeed a central line of argument made by the advocates of non-Jewish secularism. 'Jewish religion,' they tend to argue, should be categorically rejected, and not 'just' reinterpreted and selectively appropriated, as done by socialist Zionism. In its place, so the argument goes, we must take the identity built around the Israeli nation-state at face value, as any other proper, modern national identity. In other words, instead of a confused debate on secular Jewish identity, Israelis should reassert the distinction between religion and politics, forego the former and focus on the national nature of the latter. We should be talking, then, of Israeli identity, Israeli nationalism, and Israeli politics, instead of the confusing Zionist discourse on Jewish identity, Jewish nationalism, and Jewish politics.

It must be noted that some advocates of this stance would probably object to the very claim I am making, by which Israel (or Zionism) has been experiencing a Jewish identity crisis. As we saw earlier, spokespeople for this stance do not necessarily give up on their identification as Jewish, and they do not see this as conflicting with their preference of Israeli identity as the wider framework of their political identity; Jewishness for them, often understood as a matter of cultural heritage or biological origin, is simply marginal to an all-encompassing nation-statist, 'Israeli' framework of identity. Rather, they would argue that the problem at hand is a regrettable persistence of Jewish *religion*, or the incompleteness of the secularization process.

In any event, whether a fundamental crisis of identity or 'simply' a debilitating lingering of religion in realms reserved for the supposedly secular politics of the nation-state, the remedy offered by a few vocal spokespeople is seemingly straightforward: foregoing this Jewishness (or at least pushing it back to the negligible background of one's many facets of personal and collective identity), and focusing instead on the Israeli nation-statist identity.

As this chapter will show, what is probably most striking about this idea is not necessarily its merit in itself, but the resistance it encounters from within the very center of the institutionalized Israeli, Zionist, statist (and secularist) political culture. Regardless of its limited sense of national identity (among other things, it is fundamentally dependent on the nation-state for its viability, and it explicitly lacks a history beyond that of Israeli nation-statehood)[1], and irrespective of its failure to account for the role of the *Zionist* state in enabling 'Israeliness' in the first place, the argument for Israeli nationalism is thus illuminating primarily for shedding light on the Zionist indebtedness to a sense of Jewishness for its very viability. It highlights, in other words, the Israeli, Zionist inability to run away from its own Jewish predicament.

The 'Zionization' of Judaism and Non-Jewish Israeliness

The argument for non-Jewish Israeli identity is fed by the limited, nationalized sense of the meaning of Judaism promoted by the Zionist state. It quite clearly nourishes on a specifically situated (in both the historical and political terms), narrow understanding of Judaism, which is the direct outcome of the uses (and manipulations) of Jewish traditions by the Israeli, Zionist nation-state for upholding its *raison*

---

[1] In this regard, as in many others, as brilliantly argued by Faisal Devji, direct lines of comparison might be drawn between this notion of Israeli national identity and Pakistani nationalism. F. Devji, *Muslim Zion: Pakistan as a Political Idea* (Cambridge, MA: Harvard University Press, 2013).

d'être as a Jewish state. This argument fails, in other words, to account for Judaism or Jewishness independently from the Zionist construction of the meaning of these, against which it rebels.

In this frame of reference, Judaism – read to mean a distinctly exclusive, illiberal, intolerant proto-nationalism that is (all nationalist-secularist attempts at arguing otherwise notwithstanding) at its core still a matter of 'religion' – is seen as fundamentally conflicting with the values of liberal democracy. A reassertion of Israeli identity as opposed to Jewishness would then also mean a release from the illiberal and undemocratic tendencies prevalent in Israeli political culture.

This line of argument was articulated rather clearly by Gideon Levy, a long-time reporter and op-ed contributor of *Haaretz*, in the wake of yet another instance of a debate over the Israeli Left's 'problem' of Jewish identity. Levy's commentary was more immediately instigated by comments made by Avi Gabbay immediately after he was elected to lead the Israeli Labor Party in 2017. Gabbay 'criticized the Israeli Left ... saying that they have forgotten their Jewish values.' He was explicitly echoing a denigration by leaders of the Israeli Right, who have accused the Left of having 'forgotten what it means to be Jewish.' Gabbay seems to share this assessment, as he blames the Left's inability to court the Israeli voters on its alienation from Jewish identity. As he was quoted saying: 'We are Jews. We live in a Jewish state. I also think that one of the problems of Labor Party members is that [they] distanced themselves from it ... We are Jews and we need to speak about our Jewish values. It all began with our Torah, our *halakha*, and our shared heritage. It all begins there.'[2]

Gideon Levy's reaction to this leftist self-criticism questions the very premise of the Israeli or Zionist *Jewish* identity. He asks rhetorically: 'What if Labor Party leader Avi Gabbay is right and we really have forgotten how to be Jews? Would that be so terrible? Maybe it would even be better?' In Levy's liberal, secularist reading, Judaism and Jewishness can hardly amount to positive value:

---

[2] A. Ben-Zikri, 'Israel's new Labor Party leader says the Left forgot how to be Jews,' *Haaretz*, November 13, 2017; The uproar caused by Gabbay's comments was so great as to eventually force him to apologize, describing his own comments as 'a miserable choice of words.' A. Lam, 'ani maamin she'am yisrael ḥashuv yoter me'erṣ yisrael' (interview with Avi Gabbay), *Yedi'ot Aḥaronot*, August 21, 2018.

If being Jewish means a sense of belonging to a chosen people that's allowed to do anything it wishes, liberals must forget this aspect of their Jewish identities. If being Jewish means keeping religious customs, secular Jews must forget their Jewishness. If being Jewish means being a perpetual victim and thinking your people isn't only history's biggest victim but also the one and only victim, and as a result can do whatever it wants, we must free ourselves from such a Jewish identity.

If being Jewish means thinking that Hebron is yours, that Abraham your patriarch wandered around there in ancient times and bought a cave there, the Left wing isn't only entitled but is required to forget about being Jewish. If being Jewish means feeling an automatic affinity to an unenlightened Brooklyn rabbi or a corrupt LA millionaire just because they're Jewish – over a non-Jewish Israeli from Kafr Qasem – a bit of Jewish identity can be ignored. If being Jewish means allowing the offspring of a possibly Jewish grandmother the right to Israeli citizenship but not someone whose family has been in the country for generations, it's immoral to cling to such an identity.[3]

Note how Levy's sense of Judaism and Jewishness – or at least the sense of Judaism he distances himself from – is dictated by the Zionist construction of these matters. His objections are clearly aimed at the Zionist sense of Jewish nationalism, not against any other meaningful sense of Jewish tradition. Critically, he does not offer an alternative understanding of Jewishness and Judaism (for example, such that would be critical of the very abuses of Jewishness he notes above; what Brian Klug aptly titled 'Being Jewish and Doing Justice'[4]). He is either unable or uninterested to do so, clearly suggesting that these illiberal readings may be wrong, and leaving any alternative too distanced to be meaningful. The only probable remedy, he clearly suggests, is to distance oneself from this illiberal Jewishness.

Thus, for example, when Levy testifies to the very murkiness of the idea of 'a Jewish state,' the potential meanings he suggests (and rejects) are all instances of the prevalent (and, granted, problematic) Israeli-Zionist reading of Jewish politics:

When people talk about a Jewish state, it's impossible to know what they mean. Is its character determined by a statistical majority in the population

---

[3] G. Levy, 'Have Israelis forgotten how to be Jews?' *Haaretz*, November 20, 2017.

[4] B. Klug, *Being Jewish and Doing Justice: Bringing Argument to Life* (London: Vallentine Mitchell, 2011).

registry? A state governed by Jewish religious law? Is it Jewish if there's no public transportation on Shabbat and no grocery stores are open then, and not if there's civil marriage and burial? Is it Jewish if maintenance of the railway system is done on Shabbat by non-Jews, but not if it's done by Jews?

Levy's bottom line is that this Israeli-Zionist idea of Jewish politics is too confused to make sense: 'Israel has never made clear whether its Jewish identity is a matter of national or religious identity. If it's a religion, what do secular Israelis have to do with it, and if it's a nationality, what's Israeli identity?'

Like many other spokespeople of the Israeli liberal, secularist Left, it seems that Levy's secularism prevents him from offering an alternative Jewish reading, that would challenge this nationalization or 'Zionization' of Judaism. At root, his secularism determines that Judaism is a matter of religion, to which he has no affinity. Instead, he offers a combination of secular universalism and Israeli nativism as an antidote to the illiberal nature of a nationalized, xenophobic Judaism:

Secular Israelis can forget a bit about their Jewish identities, particularly if its significance is fuzzy. They can find their values from the storehouse of universal values, just as people in other countries do. And they can find their identities at a clearer address: being Israeli.

I'm an Israeli, sometimes proud, sometimes ashamed, but always Israeli.

Such reassertion of Israeli identity *against* Jewishness must inevitably undermine the sense of Jewish nationhood or peoplehood. Indeed, this has been a determined argument made against varying notions of (nationalist) Israeli nativism, suggesting that this nativism would create a historical rift within the Jewish people, and separate Israelis from non-Israeli-Jews. Levy, like other advocates of Israeli identity, does not see this inevitable outcome as a threat. From him, this rift is a matter of present reality:

The slogan 'we are all Jews' needs to be updated. There is a Jewish world that is dealing with its own issues, largely divorced from the issues that we in Israel are concerned with ... This gap will only grow. As long as its system of government isn't changed, Israel will remain open to any Jew who wishes to immigrate here. This person will gradually become an Israeli, a process that happens to immigrants in every country. That will be the case until the day when the members of both peoples, Hebrew and Arab, Jewish and

Palestinian, live here in equality – when they above all will be Israelis, or whatever their country is called then.[5]

Non-Jewish Israeliness and the State of the Jews

While Levy's is a mostly hesitant contemplation (he is still asking, rhetorically at least, whether there is a sense or justification in 'hanging on' to Jewishness; his is not a determined assertion that this is indeed not the case anymore), others before him have already stipulated the argument positively and forcefully. We have already seen in the debate between Avineri's Zionist, secular Jewishness and Fruman's non-Jewish secularism that the latter raises the notion of Israeliness exactly as the 'way out' of the ('religious') Jewish entanglement. The term 'Israeli' does indeed figure prominently in The Secular Forum's campaign against 'religionization' (or, maybe more properly put in the current context, 'Judaization'). Their vision is to create a 'secular, Israeli, and ethical [*'erki*] education.' Yet, focused as they are on rooting out religion, they offer little by way of positive explication of the idea of Israeli identity (other, that is, than celebrating their worldview as 'secular, humanist, pluralist, and Zionist.'[6])

A more systematic construction of a non-Jewish notion of Israeli identity is offered by another social union, Ani Yisre'eli (I am Israeli), which was established by Uzi Ornan in late 1998 and has been led by him ever since.[7] This organization's political activity is focused on the promotion of Israeli nationality as an alternative to what it depicts as the discriminatory politics of Jewish identity prevalent in Israel. Viewing Judaism as a sect and Jewishness as purely a matter of religiosity, Ani Yisre'eli presents its promotion of Israeli identity as offering a civil framework for civic and national equality. Their diagnosis of the present sociopolitical reality is grave: 'A regime of discriminations prevails in the State of Israel. Citizens are awarded rights and are denied rights by their being Jewish or non-Jewish, by their place inside

---

[5] Levy, 'Have Israelis forgotten how to be Jews?'
[6] The Secular Forum, 'haforum haḥiloni.'
[7] I have discussed Ani Yisre'eli's judicial initiative to promote a recognition of Israeli nationality in Yadgar, *Sovereign Jews*, 167–76.

the religious sect, and by the circumstances of their birth, which determine belonging to this or that sect [*'eda*].[8]

The term 'religious sect' is central here: The claim for inclusive Israeli nationality is based on a view of Jewishness and Judaism as particularistic religiosity, which by definition cannot be nationally uniting. Judaism and Jewishness are not, nor can they ever be, in this reading, a matter of nationality (or of politics more generally). This principled stance – which puts Ornan and his fellows in direct confrontation with the most basic notions of Zionism – argues that 'it is impossible to define all Jews in the world as belonging to a 'Jewish nation,' since Jews in all democratic states belong to the nations of the states of which they are citizens.'[9]

As Ornan argues, 'Jews,' 'Jewishness,' and 'Judaism' are all religious concepts. They are limited to the framework of sect, rendering any notion of a 'Jewish state' a senseless idea. Israel's demand to be recognized as a Jewish state (see Chapter 2), is not only misleading, but also 'totally baseless.' This is the case since a state – or, to be precise, a *nation*-state, which Ornan's evident statism sees as the only viable political frame of reference – cannot be based on familial kinship or on the religious affiliation of a sect. Hence, Israel cannot possibly be 'the nation-state of the Jewish people' but only 'the state of the Israeli nation.'[10]

Given this negation of the sectarianism of Judaism, the influence of religious Jews on matters of the state – which force on it a Jewish identity – means that

Israel was transformed into a Jewish community that directs the state's life according to the principle of Judaism, and its leaders have accepted the religious view that Jews should not 'intermingle with the gentiles' … Israel is not a 'nation like all nations,' but a Jewish community that has overtaken the country, and shuts itself from anyone who is not Jewish, either within the state or beyond it.[11]

---

[8] See the Ani Yisre'eli website at ani-israeli.org/site. For a selection of videos produced by Ani Yisre'eli see: Israel Social TV, goo.gl/J5xRv5.

[9] *Ornan et al. v. Interior Ministry*, Appeal on HP 6092/07 (2008).

[10] U. Ornan, 'Yisrael einenah 'medinat haleom shel ha'am hayehudi," Atar Hamaamarim Shel Uzi Ornan website, goo.gl/Ep6VzY.

[11] Ornan, 'Yisrael einenah 'medinat haleom shel ha'am hayehudi."

The argument for Israeli nationality, at least in Ornan's rendition, relies on a narration of political and ideological history in which a Zionist impulse has been diametrically opposed to the very notion of Jewishness. The Zionist dream, Ornan insists, has been one of a revolutionary impulse against the sectarianism of Jewish religion (which he obviously reads through a – Zionist – prism of 'negation of exile'). The driving, dominant Zionist view had been that the nationality it has been promoting 'is not a community and is not a part of a set of communities dispersed throughout the world.' Somewhat anachronistically, Ornan claims that the Zionist pioneering ideologues who settled in Ottoman and later Mandatory Palestine have viewed 'Israel [here referring to the nation-state carrying this name, not to the Jewish people] as a nation in itself.' This he learns from the role of the Hebrew language in their ideological worldview, which was much more, he insists, than a matter of linguistics: 'The revival of Hebrew speech' was part of the Zionists' 'central dream – to build 'a nation like all nations." This pitted Zionists against Jews as the main axis of the national project: 'the Jewish community [in Ottoman and Mandatory Palestine] had been the enemy of the new nationalism.'[12]

In this narration of Zionist and Israeli history, the villain is clearly the 'community' or 'sect' of religious Jews, who joined the Zionist movements as a 'hitchhiker'[13] and ended up directing the progress of the project at large. 'Once religious organizations joined the Zionist federation, they have started arguing that this [Zionist, national] revival is not a revolution. They have interpreted the yearning for the holy land as if this is Zionism. The large secular public has listened politely to the propaganda of the [religious] community, and following its liberal approach allowed it a space in public life.' This allowed the religious to exert enormous power, ultimately reaching 'a comprehensive control of our lives.' The state, directed by a religious sect (by definition, a minority), 'reinforces the opinion that the revival has not been a revolution. As if we are but a simple continuation of Jewish religion. As if our pioneering fathers who have started the revolution haven't rebelled against Judaism at all.'[14]

---

[12] Ornan, 'Yisrael einenah 'medinat haleom shel ha'am hayehudi."
[13] Ornan, 'Yisrael einenah 'medinat haleom shel ha'am hayehudi."
[14] Ornan, 'Yisrael einenah 'medinat haleom shel ha'am hayehudi."

Ornan is well aware of the fact that the Israeli-Zionist 'Proclamation of Independence' (or, in its formal name: the Declaration of the Establishment of the State of Israel) explicitly refers to 'Jews' and 'the Jewish people,' and that it unambiguously proclaims the 'establishment of a Jewish state in Eretz Israel, to be known as the State of Israel.'[15] But he sees this is as merely a rhetorical, tactical usage, meant to secure compliance with the UN's resolution to partition Mandatory Palestine between a 'Jewish state' and an 'Arab state.' The term was never meant, he argues, to be read as carrying a 'religious' meaning (note that in his terminology, Judaism can be *only* of a 'religious' meaning). Moreover, the Zionist commitment to not discriminate against non-Jews in the newly established state (also motivated by compliance with the UN's resolution) does not conform to any sense of Jewish politics, since 'Jewish religion does not maintain equality even between those who adhere to it,' and it plainly discriminates against non-Jews.[16]

Ornan offers two complementary views of the viability of Israeli nationality. Principally, or 'theoretically,' he argues that the Israeli nation has been created by the Proclamation of Independence, which constitutes Israel as a democratic state. Any meaningful adherence to democratic principles, he argues, negates the very possibility of a state that is Jewish. 'A correct reading of the Proclamation of Independence' shows, then, that it is wrong to argue that the term 'a Jewish state' was aiming at any kind of commitment or loyalty to Jewish religion. It is mistaken to argue that Israel was established in 1948 as 'the state of the Jewish people' in its wider sense; the Proclamation of Independence established 'a democratic state whose citizens are all full Israelis, and it is them who maintain and constitute the Israeli people.'[17]

This, then, is a political reasoning focused on the state. The establishment of the state (as a democracy which guarantees equal rights to all citizens, regardless of their ethnic, religious, or otherwise sectarian affiliation) means also the establishment of a new nation: the nation of the state. Israel, in this reading, cannot be other than a nation-state of all of it citizens, in which case its citizens must compose the nation embodied by the state. Ornan uses the term 'the nation of the

---

[15] The Declaration of the Establishment of the State of Israel is available at goo.gl/uSVjs3.

[16] U. Ornan, 'hakhrazat ha῾atzmaut – kummo shel leom yisre'eli' Atar Hamamarim Shel Uzi Ornan website, goo.gl/xRZdbt.

[17] Ornan, 'hakhrazat ha῾atzmaut – kummo shel leom yisre'eli.'

state' – *leom hamedina* – to denote this idea, which seems to be a deliberate word play on the prevalent term of 'nation-state,' or *medinat-leom* in Hebrew.[18] Note that this idea is (in the context of the Zionist discourse on Israel as the nation-state of the Jews) both uniquely inclusive and exclusive. The nation created with the establishment of the state 'includes all of Israel's citizens, and no other.'[19] Meaning that it is equally a state of all of its citizens, Jews and non-Jews alike, and it is *not* a state of Jews who live outside of it. Israelis are clearly distinguished, separated from Jews.

More specifically, in this political logic it is the *sovereignty* of the nation-state that brings about the birth of the new nation.

Sovereignty is the identity marker of an independent state, and the sovereign are all of the state's citizens ... The negation of the existence of an Israeli nation that includes all citizens is equal to the negation of a legitimate sovereign, to the negation of the existence of the State of Israel as a sovereign democratic state.[20]

Ornan's nation-statism dictates that for him one's right to identify with the state's nation, or, as his judicial appeal puts it with 'The People of the Israeli Nation' (English in the original; this European idea apparently does not translate easily into Hebrew), is a basic human right. Israel's refusal to acknowledge Israeli nationality thus amounts to denying its citizens their basic rights: 'A state that prevents its citizens from proudly carrying the nationality of their state is not a democratic state that respects human rights.' Moreover, by proclaiming itself a Jewish state the Israeli regime 'undermines' the very basis of the Israeli polity, since this would mean (by separating Jews from other citizens) that 'Israel is a binational or multinational state.' In contrast, Ornan and his fellow appellants 'put the loyalty to the country and state first,' designating 'secondary loyalties' (ethnic, religious, cultural, or gender) to a lower status.[21]

The second view of the viability of the Israeli nation is a sociohistorical one. Here, Ornan argues that the history of the State of Israel also brought about the practical, empirical (as opposed to the

---

[18] U. Ornan, 'haleom sheli: yisre'eli,' *Ynet*, September 3, 2008.
[19] Ornan, 'hakhrazat ha'atzmaut – kummo shel leom yisre'eli.'
[20] *Ornan et al.* v. *Interior Ministry*, Appeal on HP 6092/07.
[21] *Ornan et al.* v. *Interior Ministry*, Appeal on HP 6092/07.

'theoretical' argument presented above) formation of the Israeli nation, making it 'a reality that cannot be denied.'[22] In this line of reasoning, the existence of the Israeli nation is simply a 'fact.' This comes as part of a formal demand presented by Ornan and fellow appellants to the court, demanding that it orders the state to allow the appellants to be registered in the state's Population Registry as 'Israeli' under the category of 'Nationality' (more on this below). Given that the court has already decided in 1970, in a ruling on a similar case,[23] that the appellant was unable to prove by empirical and objective data the existence of an Israeli nation, Ornan argues that by 2006, things have changed: 'After more than 35 years have gone by since ... almost two generations – it is time to re-examine whether there is or there isn't an Israeli nation.'[24]

Here, the argument for Israeli nationality, or Israeli national identity, is an 'empirical' one: the existence of the nation is the natural outcome of more than 60 years of Israeli (nation-)statehood. This argument was forcefully echoed in *Haaretz*'s Editorial marking Israel's 66th year of statehood, in which the newspaper's Editorial Board rebukes the Israeli Supreme Court's denial of the existence of an Israeli nation. 'Does it not suffice that a group of people lives together for decades in a country called Israel, to call this people 'Israeli'?' The editorial asks rhetorically; 'The creation of Israeli literature, Israeli art, Israeli music, Israeli theater, Israeli humor, Israeli politics, Israeli sports, an Israeli accent, Israeli grief – are all of these not enough to speak of an 'Israeli people'?' The answer to this rhetorical question is empirically simple: contrary to the court's ruling, 'There is such a thing as 'Israeli.'"[25]

Ornan himself also ties the matter back to the wider politics of the Middle East, seeing the prospects of achieving peace in the region as depending on the release of Israel from the grip of Judaism. For him, a failure to 'return to our aspiration to be a people like all peoples,' a failure that would entail the 'persistence of the concept of 'a dispersed Jewish people,' which is supposedly part of Israel,' would necessary

---

[22] *Ornan et al. v. Interior Ministry*, Appeal on HP 6092/07.
[23] *Tamarin v. State of Israel*, CA 630/70 (1972).
[24] U. Ornan, 'hoda'a la'itunut 12.6.2006,' Atar Hamaamarim Shel Uzi Ornan website. goo.gl/zbupQc.
[25] *Haaretz* Editorial, 'There is such a thing as 'Israeli,"' *Haaretz*, May 5, 2014.

mean that 'we will not achieve peace in our land.'[26] Any notion of the Israeli nation-state as foundationally tied to non-Israeli-Jews (based, in Ornan's terminology, on the parochial matter of belonging to a religious sect) transforms the Middle Eastern conflict into a 'religious' one and inhibits the possibility of cohabitation.

Hebrew Nationalism and the Zionist Problem of Jewish Identity

While the idea of Israeli nationhood, in its contemporary rendition by Ornan, Fruman, Levy, and others, relies fundamentally on the existence of the nation-state, its roots can be traced back to the very core of pre-statehood Zionist ideology. As I have already suggested earlier, this non-Jewish Israeliness may be quite safely described as descending from the dominant sense of 'negation' (of 'exile,' of 'the old Jew,' of the rabbinical class, and of Judaism as a 'religion' more generally) that has propelled the Zionist rebellion against its own Jewish past. This negation has encouraged a strong sense of alienation not only from 'Judaism' but also from 'Jews' (or at least, 'old Jews,' as opposed to the Zionist 'new Jews'[27]). More specifically, this notion is a direct descendent of a distinct stream of nationalist ideology, which pushed the Zionist negation of exile into its logical conclusion, professing a 'Hebrew' nationalism that is not only distinct from 'Jewish' and 'Zionist' nationalism, but even fundamentally opposed to them.

The idea of a non-Jewish, if not anti-Jewish, Hebrew nationalism was developed most fully by the Young Hebrews, a movement founded in Mandatory Palestine in the late 1930s, gained substantial traction among Zionist youth during the 1940s, and although always small in numbers and by the 1950s also politically emaciated, has wielded a long lasting, not-insignificant influence on the political culture of the newly established State of Israel.[28] (The leader of the movement, Uriel Shelah, also known as Yonathan Ratosh, is Uzi Ornan's older brother; the latter was a member of the movement from its inception and has

---

[26] Ornan, 'Yisrael einenah 'medinat haleom shel ha'am hayehudi."
[27] A. Shapira, *New Jews, Old Jews* (Tel Aviv: Am-Oved, 1997).
[28] Y. Porath, *The Life of Uriel Shelah* (Tel Aviv: Maḥbarot Lesifrut, 1989); J. Shavit, *The New Hebrew Nation: A Study in Israeli Heresy and Fantasy* (London: Frank Cass, 1987); Kurzweil, 'The New Canaanites in Israel'; R. Vater, 'Beyond bi-nationalism? The Young Hebrews versus the 'Palestinian issue," *Journal of Political Ideologies*, 21/1 (2016), 45–60.

personified the persistence and development of its ideas throughout the history of Israeli statehood.)

The distinction of Jewish identity from 'Hebrew' nationalism and the construction of the two as mutual opposites is probably the most fundamental tenet of the movement's ideology, especially when seen in light of its opposition to the dominant Zionist understanding of the same notion of Hebrew nationalism. As Ornan put it in retrospect, the founding of the movement was motivated by the feeling that 'we, the sons of the Land of Israel, are not tied and not related to the Jews who are dispersed over the whole world.'[29] Professing 'Hebrew' nativism, the movement's guiding ideology marked a clear distinction between the native Hebrew and the diasporic Jew:

Anyone who is not a native of this land, the land of the Hebrews, cannot be a Hebrew and is not a Hebrew, and has never been a Hebrew.

Anyone coming from the Jewish diaspora … is Jewish and not Hebrew, and cannot be but Jewish …

The Jew and the Hebrew can never be identical. Whoever is Hebrew cannot be Jewish, and whoever is Jewish cannot be Hebrew. Since a member of a nation cannot be a member of a sect ['eda] who views this nation of his as a 'sect.'[30]

While a history and systematic analysis of the movement is clearly beyond the remit of the current book, the case of the Young Hebrews is nevertheless important for our purposes in clearly highlighting the presence of the Jewish identity crisis from the very foundational stages of Zionist politics in Mandatory Palestine. Moreover, as Baruch Kurzweil has perceptively noted, regardless of the movements own sense of uniqueness, the negation of Jewish religion, which is a foundational tenet of its ideology, is far from novel. Ideologically, the Young Hebrews are 'but an Israeli variation of a well-known Jewish exilic phenomenon … In its opposition to the way of the Jewish religion, the movement is far from charting a new path.'[31]

Kurtzweil's treatment of the movement is illuminating in emphasizing the indebtedness of the Young Hebrews' ideas to core Zionist notions of 'New' Jewish, national identity as 'secular,' built as it is on

---

[29] U. Ornan and Orion, Ezra, 'Anaḥnu kena'anim,' *Sevivot*, 33 (1994), 1–15.

[30] The Young Hebrews' 'Opening Call' [masa hapetiḥa], 1944, p. 45, quoted in Kurzweil, *Our New Literature*, 273.

[31] Kurzweil, *Our New Literature*, 285, 279.

the negation of Jewish 'religion.' Reviewing the Young Hebrews' ideas regarding the Jews' ahistorical character (having allegedly 'exited' history while in exile and being subjected to the dominance of religion over their life outside the Land of Israel), Kurtzweil notes:

> Indeed, all of this is not a novelty at all. This doctrine has been heard from the mouths of diasporic Jews, who also tried, in a similar fashion to that of the Young Hebrews, to strip the meaning of Jewish history off its religious content ... The Young Hebrews, who seek to install here the 'Hebrew ideology' are intertwined to a degree they do not understand in the fabric of phenomena that belong to the path of modern Jewish thought.[32]

As Kurtzweil insists, the true motivations or 'reasons' behind the emergence of the movement and its attractiveness for Israeli youth ultimately lie at the heart of Zionism with its Nietzschean rebellion against its own Jewish past.[33] (Kurtzweil's analysis also reminds us that a forceful, absolute rejection of any mention of Judaism or Jewish religion in the Israeli textbooks has been a rallying cry of the Young Hebrews already in 1950, preceding The Secular Forum's campaign against the 'religionization' of the state approved textbooks 70 years later.[34])

Yet, Kurzweil's assertion, originally made in the late 1960s, that the real importance of the movement lies not necessarily in its own (unoriginal) ideology but in the Zionist reaction to it, still holds today. The non-Jewish Hebrew/Israeli argument has clearly irritated a sensitive root of the Zionist Jewish identity 'problem.'

A Zionist Refutation of Israeliness

This came to light in, among other things, the assertive denial by both the executive and the judiciary branches of the state of the very viability, or even 'empirical existence' of an Israeli (as opposed to Jewish) nation and Israeli nationhood.

The context for this denial was an appeal (made by Ornan, who was joined by other appellants), demanding that the court instructs the Ministry of Interior to register the appellants as 'Israeli' under

---

[32] Kurzweil, *Our New Literature*, 282.
[33] Kurzweil, *Our New Literature*, 295.
[34] Kurzweil, *Our New Literature*, 280.

'Nationality' in the state's Population Registry.[35] The appeal was explicitly declarative, aiming to force the state to acknowledge the viability of Israeli nationhood or Israeli national identity – as distinct from, and ultimately opposed to Jewish national identity. (As we have already seen, the position propagated by Ornan denies the very viability of a Jewish national identity, as Judaism for him is solely a religious matter of a sect.)

Ultimately, Ornan's appeal, like the sole precedence to it from 1970,[36] failed, as the court denied the request to officially recognize the category of an Israeli nation. But it did clearly succeed in forcing the Israeli government and the court to explicate a denial of the very viability of Israeli identity. In doing so, the appeal has managed to bring the official spokespeople of the state's elite to account for the state's unresolved claim to nonreligious Jewish identity.

Much like Ornan's combination of an 'empirical' and 'theoretical' argument for the viability of Israeliness, the state and the court's refutation of Israeliness claims both that (empirically) the Israeli nation does not exist and that (ideologically) its very existence would undermine the Zionist foundation of the State of Israel.

Simply put, 'empirically,' the court has determined that an Israeli nation does not exist, or at least that the appellants have not been able to prove otherwise. Following an earlier ruling, the court was seeking an objective, scientific-like proof for the existence of an Israeli nation. The court saw 'the existence of an object – in this case, a separate Israeli nation' as a 'matter of objective circumstances';[37] It has thus set 'objective' social-scientific criteria for this objective proof and determined that the appellants failed to provide anything beyond their 'subjective' feeling that they belong to such a nation.

Beyond this 'objective' criterion, the court also considered the 'subjective' matter of how people view themselves. It thus suggested that a clear proof of the existence of a separate Israeli nation would be the factual presence of 'many people in Israel, who are of Jewish origin ... who do not identify, or no longer identify, with the Jewish nation.' This would be signaled by the lack, on their side, of 'a sense of mutual dependence and responsibility' between those Israelis and 'the

---

[35] *Ornan et al.* v. *Interior Ministry*, HP (Jerusalem) 6092/07 (2008); *Ornan et al.* v. *Interior Ministry*, CA 8573/08 (2013). For an extended consideration of this ruling see Yadgar, *Sovereign Jews*, ch. 7.
[36] *Tamarin* v. *State of Israel* (1972).   [37] *Tamarin* v. *State of Israel* (1972), 200.

members of the Jewish nation ... in any place, in the present or the future.'[38] Ultimately, this would amount to a death blow to the very foundation of Israel as the Zionist state: 'Israel will cease to be the nation-state of the Jewish people, and the constitutional definition of the state as 'Jewish and Democratic' will become a dead letter.'[39]

Similarly, the court suggested that the remedy to the appellant's 'subjective feeling' of *not* belonging to the Jewish nation would be to allow them to demand that the state leaves the 'Nationality' category blank in their cases.[40] In other words, the court was willing to accept that the appellants do not feel to be part of a Jewish nationality, but it denied both their claim that such Judaism does not amount to nationhood and their argument for Israeli nationhood.

It might be redundant to mention that the court – and the state – have not put the notion of Jewish nationhood into similar empirical tests. Rather, they have stressed the existence of the State of Israel as a Jewish state (or, less explicitly, as a state of the Jews) as the ultimate political expression of Jewish nationhood. Relying on various Zionist texts, the court has emphasized the centrality of the notion of a 'Jewish state' to the very existence of the political framework wherein the whole debate has been taking place. As put in the 1970 ruling:

The State of Israel has been established – thus has it been declared in the Declaration of Independence – as a 'Jewish state in Eretz Israel,' by power of 'natural right of the Jewish people to be masters of their own fate, like all other nations, in their own sovereign state' and 'for the realization of the age-old dream – the redemption of Israel.' It was established in Eretz Israel, since it 'was the birthplace of the Jewish people. Here their spiritual, religious and political identity was shaped.'[41]

The 2008 ruling, which quotes this text at length, adds to it just one thing: It emphasizes the word 'Jewish' throughout the text in bold letters.[42] The message is quite straightforward and clear: The matter at hand is one of Jewish statehood, Jewish peoplehood, and Jewish nationalism – not Israeli. Yet the court does not go into explicating the meaning of this Jewishness of the state, accepting as given the notion

---

[38] *Tamarin v. State of Israel* (1972), 206.
[39] Y. Z. Stern, 'ein leom yisre'eli,' *'Orekh Hadin*, January 2014, 61.
[40] *Ornan et al. v. Interior Ministry* (2013), 20.
[41] *Tamarin v. State of Israel* (1972), 221.
[42] *Ornan et al. v. Interior Ministry* (2008), 7.

that Judaism is at root a matter of nationality and the opaqueness this notion ultimately carries.

Returning to the foundational narrative of Zionist politics, a concurring judge highlights the importance of the very sense of Jewishness for Israeli politics:

> The State of Israel has been established and exists as a Jewish and democratic state as a solution for the Jewish people, who suffered severe persecutions during the generations, and was fatally beaten in the Holocaust, and this is also one of the reasons for its [the state's] definition – constitutionally – as such. There is therefore no judicial basis for the wish of the appellants to cancel the 'Jewishness' of the state and to transform all of its citizens into members of an 'Israeli nation.'[43]

There can be little doubt that the issue at hand, and the way it has been considered by all sides involved, is primarily a matter of contesting normative, ideological commitments. These reflect – or rather refract – some of the basic ideas of the Zionist project (encapsulated, as I suggested earlier, in the 'national,' 'Hebrew' or 'Israeli' negation of the 'Jewish,' 'religious' exile). A lower instance of the court saw the matter as so value-laden and ideological, that it deemed it as falling out of the bounds of judicial decision.[44] Yet the Supreme Court ultimately decided to take up the debate and provided a distinctly ideological refutation of Israeliness as posing a threat to Zionist nationalism, whose reference is the Jewish, not Israeli, people. The court's decision makes it clear that it sees the normative challenge of the appeal as demanding a determined reply.

Ideologically, then, both the government and the court insisted that any meaningful acknowledgment of Israeli nationalism would undermine the very basis of Zionist ideology and Israeli politics, by creating a rift, or differentiation, between Israelis and Jews. Both also insisted on upholding the unresolved nature of the very Zionist and Israeli claim to Jewish nationhood, preferring, as it were, to leave untouched the quandary of the unresolved nature of Israel's Jewishness.

If Ornan's appeal, claiming as it is that there is no such thing as Jewish sovereignty, only Israeli sovereignty,[45] seeks to solve the predicament by simply cutting off the problematic 'Jewish' member of the

---

[43] H. Melcer in *Ornan et al. v. Interior Ministry* (2013), 38.
[44] *Ornan et al. v. Interior Ministry* (2008).
[45] *Ornan et al. v. Interior Ministry* (2013), 24.

Israeli body politic, both the executive and the judiciary insist that it must be preserved, for without it the whole Israeli body politic will die. As stated by the representative of the state, a recognition of Israeli nationality 'undermines the foundation on which the State of Israel is constituted.'[46]

The government also referred the court to 'the writings of various thinkers, from the nineteenth century to our days, which deal with the deep controversy around the question whether Judaism is a separate nation from the nation of the state [in which a Jew is a citizen].'[47] This is an interesting admission by the state of the very controversial Zionist argument for Jewish nationalism. Indeed, as a concurring judge reminds us, apparently impatient at the state's resurrecting this (Zionist) political-philosophical quandary, the argument that the 'Jewish question' is a national one, and that the Jews are a nation has been a founding notion of the Zionist project.[48] Re-questioning it clearly amounts to undermining the very basis of Israeli, Zionist nationhood.

As summarized by one commentator, in rejecting the appeal the court has highlighted 'some of the far-reaching implications' of recognizing Israeli nationhood as viable. Such recognition would mean 'the narrowing down of Judaism into dimensions of religion, contrary to the widely accepted opinion and to foundational concepts of Zionism and its central thinkers, first among them Herzl.' It would 'break Judaism into separate nations (Israeli, American, etc.),' and will result in a rift between the Israeli-Jews and Diaspora Jews.[49]

It is interesting to note that in this reading, which insists on the Zionist understanding of Jewishness as a matter of national identification, Israeliness (as a national identity) and Jewishness are mutually exclusive. Were Israeli national identity to be recognized by the state, Jewish Israeli citizens 'would have to choose their circle of belonging – Israelis or Jews, this under the reasonable assumption that a person cannot be of two national identities.' The same applies to the Palestinian-Arabs citizens of the state, 'who will lose their distinct national identity and will be forced to be Israeli in their nationality.'[50]

---

[46] Y. Yo'az, 'hapraqlitut: leom 'yisre'eli' hoter tahat hamedina,' *Walla! News*, May 19, 2004.

[47] *Ornan et al.* v. *Interior Ministry* (2013), 5.

[48] H. Melcer in *Ornan et al.* v. *Interior Ministry* (2013), 34.

[49] Stern, ''ein leom yisre'eli,' 61.   [50] Stern, ''ein leom yisre'eli,' 61.

This last sentence is illuminating (also) in exemplifying how the Zionist rebuke of the notion of inclusive Israeli nationalism puts the blame for the lack of inclusivity in the current configuration of power, at least in part, on the Palestinian-Arab minority and its wish to preserve a distinct, separate, 'non-Jewish' national identity. This was echoed in the Israeli Supreme Court's decision, in which the judges suggest that an Israeli nationhood would result in forcing on the Palestinian-Arab minority a national identity in which members of this collective do not wish to partake.[51]

In making this argument, the court relies on a work of Zionist apologetics, which among other things presents the dominant view that 'Israeli Arabs' are members of a separate nation than that of Israeli-Jews. By this view, which can be clearly labeled as 'common-sensical' in contemporary Israeli political culture (it is surely not common-sensical when viewed from the ideological point of view of the appellants in *Ornan et al.* v. *Interior Ministry*):

Israeli Arabs are citizens whose national identity is different from that of the majority people in the state. They are therefore a national minority. Their demand to be recognized as such is justified. In fact, though there is no explicit recognition of this status of the Arab community in any official document, the state regularly refers to its Arab citizens in a way that clearly reflects recognition of the fact that this minority has a distinct national (as opposed to merely 'ethnic' or 'linguistic' identity) of its own.[52]

Note that by this reading of sociopolitical reality, it is the Palestinian-Arabs who demand to be recognized as a minority; it is not that they are positioned as such by the Zionist rendering of Jewish politics as a matter of a national (Jewish) majority versus a (non-Jewish, Palestinian-Arab minority). The problem (that is to say, the cause of the lack of inclusivity in the configuration of a Jewish nation-statehood) is that 'they,' the non-Jewish, Palestinian-Arab minority, do not wish to join in Jewish, Zionist nationhood; it is not that this nationhood precludes them by definition of their being non-Jewish. (Note also that the authors of this polemics do not say to what nation the 'Israeli Arabs' belong. They do not call them 'Palestinians,' and

---

[51] *Ornan et al.* v. *Interior Ministry* (2013), 19.
[52] A. Yakobson and A. Rubinstein, *Israel and the Family of Nations: The Jewish Nation-state and Human Rights* (New York: Routledge, 2009), 118.

they surely are aware that no single 'Arab nation-state' exists that would see these Arab Israelis as their natural co-nationals.)

Conclusion: Israeliness, Jewishness

It may be safely asserted that the guiding notion of the argument for non-Jewish Israeliness (or 'Hebrewism' in the previous rendition of the same idea) is, still, numerically at least, a fringe ideology in contemporary Israeli culture. It is quite clear that for most Israelis the whole debate over non-Jewish and anti-Jewish Israeliness would be nonsensical. Israeli-Jews (and, following their dominance, also non-Jews in Israel), tend to unreflectively uphold a conflation, if not outright identification, between Israeliness and Jewishness in a manner that would make both the idea of non-Jewish Israeliness and the questioning of the viability of Israeliness sound like utter nonsense. Israeli political culture clearly agrees that 'there is such a thing as Israeliness,' and, in the same breath, sees it as almost by definition identical to Jewishness. (Among other things, this has taken the form of a general agreement among Israeli-Jews – at least when asked about it in a survey – that Jews deserve preferential treatment in Israel.[53])

But this is not to say that this mutual identification of Israeliness with Jewishness comes without its problems. It renders non-Jewish presence in Israel menacing by definition and it fails to meaningfully account for the Jewishness of Israeli politics beyond the crude logic of upholding a 'Jewish' majority over a non-Jewish minority. The argument for non-Jewish Israeli nationhood is instrumental in highlighting this sociopolitical reality by challenging its main premises.

Beyond this use of the argument for non-Jewish Israeli nationhood for the study of the Zionist Jewish identity problem, it is clear that this argument is far from being coherent. As I have suggested above, its dependence on the configuration of power of the *Zionist* nation-state is too substantial to be ignored, as advocates of this Israeli nationhood tend to do. The argument for non-Jewish Israeli nationhood too is, in other words, derived from the same root of the unresolved (Zionist, and then Israeli) claim for Jewish identity. It tries to escape this predicament by claiming to have cut away the Jewish limb, but it ignores the

[53] Pew Research Center, 'Israel's religiously divided society,' Pew Research Center's Religion & Public Life Project, March 8, 2016.

fact that the body politic of which it wishes to be part is nevertheless based on a power distribution that is not free from the same claim to Jewishness.

Gershom Scholem is famously (and, admittedly, repeatedly) quoted as having noted, in a letter to Franz Rosenzweig, the futility of the Zionist attempt to 'secularize' Judaism. As he remarked, Zionists

> don't know what they are doing. They believe they have secularized the language, pulled out its apocalyptic thorn. But that is surely not true; this secularization of the language is only a *façon de parler*, a holy phrase. It is absolutely impossible to empty out the words filled to bursting ... God will not remain mute in a language in which he has been invoked and summoned into our existence in countless ways.[54]

Almost a half century later he repeated the same notion, remarking to an interviewer that 'History will not permit the People of Israel to be like all other nations.'[55] As we saw above, this same 'aspiration to be a people like all peoples,'[56] is what propels the paradoxical 'secularization' of the notion of 'Israel' into a non- or anti-Jewish nation-statist concept. In this, Ornan (who, like other Young Hebrews, has dedicated his lifework to the study of the Hebrew language) seems to have failed to see the futility of his and his fellow appellants' attempt at 'silencing' (in Scholem's terms) or simply erasing Judaism out of the politics of the State of Israel.

---

[54] Gershom Scholem in a letter to Franz Rosenzweig, December 26, 1926; This English translation is by Alexander Galley, quoted in W. Cutter, 'Ghostly Hebrew, ghastly speech: Scholem to Rosenzweig, 1926,' *Prooftexts*, 10 (1990), 431.

[55] G. Scholem, *Continuity and Rebellion – Gershom Scholem in Speech and Dialogue* (Tel Aviv: Am-Oved, 1994), 62.

[56] Ornan, 'Yisrael einenah 'medinat haleom shel ha'am hayehudi."

Conclusion
Israel, Judaism, and Critique

As this book argues throughout, Israel's Jewish identity crisis can be understood as a direct outcome of the Zionist ideology's unresolved claim to Jewish identity. The modernist shift spearheaded by Zionist ideology turned the focus away from the 'subjective,' historical and traditional matter of Judaism to the allegedly 'objective' and predetermined matter of 'Jews.' In this scheme, Jews are primarily identified by 'what they are' (i.e., their alleged 'natural' common biological origin, blood, ethnos, or race), and not (or only remotely) by what they believe and practice, and by how they live their collective and individual lives (i.e., Judaism, in its varied and even conflicting historical manifestations).

Now, clearly, the abandoning of a historically established, traditional Jewish way of understanding the world, including the very meaning of Jewishness (according to which it is Judaism that defines the Jews and not vice versa), demands that Zionism adopts an alternative 'language' by which to understand the world. Zionism had clearly found this language in the predominant European modernist spirit of its time. Doing so, it has adopted what I have referred to in this book as an epistemology, a way of viewing and interpreting the world, that is sustained by the European Enlightenment project, and ultimately (even if unwittingly, as might be the case of 'cultural' and 'spiritual' notions of Zionism) serves the political configuration of power beneficial to the sovereign, allegedly secular nation-state. This was especially apparent as political Zionism emerged as triumphant over other streams of Zionism.

Viewed as an enlightened secularization and politicization (or, to follow the atavistic nationalist discourse: re-politicization) of Jews, Judaism, and Jewish identity, this ideological foundation ultimately consolidated around a political, nation-statist reading of Zionist ideology, according to which the foremost, redemptive modern reincarnation of Judaism itself is to be a nation-state of Jews. Depicting two millennia of Jewish life outside of the framework of (Jewish) sovereignty as a pathology, this ideology insists that the nation-statist politicization of Jews would also amount to their 'normalization,' a healing of the Jewish collective body. Critically, this healing would mean that Jews are no longer 'unique,' but rather 'normal,' a nation 'like all other nations' of the world.

Among other things, this 'normalcy' would mean, so the ideological doctrine has determined, that once this polity (the Jews' State) comes into being, everything done in the framework of the state will be, by 'natural,' obvious political definition, 'Jewish.' Moreover, it would make the state itself 'Jewish.' To this day, Zionist ideologues and apologists repeatedly draw a (manifestly deficient) comparison to other, European nation-states suggesting that 'Jew' should be read as exactly equivalent (conceptually) to 'French,' 'Italian,' 'German,' and so forth: Just as the nation-state of the French, France, *is* French simply by virtue of being their state, so the nation-state of Jews, Israel, *is* Jewish by virtue of its being their state: The peoples' 'being' Jews (i.e., their 'natural' makeup) makes their state, *ipso facto*, Jewish.

This analogy is deficient primarily since it forces Judaism, Jews, and Jewishness into the straitjacket of a historically situated and politically embodied conceptual scheme – that of the modern, sovereign, allegedly secular European nation-state. Yet, alas, Judaism, Jews, and Jewishness, so variedly understood throughout history, seem to refuse to fit easily, if ever, into the predominant nation-statist discourse of the time.

In any event, the most immediate implication of this analogy ('a nation like all other nations'), given the historical context of the establishment of the State of Israel, has been the logic produced by the reversing of the analogy: Israel is Jewish only in-so-far-as it is a state of Jews. Were the population it rules over not to be seen as Jewish, the Jews' State will cease to exist as such. Alternative potential understandings of Jewish nation-statism, according to which it is a Jewish constitution of the state (whatever this notion may amount to) that determines its Jewishness, regardless of the biological, racial, or ethnic origin of the members of its population, are simply not considered viable.

Furthermore, it is important to remember that unlike the so-called precedents of other national (European) movements and nation-states, Zionism and Israel have not emerged 'organically' as the political self-determination of a (newly defined, realized, or invented) nation living on a shared territory. Rather, Israel's history is such that the nation-state (itself being the culmination of an ideological and political pro-ject) preceded the formation of the 'state's nation.' In actuality, the state itself has played a most central role in bringing Jews from all over the world under its sovereignty and shaping this newly created collect-ive as 'new,' national Jews. And just as crucially, the territory over which the state is sovereign has been historically settled by non-Jews.

These foundational parameters have determined a historical course by which the state is bound (by its own guiding logic) to manufacture and maintain a Jewish majority – or, to be precise, a majority of Jews – in its population. This necessitates the ceaseless arithmetic of 'demog-raphy' where a necessary majority of Jews is continually counted against a minority of non-Jewish Palestinian-Arabs, rendering the latter an immediate threat to the very notion of the sovereignty of Jews.

Yet most crucially, as I have argued throughout the book, both the Zionist ideological foundation and its political embodiment, the State of Israel, have failed to offer their own (modern, enlightened, secular, 'natural,' etc.) definition of Jewish identity. Instead, either as a stopgap or as a somewhat self-denying, almost Freudian-slip-like manifestation of adherence to a mythical, essentialist notion of Jewishness, the state (under the dominance of the socialist-Zionist party, it must be recalled) has chosen to rely on rabbinical, Orthodox gatekeepers for the foun-dational maintenance and upholding of the line separating Jews from non-Jews. The prevalent discourse that blames this reality on the Orthodox minority's alleged 'coercion' of the non-Orthodox majority of Israeli-Jews is indeed helpful for this majority's upholding of an enlightened, liberal-democratic self-image. But it should not distract us from seeing how important is the role of the rabbinical gatekeepers for the state's upholding of its most basic of premises: that it is a Jews' State. These gatekeepers help maintain the most fundamental param-eter of all that differentiates Jews from non-Jews in Israel, thus allowing the state to preserve the proper demographic balance between Jews and non-Jewish Palestinian-Arabs. To put it rather crudely: How can you (or rather the state) 'Judaize the Galilee' (or otherwise), by way of tilting the demographic balance in the region in favor of Jews (as has been the state's declared policy) without having a prior demarcation separating Jews from non-Jews?

The Israeli Jewish identity crisis is further compounded by another basic failure of the Zionist prognosis. Contrary to the secularist prediction that the nation-state of Jews would become not only the center of Jewish life but also the very embodiment of modern Jewishness (rendering non-Israeli Jewish identities pathologically incomplete, if not outright inauthentic), Jews throughout the world, and Israeli-Jews in particular, have kept on insisting (as has been historically the case) that 'Jewish blood' alone does not suffice.[1] Or, to put it politically, that a positively meaningful Jewish identification demands more than just being subjected to the sovereignty of the state of Jews. This, of course, is further emphasized by the fact that there are also non-Jews who are subjects of this sovereignty: Contrary to the statist Zionist prognosis, Israeli political culture does not accept the designation of these people (or their creations) as 'Jewish' simply by virtue of their being citizens of the Jews' state, descendants of the Land of Israel, and even speakers of Israeli Hebrew.

Moreover, the political culture sponsored and propagated by the state itself (through its various institutions and branches) echoes this normative understanding of Jewishness, even if it does so clumsily, to say the least. This is manifested primarily in what has been historically labeled 'the status quo,' and what recent misguided secularist protestations decry as 'religionization': namely, the propagation by the state of (an admittedly narrow and problematic) sense of Jewish identity, mostly through the statist educational system and via the legal enforcement of certain decrees (as a matter of civil, i.e. 'secular,' law) that color the Israeli public sphere in Jewish 'hues.' These governmental measures, while far from instilling one's identity with a positively meaningful knowledge of Jewish history, tradition, ethics, and identity, have one fundamental trait: They are reserved for Jews alone; hence, they reiterate the basic fault lines of Israeli nationhood.

Recent attempts at 'bolstering' Israeli-Jews' Jewish identity and 'anchoring' Israel's own Jewish identity, and the fierce controversy they have instigated have only further highlighted the depth of this identity crisis. Driven by the nation-statist concern over demographics, or more accurately the balance between Israeli-Jews and non-Jewish Palestinian-Arabs, these various legal measures and initiatives by the executive branch tend to use a shallow, politically manipulated notion of Jewish normativity in order to reassert the sovereignty of Jews and to deny Palestinian-Arabs similar claim for national self-determination.

---

[1] See my discussion in the Introduction.

The State of Jews and the Jewish Challenge

There are many ways in which Israel's Jewish identity crisis might conceivably develop. It is not too difficult to conceive of potential realignments that would either backtrack or reorient the current course of the Israeli problematic construction of Jewish politics. Yet, the publication in March 2018 of a report by a special committee appointed by Israel's Diaspora Affairs Ministry suggests that the current impetus in Israel is driven toward doubling down on the sense that it is 'blood' and the 'demographics' of a majority of Jews versus a minority of non-Jews that define and guarantee Israeli sovereignty as Jewish. To judge by this report, the Israeli Jewish identity crisis only seems to deepen even further, and to spread far beyond the limits of the Israeli polity, reinventing, if its logic would have its way, the whole Jewish world.

This report is noteworthy since it attests to the quite staggering degree to which the political interests of the sovereign nation-state of the Jews might intervene – and even interfere – in the ongoing configuration and reconfiguration of the very sense of Jewishness both inside and outside of the state. The report captures vividly the political logic by which a continuous, proactive mission aimed at increasing the number of Jews in Israel (and progressively so also outside of the state) is of an existential necessity for the state.

The committee that produced the report was set up in 2016 to study what the Diaspora Affairs Ministry has identified as a recently formed 'new and unprecedented reality ... regarding the limits of the Jewish people and its size;

The centuries-old situation, where the Jewish people is a highly defined group, which is mostly discriminated against ... and whose desertion causes assimilation and a rapid disappearance of those leaving the group, is no longer the case in many places. On the contrary, there are growing publics in the world for whom belonging to, or at least having an affinity with the Jewish people, are worthy and even desired. This deep change demands rethinking on and a reconfiguration of matters pertaining to the limits of the Jewish people and their definition, the Jewish people's attitude to those who leave it and those who wish to join it, and the role of the State of Israel vis-à-vis publics who have an affinity to the Jewish people.[2]

---

[2] O. Ha'ivri, B. Ish-shalom, Z. Hauser, R. Yadlin, and P. Nirnstein, 'duaḥ hava'ada haṣiburit hameya'eṣet livḥinat yaḥasah shel yisrael leṣiburim ba'olam

The committee sees this new reality as an 'unprecedented strategic opportunity to draw closer to the Jewish people those publics that have an affinity to it.'[3] This would involve both charting a clear path for joining the Jewish people (going back, the report suggests, to a notion of a national-religious form of *giyyur*), and building on this affinity to bolster's Israel's position in the world with the help of those – Jews and non-Jews alike – 'who wish to be tied to the Jewish people and to assist it and its state.'[4]

Identifying a population of 123 million (!) people worldwide as having varying degrees of positive affinity to the Jewish people, the committee sees the State of Israel – being, as the very first sentence of the report itself makes a point of stressing (clearly echoing the ongoing debate on the matter) 'the nation-state of the Jewish people'[5] – as obligated to chart the path for this reconfiguration of the Jewish people.

This abovementioned, overwhelming number – to reiterate: 123 million – is an illuminating exercise in the nation-statist arithmetic of the Jewish 'blood,' now redefined not only as a matter of 'biological origin' but also as a sentiment of empathy to Jews and support of Israel. The committee has identified five 'circles of belonging [or affinity]' to the Jewish people. The image offered by the committee is an onion-like layered spheres of 'affinity,' at the core of which are Israeli-Jews. These layers/spheres are as follows:

- A 'core' of 14 million people who are 'known as Jews by all accounts,' 8 million of whom live outside of Israel.
- A second sphere includes 9 million non-Jews who are eligible for immigration to Israel under the Law of Return. These are second and third generation descendants of Jews and their families.

---

ba'alei ziqa la'am hayehudi,' Report (Jerusalem: Ministry of Diaspora Affairs, 2018), 124.

[3] Ha'ivri, Ish-shalom, Hauser, Yadlin, and Nirnstein, 'duah hava'ada hasiburit hameya'eset livhinat yahasah shel yisrael lesiburim ba'olam ba'alei ziqa la'am hayehudi,' 124.

[4] Ha'ivri, Ish-shalom, Hauser, Yadlin, and Nirnstein, 'duah hava'ada hasiburit hameya'eset livhinat yahasah shel yisrael lesiburim ba'olam ba'alei ziqa la'am hayehudi,' 125.

[5] Ha'ivri, Ish-shalom, Hauser, Yadlin, and Nirnstein, 'duah hava'ada hasiburit hameya'eset livhinat yahasah shel yisrael lesiburim ba'olam ba'alei ziqa la'am hayehudi,' 12.

- The third sphere is composed of 5 million people 'who might be defined as distant relatives, [non-Jewish] descendants of Jews from a fourth generation and above, and of Jews who have converted [out of Judaism] in recent generations.' These people have a claim to Jewish descent but are not eligible for immigration to Israel under the Law of Return.

- The fourth circle is composed of 'people and communities who pronounce, one way or another, their affinity to the Jewish people,' numbering by the committee's account a total of 35 million. This group includes 15 million descendants of *conversos*, those Jews who were forced to convert to Christianity in the Middle Ages. The committee sees these individuals – 'and especially those of Iberian descent' as 'the biggest and most important' of those who have 'an affinity' to the Jewish people, and recommends that the government focuses its attention in the shorter run primarily on this group. In addition to them, 15 million others are 'lost tribes,' i.e., alleged descendants of the ten tribes of the Kingdom of Israel (Samaria), who were 'lost' as members of the Israelite/Hebrew people following the Assyrian occupation and exile in 720 BCE. The remaining 5 million in this group are what the committee calls 'newcomers': people who are part of an alleged growing movement of 'joining on this or that level the circles of the Jewish people – and in many senses are not Jewish and are not converts to Judaism.' An Israeli sociologist whom the committee heard as an expert witness suggests that these individuals 'might be defined as 'assimilating into Jewry.'' This group includes 'those who joined the Jewish people, and even take part in the activity of a Jewish community, but have never gone (and apparently also do not intend to go) through a conversion of any kind.'[6] In most cases, he explains, these are (non-Jewish) spouses of Jews who raise their kids as Jewish.

- The fifth and last sphere hosts 60 million people whom the committee defines as 'future potential.' These are people 'who have an affinity to the Jewish people [yet] do not pronounce it for various

---

[6] Eliezer Ben-Rafael in Haʿivri, Ish-shalom, Hauser, Yadlin, and Nirnstein, 'duaḥ havaʿada haṣiburit hameyaʿeṣet livḥinat yaḥasah shel yisrael leṣiburim baʿolam baʿalei ziqa laʿam hayehudi,' 100.

reasons, or are not aware of it, and there is the possibility that they will be exposed to such information in the coming years.'[7]

As critics were quick to note, the report manifests – its text's and the Ministry's triumphant tone notwithstanding – the long-standing Israeli anxiety regarding the numerical balance between those whom the state counts as Jews and non-Jewish Palestinian-Arabs. One such critical reaction sees the report as emanating from a 'demographic panic rooted in the fear of losing Israel's Jewish majority.'[8] This panic was apparently reinforced by a contemporaneous publication of a report by the Israeli military, according to which 'more Arabs than Jews live in Israel, the West Bank and Gaza.'[9]

Tellingly, the same critical reaction – by *Haaretz*'s lead editorial – fails to suggest a breaking away from the demographic mind-set. It thus further stresses the centrality of the notion of Jewishness as a matter of 'blood' in the liberal-Zionist worldview, too – the vehement tone of its criticism of the right-wing's rendering of the same logic notwithstanding. Indeed, this liberal-Zionist worldview's indebtedness to European notions of secularity seems to force it to remain trapped in this demographic-thinking straitjacket.

As the editorial makes clear, the solution to the demographic parity between Jews and Arabs in the territory between the river Jordan and the Mediterranean – a parity which amounts to what all (Zionist) parties agree is a demographic threat to the sovereignty of Jews – can only be conceived of in a framework that perpetuates the very same outlook that brought this 'demographic panic' to light in the first place. The difference between the (right-wing Zionist) report and its (left-wing liberal-Zionist) critics lies in the tactics they advocate to serve the unchallenged strategy of preserving a Jewish majority. If the Ministry of Diaspora Affairs (headed at the time by right-wing politicians) engages in the troubling attempt at artificially (or, if you like, 'innovatively') increasing the number of Jews worldwide, the liberal-Zionist stance insists that only a separation between Jews and

---

[7] Ha'ivri, Ish-shalom, Hauser, Yadlin, and Nirnstein, 'duaḥ hava'ada haṣiburit hameya'eṣet livḥinat yaḥasah shel yisrael leṣiburim ba'olam ba'alei ziqa la'am hayehudi,' 126.

[8] *Haaretz* Editorial, 'The Jewish mission,' *Haaretz*, March 28, 2018.

[9] Y. Berger, 'Figures presented by army show more Arabs than Jews live in Israel, West Bank and Gaza,' *Haaretz*, March 26, 2018.

Palestinian-Arabs (in the form of 'two states for two peoples') would service the shared goal of preserving a Jewish majority:

The latest demographic data isn't surprising. Supporters of the two-state solution have long warned that the only ethical and effective way to maintain Israel's Jewish majority is to divide the land. But because the current government is working instead to annex the territories, with their residents, en route to an apartheid system, it must concoct delusional plans to import a pseudo-Jewish population. It would do better to recognize that only a two-state solution can guarantee the future of the Zionist project.[10]

This liberal-Zionist stance does not offer, in other words, a challenge to the 'demographic' outlook. Such a challenge would offer, for example, alternative ways for understanding the notion of Jewish sovereignty, such that do not rely on the number of Jews but rather on some core Jewish constitutive normative infrastructure. Rather, as this book has discussed throughout, the foundational Zionist, ethno-nationalist sense by which the Jew precedes Judaism, meaning that descent trumps normative outlooks and traditions, has been a mainstay of (political-Zionist) 'Jewish politics,' as this notion is understood and maintained by all major streams of Israeli political thought.

It is indeed disheartening to note the degree to which those liberal-Zionist, secularist critics who decry the Ministry of Diaspora Affair's report, as well as a whole range of executive measures that nourish on the same motivation – rightly noting these measures' obvious contradiction with and negation of basic liberal-democratic principles of governance – share the same basic view, by which these measures are an authentic expression of *Jewish* politics. These critics' adherence to a secularist, 'enlightened,' and nation-statist framework leads them to reassert the same false binary that reads these 'bolstering' and 'anchoring' of Jewish identity as the authentic manifestation of Jewish normativity. Their critiques are thus misguidedly aimed at an alleged encroaching process of 'religionization' which is in effect but a recent manifestation of the continuous, political, nationalist determination of the state to reassert its most basic (demographic) premise (which the critics share) as a Jews' state. Failing to see how these questionable understandings of Jewish normativity in effect serve the theopolitics of the state, the liberal-Zionist critics seem to be trapped in their own

---

[10] *Haaretz* Editorial, 'The Jewish Mission.'

claim to a secular 'Israeli' (Jewish) identity. The obvious shortcomings of the logical solution of exiting the Jewish-identity bind altogether (by way of asserting non-Jewish 'Israeliness' as a supposed nondenominational national identity) only further highlight this predicament.

This bind, in other words, is an outcome of the Israeli-secularist, liberal-Zionist failure to engage in a *Jewish* critique of the state and the Zionist rendition of Jewish politics. This failure is the result of two primary reasons: First, as already noted, on a more immediate level the secular, liberal-Zionist critique shares the most basic premise of all, by which modern Jewish politics must take the form of a European-like nation-state, which is defined as 'Jewish' by virtue (and, these critics will often insist, *only* by virtue) of a demographic disparity between a Jewish majority vs. a non-Jewish minority under the state's sovereignty (i.e., this failure is an outcome of the political-Zionist worldview, which the critics ultimately share). Second, on another, more foundational level, the problem has to do with the binary way in which the secular worldview sees Judaism (i.e., this failure is an outcome of the critics' secularist worldview). Secularism's dichotomous worldview feeds a series of oppositions that buttress each other: secular-religious, enlightened-benighted, modern-primitive, rational-irrational, universal-parochial, and so forth. It assumes that if one (person, idea, argument) is to be found on one side of this chain of binaries, one must remain so throughout: one cannot, by this logic, be both religious and rational, enlightened and parochial, etc.

Regrettably, in the liberal-Zionist Israeli case, as we have seen, the dichotomy is even further stretched to force a misconception by which 'Jewish' is identified with 'religious.' Hence, Judaism itself is read as essentially having to do with the 'other side' of this foundational dichotomous worldview: It is, at root, irrational, benighted and primitive – by (modern, secularist, rational, and enlightened) definition; it is, in a deep sense, alien to the liberal-Zionist world. This rather crude rendition of secularism further leads many liberal-Zionist spokespeople to unreflectively equate Judaism/religion and Jewishness with the Israeli Right, 'forgetting' as it were the historical manifestations of secularist streams among the Zionist Right, and foregoing the possibility of a Jewishly informed critique of the status quo.

Indeed, an insistence on the notion that it is exactly the arithmetic of a (Jewish) majority vs. (non-Jewish) minority, and *only* this arithmetic that may define Israel as Jewish has become a rallying cry of secularist liberal-Zionism. This becomes especially apparent in contexts in which the secularism of this liberal stance reasserts itself vis-à-vis what it sees as religious coercion. Thus, on one such occasion, *Haaretz*'s columnist sees the assertion by some members of the secular (Zionist) parties of the Left that 'the Sabbath must be a meaningful part of the definition of Israel's Jewishness,' as attesting to the surrender of 'the secular public' to the 'Ultra-Orthodox public.' For this commentator, the very assertion that 'the Sabbath must carry a Jewish character and be loaded with Jewish content' amounts to a betrayal of what he presents as the only truly liberal-secularist notion of Jewish politics, namely, 'that Israel is a Jewish state only in the sense of it being a state in which a solid majority of people from a Jewish origin live, and not in any other sense.' (Interestingly, in this self-proclaimed liberal-secularist view, only the market's dictates can override all other considerations, clearly betraying the liberal indebtedness to capitalism. As the columnist puts it: 'A truly secular and liberal [person] positions above all other things the value of freedom, which includes the freedom to commerce in any day. No restriction from religious reasons can be acceptable in any day of the week.') The bottom line, then, is that Israel's Jewishness can – and should – be solely a matter of 'blood' or 'descent': 'Israel will be a Jewish state only if the majority of its citizens will be of a Jewish origin, and not because of rules that dictate ways of life.'[11]

In a dichotomous view, where 'the secular' and 'the religious' (people, views, worlds) are seen as absolute opposites trapped in a zero-sum game over the character of Israeliness, while Judaism is equated with religion, any insistence on a positively meaningful understanding of the Jewishness of Israeli politics beyond matters of 'demography' becomes anathema to the secularism of the liberal-Zionist stance. The latter's Zionism is thus distilled down to an insistence on the view of Israel as a state of Jews, not as a Jewish state. And this, as I have argued throughout, leaves the arithmetic of the Jewish 'blood' as the sole viable notion of Jewish politics.

Yet it would be wrong to conclude that the Jewish identity crisis entailed in Israeli political thought is the property of the liberal-Zionist Left alone. Granted, the manifestations of this crisis are all the more pronounced in the case of the Israeli Left, due to its manifest

---

[11] R. Alpher, 'ḥoq hamarkolim mokhiaḥ shehaḥilonim sovlim mirigshei neḥitut,' *Haaretz*, September 1, 2018.

indebtedness to notions of secularity and principles of freedom and democracy. This, I should stress, is *not* to suggest that the Zionist Israeli Right has either overcome this crisis or holds a remedy to it that is inaccessible to the liberal-Zionist Left. By subjecting democratic principles of equality, civil and human rights to the primacy of ethno-national sovereignty, the Right does not offer what could be honestly considered a genuine, *Jewishly* concerned solution to the root cause of the crisis, namely the failed Zionist attempt at claiming Jewish politics without offering a viable, meaningful reconfiguration or redefinition of Jewish identity.

To a large extent, the liberal-Zionist discourse takes place in reaction to the growing dominance of the Israeli Right. The clear marks of this dominance and the Left's reaction to it can be seen throughout the book. The dominance of the Right is manifested in, among other things, various legislative and executive measures and initiatives that aim at solving the tension or crisis at hand by explicitly preferring the (Zionist reading of) 'Jewishness' of the state over its commitment to principles of democracy and civil rights.[12]

This still leaves open the question of how the Right views (and reads, or misreads) this Jewishness. The Right's 'nationalization' of Judaism/Jewishness tends to follow in recent decades the ideological drumbeat of religious Zionism (or, to call the movement and ideology as Yakov Rabkin[13] convincingly insists we do, 'National Judaism'). The prevalent terminology and nomenclature in Israel may indeed be misleading, but they should not distract us: Much of what is seen as 'religious' Zionism is at bottom a subjugation of certain elements prized out of Jewish tradition to the supremacy of the concerns of the modern, sovereign nation-state, with its obsession for a total, 'pure' confluence between territory and identity, and the derived political arithmetic of majority and minority.

In this framework, the meaning of Judaism is reread under the heavy shadow of the primary commitment to the (European) ideology of

---

[12] As Ayelet Shaked, Israel's justice minister, is reported to have said, her determining view is that Israel must keep a Jewish majority even at the price of violation of rights; R. Hovel, 'Justice Minister: Israel must keep Jewish majority even at the expense of human rights,' *Haaretz*, February 13, 2018.

[13] Y. M. Rabkin, *What Is Modern Israel?* (London: Pluto Press, 2016).

modern nationalism. This rereading tends to view the nation-state, or its political theology, in the colors of 'religious' theology; everything that is understood to be promoting the interests of the nation-state of the Jews is also understood to be *ipso facto* 'Jewish,' i.e., as promoting the true essence and meaning of Judaism and Jewishness. In this framework, Judaism itself is indeed nationalized, so as to serve the interest of the nation-state. Indeed, from an intellectual point of view this may be considered the less interesting rendition of Jewish nationalism, as so much of it is focused on the worshiping of the sovereign state.

Yet I do find the expressions and articulations of the crisis at hand to be more pronounced – and hence more intriguing and illuminating – among the Israeli Left, making it much more attractive as an object of analysis and study. This is so partially because the liberal-Zionist discourse, attentive as it is at least to the rhetoric (if not always to the substance) of democratic principles, human and civil rights, and – well, ultimately, secularism as a value in and of itself – is also more attentive to some of the 'problematical' implications of a political, nation-statist reading of Jewishness and Judaism. It is less capable of repressing the symptoms of this identity crisis, as seems to be the case with the Israeli Right.

Beyond the Israeli Case

Now, while this discussion is obviously focused on a specific Israeli rendition of the secularist epistemology, I would argue (as I have already noted earlier) that in a deep sense this is but a sociohistorically specific appearance of a prevalent, predominant understanding of the politics of the modern nation-state. To understand this, let me go back one last time to the debate over the nation-state bill:

In the aftermath of the Israeli Parliament's passing of the nation-state bill into a basic-law of the land, amidst a barrage of celebrations and condemnations (on both the national and international level), one critical comment stood out in the clarity of its almost un-self-reflective insistence to reassert the basic Zionist premise. It came from Dan Meridor, a former member of the Likud leadership, who, among other posts, was justice minister in the early 1990s, overseeing the passage of those basic laws that have come to be seen as the core of Israel's 'constitutional revolution.'

In his comments on the recently passed basic law, Meridor argues against a prevalent political view, according to which the liberal-democratic model for the nation-state (here code-named 'a state of all of its citizens') stands in direct opposition to an explicit preference of a certain group (ethnos, race, etc.) over others by the polity (here code-named 'the state of the Jewish people'). In Meridor's view, the two models are far from mutually exclusive:

> Is Israel the state of the Jewish people, or a state of all of its citizens? This question has been raised time and again in recent years, and one is demanded to choose between the two options. I wish to argue that there is no contradiction between the two. Moreover, the Zionist vision is founded on the State of Israel's being both the nation-state of the Jewish people and a state of all of its citizens.[14]

In this reading, 'Zionism was never satisfied with the argument for the right over the land alone.' The territorial claim 'was always accompanied by an essential condition: a Jewish majority. We will exercise our right [over the land] by a Jewish majority. With no majority, there is no Jewish state.' As Meridor goes on to explain the pivotal importance of this insistence on the construction and preservations of a Jewish majority, he makes it clear that the very notion of Israel's being a liberal-democracy is premised exactly on this demographic arithmetic:

> Why did Zionism fight for a Jewish majority? Because according to the Zionist vision, the state to be established shall be democratic. It will hold equal rights, and everyone – Jews and Arabs – will have the right to vote. In order for it to be a Jewish state, it is required that Jews will be a large and stable majority of its citizens.

Moreover, in this reading it is exactly the insistence on a Jewish majority that proves the Israeli, Zionist adherence to democracy: 'After all, if Zionism had believed that only Jews will be the citizens of the Jewish state, and only they will have the right to determine its fate, there would not have been a need to fight for a Jewish majority.'

In Meridor's view, then, the notions of 'a Jewish state' and the principle of 'a democratic state' (which he reads as amounting in essence to 'a state of all of its citizens') are of two different orders.

---

[14] D. Meridor, 'en kol setira ben medinat leom limdinat kol ezraḥeha,' *Haaretz*, September 13, 2018.

One is 'national, historical, cultural and moral.' The other is procedural, a matter of the (liberal-democratic) rules of the game. The two
orders are not in conflict, he argues, since (and only if) the state holds a
Jewish majority under its sovereignty. 'Indeed, only because in an
essential manner all human beings are equal in their rights ... a Jewish
majority is required.' With no Jewish majority, he insists, the notion of
a nation-state of the Jewish people will irrecoverably contradict the
most basic democratic principles or equality and human rights. Ultimately, then, 'there is a Jewish majority, so there is no contradiction
between the two concepts.'[15]

Meridor does go on to stress that the state must avoid a despotic rule
of the majority. But as he makes a point of repeating, this, too, can only
be guaranteed if there is an a priori distinction between a Jewish
majority and a minority of non-Jewish Palestinian-Arabs. This demographic distinction, achieved by immigration laws (i.e., the Law of
Return), he insists, does not amount to a discriminatory practice within
the state, since it is but a 'regulation of entrance to the state.' Meridor
seems to avoid the tautological nature of this argument: after all, the
Law of Return, which is aimed (among other things) to guarantee a
Jewish majority in Israel is the law of the land only thanks to the Jewish
majority, which in turn this law secures.

Ultimately, Meridor's is but a reiteration (by a politician from the
Right, at that) of the basic Zionist premise, by which Israel is primarily
a (democratic) state of Jews (by makeup of its population). Its 'Jewishness' is only a natural derivative of this foundational fact. Indeed, as we
have seen throughout, this is an argument repeated by liberal-Zionists
commentators. And as they would often restate, this basic tenet of
Israeli politics should not be read as discriminatory, since it is but a
specific iteration of a global system of governance, namely nationalism
and nation-statism.

One may indeed wonder how is it that these commentators so often
fail to see the limits of the application of (European, historically
Christian) notions of politics, religion, nation, ethnos, race, and
nation-state to the case of Jew, Jewishness, and Judaism. But beyond
this, it seems hard to refute that they do point to an essential matter
regarding the secularist nation-statist (liberal-democratic or otherwise)
order of the world. The nation-statist rules of the game assume (if they

---

[15] Meridor, 'en kol setira ben medinat leom limdinat kol ezraḥeha.'

are not outright enabled by this) an infrastructure of collective, political preferences that are clearly of an order that may be described (at least in the European case) as ethnic, religious, cultural, and even racial. A liberal-democratic polity that is built on this nationalist infrastructure does not erase or overcome this infrastructure, but rather assumes it and is ultimately enabled by it.

If anything, the contested politics of immigration, multiculturalism, religion, and secularism in Europe during the past few decades have stressed this point to an alarming degree. This contested, bitter politics seems to expose the high degree to which the liberal-democratic state (in the context of a global nation-statist division of the world, of course) assumes a preexisting particularistic infrastructure – of values, preferences, worldview, ways of living in the world, etc. – as the foundational bed on which liberal-democracy is enabled. A challenge against these particularistic presumptions (in the form of adherence to a different set of cultural values or the practice of other ways of being in the world, for example), is too often taken to be not only an inconvenience, but a direct threat to the very viability of the polity.

Take, as one obvious example, the various bans on women's apparel presented in France (among other places), the enforcement of which led to the quite staggering images of (male) policeman forcing women beachgoers to undress. The justification for this obvious restriction if not outright infringement of basic human rights was the women's clothing's alleged failure to demonstrate respect for 'good morals and secularism.'[16] Beyond reinforcing William Connolly's judgment that 'secular models of thinking, discourse and ethics are too constipated to sustain the diversity they seek to admire,'[17] these cases betray the degree to which this secularism is dependent on a nation-statist configuration of power.

Seen against this background (as it is indeed often argued by Israeli and Zionist spokespersons) there is very little that is especially unique – conceptually at least – in the Israeli (nation-statist) striving for an upholding both and at the same time of a liberal-democratic self-image and the explicit preference of one group – that of 'Jews,' in this case – over others. What is unique in the Israeli case, of course, is the degree

---

[16] B. Quinn, 'French police make woman remove clothing on Nice beach following burkini ban,' *The Guardian*, August 23, 2016.
[17] W. E. Connolly, *Why I Am Not a Secularist* (Minneapolis: University of Minnesota Press, 1999), 6.

to which the state itself is conflicted as to its own very claim to a 'Jewish identity' and its understanding of 'Jewish politics.' The Israeli case is thus conducive in pointing to the ways in which a secularist discourse, built on the premise of the religious-secular dichotomy, works to preserve the 'enlightened' self-image of the secularist order by blaming its own inability to sustain the diversity it purportedly admires on a 'religious' or 'reactionary' minority. It is, in other words, yet another manifestation of the self-reinforcing 'network of binary oppositions,'[18] where an almost instinctive association is established between the religious-secular opposition and other, self-reinforcing oppositions. This 'endlessly circular chain of reference'[19] functions in effect to veil a secularly or liberal-democratically palatable reality, in which the 'enlightened' order is premised on an unpalatable system of particular preferences.

Toward a *Jewish* Critique of the Nation-State of Jews

It is my argument that as far as Jews, Jewishness, and Judaism are involved, the hoped-for overcoming of the Israeli predicament – and more generally of the un-self-reflective nature of the secularist ideology of nation-statism – would greatly benefit from a constructive dialogue with Jewish traditions as a source for critiquing the present and rethinking its alternatives. Yet, the attentive reader must be aware of the fact that I have yet to offer such an alternative – Jewishly aware or otherwise – framework for the understanding, or even construction, of Jewish politics.

I will not pretend to have a clear view of what a positively Jewishly informed concern for politics may amount to. This, obviously, is a colossal task, that must be carried by a community that shares this concern.

But I do wish to point to two complementary elements, which I believe may support this task. These have to do with (a) a proper understanding of the notion of tradition, and (b) the importance of being attentive to the conceptual – or epistemological – infrastructure of our discussion.

---

[18] J. Jakobsen and A. Pellegrini, 'Times like this,' in J. Jakobsen, and A. Pellegrini (eds.), *Secularisms* (Durham, NC: Duke University Press, 2008), 6.

[19] C. M. Bell, *Ritual Theory, Ritual Practice* (Oxford: Oxford University Press, 1992), 101.

Let me start with tradition: I would argue that the Israeli-Zionist Jewish identity crisis is fed by a basic failure to understand the concept of tradition and our attitudes, as humans, toward it. And the overcoming of this crisis would necessarily amount to (also) a reevaluation of the role of tradition in human life. In other words, a reclaiming, as it were, of the concept of Jewish politics, should be built on an instructive dialogue with the vast ocean of Jewish traditions, which is premised on a careful evaluation of the meaning of tradition and our (its carriers) relation to it.

The misunderstanding of the very notion of tradition and the relationship between tradition and its carriers is not unique to Zionism or to Israeli-Jews. In effect, the Zionist failure in this regard is but the outcome of the adoption by European Jews of the more general, prevalent (modernist, European, Enlightenment-fed) misconception of tradition. Without diving too deep into a socio-philosophical discussion of the matter,[20] it may suffice to note the degree to which the modernist self-image of the Enlightenment is based on a sense of a sovereign self that is released from the shackles of tradition. In this scheme of thought, there is a rather stark sense of an antinomy between tradition and the liberty of the individual, which in turn motivates a complementing opposition, between tradition and truth.

This feeds a suspicion of tradition that has propelled various projects of so-called liberation from the dictates of the past. This is most prevalent among certain influential Zionist ideologues, who tended to follow the Nietzschean call for the 'destruction' of the 'old temple' (i.e., in this case, what the liberated individuals have viewed as a suffocating Jewish religious tradition), as a precondition for the building of the 'new temple,' that is, the modern incarnation of Jewish identity, collectivity, and nationhood. For these ideologues, tradition has very little constructive to offer, as it is primarily an impediment to individual liberty. As M. Y. Berdyczewski put it, 'the pain of our ancient heritage burdens us, and its weight is heavy. Everything that our heart wants and our brain contemplates is covered by a cloud of traditional and religious concepts, so much so that we cannot breathe.'[21] The only way

---

[20] I have offered a more detailed consideration of the concept in: Yadgar, 'Tradition.'

[21] M. Y. Berdyczewski, *Maamarim, baderekh. Part 2: Shinui arakhin* [Articles, on the way. Part 2: Transvaluation] (Leipzig, Germany: Stiebel, 5682/1922), 25.

forward, he argued, is to reassert the individual will to life against the dictates of this suffocating tradition.

Driven by this sense of a liberation conditioned on a breaking away from the past, much of the impetus of the Zionist project was colored in the hues of a rebellion against tradition, which, at least in its initial stages, was fed by an intimate knowledge of this tradition. This is what allowed for the designation of Zionism as a 'secularist' movement, a designation that is oblivious not only to the persistence of certain traditional Jewish (if not outright 'religious') elements within the Zionist worldview and practice, but also, more importantly, to the obvious *theopolitical* or national-theological character of the movement and its ideology.

It was another Zionist ideologue, Aḥad Haʿam, who perceptively understood the futility of such an endeavor to run away from one's tradition, and highlighted the importance of a constructive reengagement with tradition as a precondition for the construction of a meaningfully *Jewish* modern polity, which he nevertheless read in the predominant terminology of European nationalism. (This insistence on the constructive role of tradition led one socialist-Zionist critic of Aḥad Haʿam to derogatorily call his a 'National Theology.'[22]) But the triumphant political, nation-statist interpretation of Zionism is clearly premised on the sense of a foundational antinomy between modernity and tradition. Its construction of the meaning of Jewish politics was thus driven by a secularist self-image, in which tradition is identified with the foregone 'religion,' and the national reincarnation of the Jewish people is read as premised on an active negation of this tradition (titled under 'exile').

Following the cue of a vast body of literature that highlights the shortcomings and misconceptions of the modernist, secularist construction of tradition, I would argue that a (Jewish) thinking and rethinking of the meaning of Jewish politics must begin with a careful understanding of the dynamic, dialogical nature of tradition and our relation to it.

I once suggested that such a stance (which may be titled 'traditionist,' but ultimately aims to be understood simply in terms of a humane

---

[22] Y. Elʿazari-Volcani, *Kitvey Yitzḥak Elʿazari-Volcani. Volume 2: Sefirot* [Elʿazari-Volcani's writings, Vol. 2] (Tel Aviv: N. Taberski, 5710/1950), 13–68.

being in the world) may be better understood if seen as standing outside of the secularist-conservative dichotomy.[23] It is a dialogical stance in relation to tradition, in which the 'unequal' nature of the dialogue is clearly stated; in other words, it does not presume to put tradition and its carriers on an equal footing in conducting this dialogue, as tradition is understood to be constitutive of those who carry it. This is a loyal yet reflective stance of the individual and her community vis-à-vis their tradition(s). It upholds a basic favorable, sanctifying even view of tradition, that is at the same time interpretive, critical, and selective in practice.

This stance is based on an understanding of tradition in which it is not seen as negating liberty, but as constitutive of our being in the world. As so eloquently put by Edward Shils:

Tradition is not the dead hand of the past but rather the hand of the gardener, which nourishes and elicits tendencies of judgment which would otherwise not be strong enough to emerge on their own. In this respect tradition is an encouragement to incipient individuality rather than its enemy. It is a stimulant to moral judgment and self-discipline rather than an opiate.[24]

A critical reimagining of the meaning of Jewish politics (as against the prevalent political-Zionist, nation-statist understanding of this concept, that feeds so much of the identity crisis outlined above) would seek, then, to engage in an informed dialogue with the vast ocean of Jewish traditions and histories in order to instill the notion of Jewish politics with meaning. Given the diverse, often conflicting nature of these traditions, this is bound to be a project focused on argumentation, dialogue, and disputation more than on dictation and consensus. Yet, as Alisdair MacIntyre would insist, this is exactly the nature of a traditionist engagement, as tradition itself, 'is an argument extended through time in which certain fundamental agreements are defined and redefined in terms of two kinds of conflict: those with critics and enemies external to the tradition who reject all or at least key parts of those fundamental agreements, and those internal, interpretive debates through which the meaning and rationale of the fundamental

---

[23] Yadgar, 'Traditionism.'

[24] E. Shils, 'Tradition and liberty: Antinomy and interdependence,' *Ethics*, 68/3 (1958), 156.

agreements come to be expressed and by whose progress a tradition is constituted.'[25]

I do not know what this argumentation may ultimately yield.[26] But it seems apparent to me that this discussion or argument must be based on a conceptual or epistemological bed that would be judged by those participating in it as historically, traditionally authentic to the Jewish traditions under discussion. In other words, it cannot begin with the adoption of historically embodied, culturally specific concepts, terms, and ideologies that emerge largely from outside of Judaism (as was the case with the modern uses of 'religion,' 'secularism,' 'nationalism,' 'nation-statism,' and so forth).

A good case in point, a negative example of sorts, is a relatively recent emergence (and, it seems, already at this point waning) of an academic field of the study of Jewish political thought, or the Jewish political tradition.[27] As Julie Cooper convincingly shows in her review of the field, the indebtedness of the philosophers and political scientists carrying this project to the modern notion of the sovereign nation-state has been detrimental to the discussion they have held. Given that historically, traditionally, 'Jewish political thought is decisively marked by the experience of statelessness,' and especially the lack of sovereignty, the players in this field, who seem to have adopted the modern-European, nation-statist conceptual scheme as given, found themselves in a bind; 'Although the pervasiveness of politics is the field's animating conviction, scholars have yet to mount a sufficiently forceful challenge

---

[25] A. MacIntyre, *Whose Justice? Which Rationality?* (Notre Dame, IN: University of Notre Dame Press, 1988), 12.

[26] David Novak has offered an attempt to reimagine Zionism from a Jewishly concerned point of view: D. Novak, *Zionism and Judaism: A New Theory* (New York: Cambridge University Press, 2015).

[27] The main protagonists of this field seem to cluster around two institutions in Jerusalem: the Hartman Institute and the Shalem Institute. Probably the most famous of the field's products is a multivolume collection on Jewish political tradition and thought: M. Walzer, M. Lorberbaum, N. Zohar, and Y. Lorberbaum (eds.), *The Jewish Political Tradition. Volume 1: Authority* (New Haven, CT: Yale University Press, 2003); M. Walzer, M. Lorberbaum, N. Zohar, and A. Ackerman (eds.), *The Jewish Political Tradition. Volume 2: Membership* (New Haven, CT: Yale University Press, 2003); M. Walzer, M. Lorberbaum, N. J. Zohar, and M. Kochen (eds.), *The Jewish Political Tradition. Volume 3: Community* (New Haven, CT: Yale University Press, 2018). For a comprehensive review of the field see: Cooper, 'The turn to tradition in the study of Jewish politics.'

to sovereignty's conceptual and political priority.' Cooper finds them to be 'reluctant to pursue alternative, diasporic conceptions of the political,' concluding that 'developing a more ambitious conception of the Jewish political tradition is a prerequisite for encouraging political debate about sovereignty's importance for Jewish political agency.'[28] I would argue that this must extend also to other prominent concepts of the modern-European political discourse, such as nation, ethnos, secularism, and religion.

This, then, is the second element I would stress as essential for a successful Jewish critique of the nation-state of Jews: the reconstruction or reclaiming of an epistemology that is not bound to the configuration of power of the modern nation-state.

* * *

Facing the nationalization of Judaism by the Zionist ideology and the sovereign state it has formed and the Jewish identity crisis it has instigated, some might be tempted to see the only viable reaction or solution in foregoing Judaism or Jewishness altogether. If this is what Judaism has become, it would be better to leave it behind and to reassert our commitment to values of human rights and democracy. This indeed may seem to be a 'more consistent' secularist, supposedly universalist way of handling the Jewish identity crisis.[29]

Yet, as the discussion in this book has shown, deserting Judaism or Jewishness altogether may very well end up in further emphasis of nationalist ideas and a racial worldview. Paradoxical as it may be, it is the State of Israel itself that has proven the point. As Brian Klug

---

[28] Cooper, 'The turn to tradition in the study of Jewish politics,' 67.

[29] Indeed, in the understanding of one *Haaretz* commentator, this may amount to a preference of assimilation:

> The opposition to assimilation is racist and purely nationalistic. Again it's the superior and pure Jewish blood that mustn't be mixed, heaven forbid, with any Christian, Muslim or other impurity. After a long history living as a minority under threat, the people can't shake that survival instinct. But let's advance one step and ask: What for? The state of Israel is the embodiment of Judaism and its values. Here the Jews are a majority, they're the sovereign, there's nothing to stop them from achieving their wishes ... The Jewish state has already crystallized an identity, which can only be enriched by assimilation, which is a normal, healthy process.

> G. Levy, 'What's so bad about assimilation?' *Haaretz*, October 13, 2018.

articulates this observation in his manifestly Jewish critique of Israeli politics, we have reached a point in time in which 'Many Jewish Israelis feel no affiliation whatsoever to Judaism and even repudiate it totally. They are *Jewish people* but they do not see themselves as part of 'the Jewish people,' *am Yisroel*, the People of the Book.'[30] And they clearly have not come to offer, if they ever saw the need to do so, a viable solution to the Zionist Jewish identity predicament. It seems reasonable to suggest that it is exactly the conflation of this identity crisis with a political configuration of power that is based on the notion of the sovereignty of Jews, and the implied preference of Jews over non-Jews, that brings to life some vehemently anti-Jewish positions in defense of the state of Jews.

Moreover, beyond the manifestly unhealthy tendency of running away from the problem instead of going through the (often painful) course of seeking a remedy to it, the defeatist course by which the solution to the Jewish problem at hand is to 'stop being a Jew' also seems to be ignoring a grave historical (admittedly European) lesson regarding the futility of such Jewish escapism.

In any event, for those who do not wish to throw out the Jewish baby with the nationalized, racialized bath water, there seems to be only one viable course of action: a *Jewish* constructive critique of the current meaning and future outlook of Jewish politics. This critique must overcome the limited, narrow and one-dimensional frame of reference, in which one is either 'pro-Israel' and passively, unreflectively accepts the state's rendition of Jewish politics, or she is 'anti-Israel,' adopting a discourse that justifiably or not may very well end up being labeled 'anti-Jewish,' hence excluded a priori from an intra-Jewish conversation.

I would not pretend to suggest that I have the key to this solution. The task of searching for such a key must be a collective effort, and any attempt at approaching it must be put in dialogue with competing and complementing ideas (as has been the case, one is tempted to note, throughout Jewish history). It seems to be that whatever Jewish critique we may consider, it would have to begin with a refutation of the modern, racialized, and nationalized arithmetic of a Jewish majority vs. a non-Jewish minority. Instead, it would be wise to reclaim a normative sense of Jewishness and Judaism as guiding the meaning

---

[30] Klug, *Being Jewish and Doing Justice*, 25.

of Jewish politics. As Klug perceptively reminds us, the constitutive 'concept of *am Yisroel*, the people of Israel, the Jewish people,' has been the Jews' 'commitment to an ethic.' This concept is, indeed, anathema to the politics of the modern nation-state, as '[t]his commitment constitutes a way of life, not a modern state ... For the whole idea of Israel in the Torah is conditional – conditional upon the people keeping their side of the bargain, living up to their billing as a 'light of nations' (Is. 49:6).'[31]

---

[31] Klug, *Being Jewish and Doing Justice*, 24.

Bibliography

Aadel Ka'adan v. Israel Lands Administration, HCJ 6698/95 (2000).

Abramson, Y., 'Making a homeland, constructing a diaspora: The case of Taglit-Birthright Israel,' *Political Geography*, 58 (2017), 14–23.

Academy of the Hebrew Language, The, 'Hadata' (2006). Website. https://hebrew-academy.org.il/?p=22525.

Adalah, 'Arab leadership takes action against Israel's new Jewish Nation-State Law,' Adalah – The Legal Center for Arab Minority Rights in Israel, August 7, 2018. www.adalah.org/en/content/view/9574.

Agence France Presse, 'Benjamin Netanyahu says Israel is 'not a state of all its citizens,'' March 10, 2019.

Aḥad Ha'am (Asher Ginzburg), 'Altneuland', *Hashiloah*, 10/6 (1902).

'Al Parashat Derakhim [On a crossroad], Vol. 2 (Berlin: Judischer Verlag, 5690/1930).

Words of Fire: Selected Essays of Ahad Ha'am (Devon, UK: Notting Hill Editions, 2015).

Alcalay, A., *After Jews and Arabs: Remaking Levantine Culture* (Minneapolis: University of Minnesota Press, 1992).

Al-e Ahmad, J., *Plagued by the West*, trans. Paul Sprachman (Delmor, NY: Center for Iranian Studies, Columbia University, 1982).

Occidentosis: A Plague from the West, trans. Robert Campbell (Berkeley, CA: Mizan Press, 1984).

Gharbzadegi [Weststruckness], trans. John Green and Ahmad Alizadeh (Costa Mesa, CA: Mazda Publishers, 1997).

Alpher, R., 'The reading list for learning fascism in second grade,' *Haaretz*, December 11, 2016.

'Hiṭler, hayehudim hitkavṣu,' *Haaretz*, December 21, 2016.

'ḥoq hamarkolim mokhiaḥ shehaḥilonim sovlim mirigshei neḥitut,' *Haaretz*, September 1, 2018.

Amsellem, Ḥ., *Meqor Yisrael* (Jerusalem: Mekhon Meqabeṣ Nidḥe Yisrael, 5770/2010).

Zera' Yisrael (Jerusalem: Mekhon Meqabeṣ Nidḥe Yisrael, 5770/2010).

Arens, M., 'Israel's Jewish nation-state bill is not just useless – it's harmful,' *Haaretz*, May 14, 2017.

'The Jewish nation-state bill alienates Israel's Arab citizens for nothing,' *Haaretz*, July 16, 2018.

Arian, A. and A. Keissar-Sugarmen, *A Portrait of Israeli Jews: Beliefs, Observance, and Values of Israeli Jews, 2009* (Jerusalem: Israel Democracy Institute and Avi Chai Foundation, 2011).

Asad, T., *Genealogies of Religion: Discipline and Reasons of Power in Christianity and Islam* (Baltimore, MD: Johns Hopkins University Press, 1993).

Formations of the Secular: Christianity, Islam, Modernity (Stanford, CA: Stanford University Press, 2003).

Avineri, S., 'New 'Jewish identity' bill will cause chaos in Israel,' *Haaretz*, November 21, 2011.

'neged ḥiloniyut ḥalula,' *Haaretz*, January 5, 2017.

'neged ḥiloniyut ḥalula (2),' *Haaretz*, February 2, 2017.

'neged ḥiloniyut ḥalula (3),' *Haaretz*, February 23, 2017.

'neged ḥiloniyut ḥalula (4),' *Haaretz*, April 14, 2017.

'Herzl veḥoq haleom,' *Haaretz*, September 19, 2017.

Avneri, U., 'Yair Lapid hu dugma lahitrapsut haḥilonit,' *Haaretz*, December 27, 2016.

Barak, A., 'A constitutional revolution: Israel's basic laws,' *Constitutional Forum*, 4/3 (1993), 83–4.

'The constitutionalization of the Israeli legal system as a result of the basic laws and its effect on procedural and substantive criminal law,' *Israel Law Review*, 31/1–3 (1997), 3–23.

The Judge in a Democracy (Princeton, NJ: Princeton University Press, 2006).

'The values of the State of Israel as a Jewish and democratic state,' *Baacademia*, 24 (2012), 58–66.

Barakeh, M., H. Sweid, D. Khenin, and A. Agbaria, 'Basic Law proposal: Israel – a democratic and egalitarian state,' The Knesset, Pub. L. No. P/19/2913 (2014).

Barak-Erez, D., 'Law and religion under the status quo model: Between past compromises and constant change,' *Cardozo Law Review*, 30 (2008), 2495–508.

Baron, I. Z., *Obligation in Exile* (Edinburgh: Edinburgh University Press, 2014).

Bar-Yosef, E., *A Villa in the Jungle: Africa in Israeli Culture* (Jerusalem: Van Leer Institute, 2013).

Barzilai, G., 'Fantasies of liberalism and liberal jurisprudence: State law, politics, and the Israeli Arab-Palestinian community,' *Israel Law Review*, 34/3 (2000), 425–51.

Batnitzky, L. F., *How Judaism Became a Religion: An Introduction to Modern Jewish Thought* (Princeton, NJ: Princeton University Press, 2011).

Bauman, Z., *Modernity and Ambivalence* (Oxford: Polity Press, 1993).

Begin, B., 'Law proposal: The essence of the State of Israel, 2016/5777,' The Knesset, Pub. L. No. P/20/3541 (2016).

Beḥadrei, ḥaredim, 'forum: beḥadrei ḥaredim – diyun be'iqvot ishur ḥoq haleom'. November 23, 2014. https://goo.gl/FjZJHe.

Bell, C. M., *Ritual Theory, Ritual Practice* (Oxford: Oxford University Press, 1992).

Bender, A., 'Rivlin shiger mikhtav ḥarig laknesset: ḥoq haleom 'alul lifgo'a ba'am hayehudi,' *Maariv*, July 10, 2018.

'Berov shel 62 tomkhim mol 55 mitnagdim: ḥoq hlaeom ushar baknesset,' *Maariv*, July 19, 2018.

Ben-Eliezer, U., *The Making of Israeli Militarism* (Bloomington: Indiana University Press, 1998).

Ben-Rafael, E. (ed.), *Reconsidering Israel–Diaspora Relations* (Leiden, Netherlands: Brill, 2014).

Ben-Zikri, A., 'Israel's new Labor Party leader says the Left forgot how to be Jews,' *Haaretz*, November 13, 2017.

Berdyczewski, M. Y., *Maamarim, baderekh. Part 2: Shinui arakhin* [Articles, on the way. Part 2: Transvaluation] (Leipzig, Germany: Stiebel, 5682/1922).

Berger, Y., 'Figures presented by army show more Arabs than Jews live in Israel, West Bank and Gaza,' *Haaretz*, bhol.co.il, March 26, 2018.

Blum, R., 'In wake of Paris attacks, Roseanne Barr blasts *Haaretz* writer for bashing Israel,' *Algemeiner.com*, November 23, 2015. www.algemeiner.com/?p=298294.

Brenner, Y. Ḥ., *Ketavim* [Writings] (Tel Aviv: Sifriyat Po'alim and Haqibutz Hameuḥad, 5738/1978).

Brubaker, R. and F. Cooper, 'Beyond 'identity,'' *Theory and Society*, 29/1 (2000), 1–47.

Calderon, R., A. Mitzna, R. Frenkel, S. Solomon, E. Stern, R. Hoffman, D. Tzur, B. Toporovsky, and B. Ben-Eliezer, 'Basic Law proposal: The Israeli declaration of independence and the Jewish and democratic state, The Knesset, Pub. L. No. P/19/1939 (2013).

Cavanaugh, W. T., *Theopolitical Imagination: Christian Practices of Space and Time* (Edinburgh: Bloomsbury T&T Clark, 2003).

The Myth of Religious Violence: Secular Ideology and the Roots of Modern Conflict (New York: Oxford University Press, 2009).

Cohen, A., *Non-Jewish Jews in Israel* (Jerusalem: Keter Publishing House, 2006).

Cohen, A. and B. Susser, *Israel and the Politics of Jewish Identity: The Secular-Religious Impasse* (Baltimore, MD: Johns Hopkins University Press, 2000).

Cohen, G., 'Outcry prompts army to change its policy. IDF backtracks: Last fallen soldier will be honored in ceremony, regardless of Jewish status,' *Haaretz*, April 11, 2013.

Cohen, Y., 'gam eichler: yahadut hatora titmokh be'ḥoq haleom,' *Kikar Hashabat*, July 18, 2018. https://goo.gl/hbc64i.

Connolly, W. E., *Why I Am Not a Secularist* (Minneapolis: University of Minnesota Press, 1999).

Cooper, J. E., 'The turn to tradition in the study of Jewish politics,' *Annual Review of Political Science*, 19 (2016), 67–87.

Cutter, W., 'Ghostly Hebrew, ghastly speech: Scholem to Rosenzweig, 1926,' *Prooftexts*, 10 (1990), 413–33.

Devji, F., *Muslim Zion: Pakistan as a Political Idea* (Cambridge, MA: Harvard University Press, 2013).

Dichter, A. et al., 'Basic Law proposal: Israel is the nation-state of the Jewish people,' The Knesset, Pub. L. No. P/18/3541 (2011).

Dichter, A., A. Neguise, T. Ploskov, M. Yogev, Y. Kish, N. Boker, B. Smotich, O. Levy-Abekasis, R. Ilatov, D. Amsalem, and D. Bitan, Basic Law proposal: Israel – the nation-state of the Jewish people, The Knesset, Pub. L. No. P/20/1989 (2018).

Don-Yehiya, E., 'The negation of Galut in religious zionism,' *Modern Judaism*, 12 (1992), 129–55.

Religion and Political Accommodation in Israel (Jerusalem: The Floersheimer Institute for Policy Studies, 1999).

Don-Yehiya, E. and C. S. Liebman, 'The symbol system of Zionist-socialism: An aspect of Israeli civil religion,' *Modern Judaism*, 1/2 (1981), 121–48.

Dubnov, A. M., 'Notes on the Zionist passage to India, or: The analogical imagination and its boundaries,' *Journal of Israeli History*, 35/2 (2016), 177–214.

The Economist, 'Who is a Jew?' January 11, 2014.

Eilam, Y., 'emuna datit he beriḥa meaḥrayut,' *Haaretz*, January 23, 2017.

Elʿazari-Volcani, Y., *Kitvey Yitzḥak Elʿazari-Volcani. Volume 2: Sefirot* [Elʿazari-Volcani's writings] (Tel Aviv: N. Taberski, 5710/1950).

Eldad, A., Basic Law proposal: Israel – the nation-state of the Jewish people, The Knesset, Pub. L. No. P/18/4096 (2012).

El-Haj, N. A., *The Genealogical Science: The Search for Jewish Origins and the Politics of Epistemology*, repr. ed. (Chicago: University of Chicago Press, 2014).

Eli, Y., 'Hamedina moda: Bedikot DNA hokhiku yahadut,' nrg.co.il, July 29, 2013. https://goo.gl/JnUxw3.

Elkin, Z., Basic Law proposal: Israel – the nation state of the Jewish people, Pub. L. No. P/19/2502 (2014).

Ettinger, Y., 'Ex-IDF chief rabbi takes over Israel's new Jewish identity administration,' *Haaretz*, May 21, 2013.

Falah, G., 'Israeli 'Judaization' policy in Galilee,' *Journal of Palestine Studies*, 20/4 (1991), 69–85.

Firro, K., *The Druzes in the Jewish State: A Brief History* (Leiden, Netherlands: Brill, 1999).

'Reshaping Druze particularism in Israel,' *Journal of Palestine Studies*, 30/3 (2001), 40–53.

Fisher, N., *The Challenge of Conversion to Judaism in Israel: Policy Analysis and Recommendations* (Jerusalem: The Israel Democracy Institute, 2015).

Fitzgerald, T., *Discourse on Civility and Barbarity* (New York: Oxford University Press, 2007).

Friedman, M., 'And this is the history of the status quo,' in V. Pilovsky (ed.), *The Transition from Yishuv to Statehood 1947–1949: Continuity and Changes* (Haifa: Herzl Institute, 1990), pp. 47–79.

Fruman, R., 'hilonim, matai tavinu eifu atem hayim?,' *Haaretz*, July 4, 2016.

'hapitaron ho qodem kol yisre'eli,' *Haaretz*, February 9, 2017.

'ma 'im haherut le'ekhol hames bepesah?,' *Haaretz*, April 9, 2017.

'hiloniyut hadasha veatraqtivit,' *Haaretz*, August 1, 2017.

Gavison, R., 'Zionism in Israel: After the Ka'adan case,' *Law and Government*, 6 (2001), 25–51.

The Law of Return at Sixty Years: History, Ideology, Justification (Jerusalem: The Metzilah Center for Zionist, Jewish, Liberal and Humanist Thought, 2010).

A Constitutional Anchoring of the State's Vision: Recommendations to the Justice Minister (Jerusalem: Metzilah, 2014).

'Defining Israel, Part I: Constitutional anchoring of Israel's vision: Recommendations submitted to the Minister of Justice – with an introduction by Simon Rabinovitch,' *Marginalia Review of Books* [forum], December 30, 2014. https://marginalia.lareviewofbooks.org/?p=6711.

Golan, Y., 'Hasbarat shitat harav Hayim Amsellem benose hagiyur,' Shoresh.org.Il (blog), September 23, 2009. https://goo.gl/anj62y.

Goodman, M., *A History of Judaism* (London: Allen Lane, 2017).

Goodman, Y., 'Citizenship, modernity and belief in the nation-state: Racialization and de-racialization in the conversion of Russian immigrants and Ethiopian immigrants in Israel,' in Y. Shenhav and Y. Yonah (eds.), *Racism in Israel* (Jerusalem: Van Leer Jerusalem Institute, 2008), pp. 381–415.

Greenberg, Y., 'Mi sheroṣe liḥyut beshalom ʿim hadatiyim ṣarikh lehakhriaḥ otam, ṣarikh lishbor otam,' *Haaretz*, November 29, 2017.

Greenwood, Ḥ., 'ḥasifa: mikhtav bekhirey harabanim neged hasefer zeraʿ yisrael shel harav amsellem,' Kipa.co.il. https://goo.gl/borrG5.

Haaretz, "Israel is the nation-state of Jews alone': Netanyahu responds to TV star who said Arabs are equal citizens,' *Haaretz*, March 11, 2019.

Haaretz Editorial, 'The Jewish Coercion Administration,' *Haaretz*, May 22, 2013.

'Basic Law: Apartheid in Israel,' *Haaretz*, May 30, 2013.

'There is such a thing as 'Israeli,'' *Haaretz*, May 5, 2014.

'Prescribing Jewish law in absence of legal precedent sacralizes Israel's judicial system,' *Haaretz*, September 18, 2017.

'The Jewish mission,' *Haaretz*, March 28, 2018.

'A state for some of its citizens,' *Haaretz*, March 11, 2019.

'DNA testing to 'prove' Jewishness is spine-chilling,' *Haaretz*, September 1, 2019.

Habib, J., *Israel, Diaspora, and the Routes of National Belonging* (Toronto: University of Toronto Press, 2004).

Haʿivri, O., B. Ish-shalom, Z. Hauser, R. Yadlin, and P. Nirnstein, 'duaḥ havaʿada haṣiburit hameyaʿeṣet livḥinat yaḥasah shel yisrael leṣiburim baʿolam baʿalei ziqa laʿam hayehudi,' Report (Jerusalem: Ministry of Diaspora Affairs, 2018).

Helman, D. and A. Arbel, 'doresh ʿiggun,' Institute of Zionist Strategies, July 2009. https://goo.gl/SvW5cx.

'Jewish national home,' Institute of Zionist Strategies, December 30, 2015. http://izs.org.il/?p=3924.

Herzl, T., *The Jewish State*, trans. Louis Lipsky (New York: Dover Publications, 2008).

High Follow-Up Committee for Arab Citizens, the National Committee of Arab Mayors, and the Joint List Members of Knesset v. The Knesset HJC 5866/18 (2018).

Hovel, R., 'Justice minister slams Israel's top court, says it disregards Zionism and upholding Jewish majority,' *Haaretz*, August 29, 2017.

'Justice Minister: Israel must keep Jewish majority even at the expense of human rights,' *Haaretz*, February 13, 2018.

Hurd, E. S., *Beyond Religious Freedom: The New Global Politics of Religion* (Princeton, NJ: Princeton University Press, 2015).

Institute for Zionist Strategies, The, 'About us.' http://izs.org.il/about-3.

Israel Democracy Institute, 'IDI – Israel's Leading Think Tank, 'Do Tank,' and Policy Institute.' https://goo.gl/o25tkN.

'Religion and state in Israel.' https://goo.gl/y1v8kW.

Jakobsen, J. and A. Pellegrini, 'Times like this,' in J. Jakobsen, and A. Pellegrini (eds.), *Secularisms* (Durham, NC: Duke University Press, 2008), pp. 1–35.

Jaradat, M. G., *The Unchosen: The Lives of Israel's New Others* (London: Pluto Press, 2017).

Jewish Agency, The, 'Community Shlichim.' Website. www.jewishagency .org/shlichim-israeli-emissaries/program/287.

Kashti, O., '"Judaism facilitators' will strengthen religious values among seculars across the country,' *Haaretz*, March 2, 2014.

'Group seeks to counter religious 'coercion' in Israeli public schools,' *Haaretz*, January 5, 2016.

'behemot tehorot vesiyur bebeit hamiqdash,' *Haaretz*, April 20, 2017.

'Jews' advantages to non-Jews': Religious indoctrination seeping into Israeli textbooks,' *Haaretz*, April 22, 2017.

Kedar, N., 'Ben-Gurion's mamlakhtiyut : Etymological and theoretical roots,' *Israel Studies*, 7/3 (2002), 117–33.

Mamlachtiyut: Ben-Gurion's civilian conception (Beersheba, Israel: Ben-Gurion University Press, 2009).

Kelner, S., *Tours That Bind: Diaspora, Pilgrimage, and Israeli Birthright Tourism*, (New York: New York University Press, 2012).

Klein, I., 'yahadut hatora monaʿat et qidomo shel 'hoq haleom," *Actuaclic*, May 23, 2017. http://actualic.co.il/?p=346034.

Klug, B., *Being Jewish and Doing Justice: Bringing Argument to Life* (London: Vallentine Mitchell, 2011).

Kravel-Tovi, M., *When the State Winks: The Performance of Jewish Conversion in Israel* (New York: Columbia University Press, 2017).

Kreisel, H., 'Maimonides political philosophy,' in K. Seeskin (ed.), *The Cambridge Companion to Maimonides* (New York: Cambridge University Press, 2005).

Kurzweil, B., 'The new Canaanites in Israel,' *Judaism*, 2 (1953), 3–15.

Our New Literature: Continuation of Revolution? (Tel Aviv: Schocken, 1971).

Lam, A., 'ani maamin she'am yisrael ḥashuv yoter me'erṣ yisrael' (interview with Avi Gabbay), *Yediʿot Aharonot*, August 21, 2018.

Latour, B., *We Have Never Been Modern* (Cambridge, MA: Harvard University Press, 1993).

Levy, G., 'Have Israelis forgotten how to be Jews?' *Haaretz*, November 20, 2017.

'What's so bad about assimilation?' *Haaretz*, October 13, 2018.

'It's Leftism or Zionism – you can't have both,' *Haaretz*, February 10, 2019.

Levy, S., H. Levinsohn, and E. Katz, *A Portrait of Israeli Jews: Beliefs, Observance, and Values of Israeli Jews, 2000* (Jerusalem: Avi Chai and the Israel Democracy Institute, 2002).

Liebman, C. S. and E. Don-Yehiya, *Civil Religion in Israel: Traditional Judaism and Political Culture in the Jewish State* (Berkeley: University of California Press, 1983).

Liebman, C. S. and Y. Yadgar, 'Secular-Jewish identity and the condition of secular Judaism in Israel,' in Z. Gitelman (ed.), *Religion or Ethnicity? Jewish Identities in Evolution* (New Brunswick, NJ: Rutgers University Press, 2009), pp. 149–70.

Lilla, M., *The Once and Future Liberal: After Identity Politics* (New York: Harper, 2017).

Lis, J., 'Dichter replaces 'Jewish identity' bill with equally contentious draft law,' *Haaretz*, November 15, 2011.

'Netanyahu: Abbas' refusal to recognize Israel as Jewish state is 'absurd,'' *Haaretz*, February 3, 2014.

'beoulam male uvli yesh 'atid: hushka hashedula haḥilonit baknesset,' *Haaretz*, January 17, 2018.

'Knesset set to give initial approval of bill allowing Jewish-only communities,' *Haaretz*, April 30, 2018.

Livni, R., 'Three reasons Israelis stopped being secular,' *Haaretz*, January 2, 2017.

The End of Hebrewness (Jerusalem: Carmel, 2018).

Loveday, M., 'Deluge of opposition to Israel's nation-state law builds with new court petition,' *The Washington Post*, August 7, 2018.

Lustick, I. S., 'Israel as a non-Arab state: The political implications of mass immigration of non-Jews,' *Middle East Journal*, 53/3 (1999), 417–33.

MacIntyre, A., *Whose Justice? Which Rationality?* (Notre Dame, IN: University of Notre Dame Press, 1988).

Magnezi, A., 'Rivlin: What is the point of the 'Nationality Law'?' *Ynetnews*, November 25, 2014. https://goo.gl/WVp6cA.

Maltz, Judy. 'Israel rabbinate accused of using DNA testing to prove Jewishness,' *Haaretz*, February 4, 2019.

McGonigle, I. V., ''Jewish genetics' and the 'nature' of Israeli citizenship' *Transversal*, 13/2 (2015), 90–102.

McGonigle, I. V. and L. W. Herman, 'Genetic citizenship: DNA testing and the Israeli Law of Return' *Journal of Law and the Biosciences*, 2/2 (2015), 469–78.

Mendel, Y., *The Creation of Israeli Arabic: Security and Politics in Arabic Studies in Israel* (Basingstoke, UK: Palgrave Macmillan, 2014).

Mendel, Y., D. Yitzhaki, and M. Pinto, 'Official but not recognized: The precarious status of the Arabic language in Israel and the need to redress this,' *Giluy Da'at*, 10 (2016), 17–45.

Meridor, D., 'en kol setira ben medinat leom limdinat kol ezraḥeha,' *Haaretz*, September 13, 2018.

Michael, S. and Others v. The Knesset, (2019).

Ministry of Religious Services, 'Jewish identity administration.' Website. www.dat.gov.il/About/Units/Pages/JewishIdentity.aspx.

Misgav, U., 'kefiya datit? teror dati,' *Haaretz*, December 4, 2015.

'For God's sake, enough with this obsession over Judaism,' *Haaretz*, November 16, 2017.

Moṣafi, B., 'Question #1655,' Doresh Ṣion (blog). https://goo.gl/pnbXHi.

Na'alamim, TV film, presented by Y. Limore. Keshet, Channel 2, Mako.co.il, 2016.

The National Committee for the Heads of the Arab Local Authorities in Israel, 'The future vision for the Palestinian Arabs in Israel' (2006). https://goo.gl/DBqzW9.

Newman, M., 'Begin breaks ranks to oppose Jewish nation-state bill,' *The Times of Israel*, July 26, 2017. www.timesofisrael.com/begin-breaks-ranks-to-oppose-jewish-nation-state-bill.

Nongbri, B., *Before Religion: A History of a Modern Concept*, (New Haven, CT: Yale University Press, 2015).

Novak, D., *Zionism and Judaism: A New Theory* (New York: Cambridge University Press, 2015).

Noy, O., 'Israel's nation-state law also discriminates against Mizrahi Jews,' +972 *Magazine* (blog), January 2, 2019, https://972mag.com/?p=139541.

Ohana, D., *Messianism and Mamlachtiyut: Ben Gurion and the Intellectuals between Political Vision and Political Theory* (Beersheba, Israel: Ben-Gurion University Press, 2003).

Oppenheimer, J., 'The Druze in Israel as Arabs and non-Arabs: Manipulation of categories of identity in a non-civil state' in A. Weingrod (ed.), *Studies in Israeli Ethnicity: After the Ingathering* (New York: Gordon and Breach, 1985), pp. 259–80.

Ornan, U., 'haleom sheli: yisre'eli,' *Ynet*, September 3, 2008. https://goo.gl/D5K5Pi.

'hakhrazat ha'atzmaut – kummo shel leom yisre'eli,' Atar Hamamarim Shel Uzi Ornan. Website. https://goo.gl/xRZdbt.

'hoda'a la'itunut 12.6.2006,' Atar Hamamarim Shel Uzi Ornan. Website. https://goo.gl/zbupQc.

'Yisrael einenah 'medinat haleom shel ha'am hayehudi,'' Atar Hamamarim Shel Uzi Ornan. Website. https://goo.gl/Ep6VzY.

Ornan, U. and Orion, E., 'Anaḥnu kena'anim,' *Sevivot*, 33 (1994), 1–15.

Ornan et al. v. Interior Ministry, HP (Jerusalem) 6092/07 (2008).

Ornan et al. v. Interior Ministry, 'Appeal on HP 6092/07' (2008).

Ornan et al. v. Interior Ministry, CA 8573/08 (2013).

Peled, Y. and H. Herman Peled, *The Religionization of Israeli Society* (London: Routledge, 2018).

Peleg, B., 'Druze protest nation-state law outside Israeli party leaders' homes; politicians vow to 'fix' legislation,' *Haaretz*, January 16, 2019.

'In first public statement, Benny Gantz vows to 'fix' nation-state law,' *Haaretz*, January 14, 2019.

Pew Research Center, 'Israel's religiously divided society,' Pew Research Center's Religion & Public Life Project, March 8, 2016. pewrsr.ch/1QDNS2O.

Plamenatz, J., 'Two types of nationalism' in E. Kamenka (ed.), *Nationalism: The Nature and Evolution of an Idea* (London: Edward Arnold, 1978), pp. 22–36.

Porath, Y., *The Life of Uriel Shelah* (Tel Aviv: Maḥbarot Lesifrut, 1989).

Qam, Z., ''al pi derishat heḥaredim: halikud yiqbor et ḥoq haleom,' nrg.co.il, April 9, 2015. https://goo.gl/25AzVC.

Quinn, B., 'French police make woman remove clothing on Nice beach following burkini ban,' *The Guardian*, August 23, 2016.

Rabinowitz, A., 'Israel's rabbinical courts begin to recognize DNA tests, potentially opening gateway to proving Jewishness,' *Haaretz*, August 30, 2019.

Rabinovitch, S., 'Defining Israel, Part II: Jewish and democratic according to the law,' *The Marginalia Review of Books* [forum], February 2, 2015. https://marginalia.lareviewofbooks.org/?p=6705.

Rabkin, Y. M., *A Threat from Within: A Century of Jewish Opposition to Zionism* (London: Zed Books, 2006).

'The problem, Benny Morris, is Zionism,' *The Jerusalem Post*, January 29, 2007.

What Is Modern Israel? (London: Pluto Press, 2016).

'Conflating Zionism and Judaism leaves Jewish students exposed,' +972 *Magazine*, December 8, 2017. https://972mag.com/?p=131244.

Raz-Krakotzkin, A., 'Exile within sovereignty: Toward a critique of the 'negation of exile' in Israeli culture, Part 1,' *Theory and criticism*, 4 (1993), 23–55.

'Exile, history and the nationalization of Jewish memory: Some reflections on the Zionist notion of history and return,' *Journal of Levantine Studies*, 3/2 (2013), 37–70.

Regev, M., Basic Law proposal: Israel is the nation-state of the Jewish people, The Knesset, Pub. L. No. P/19/2530 (2014).

Roth, L., *Judaism: A Portrait* (New York: Viking Press, 1968).

Rudnitzky, A., *The Arab Minority in Israel and the 'Jewish State' Discourse* (Jerusalem: The Israel Democracy Institute, 2015).

Rudoren, J., 'Sticking point in peace talks: Recognition of a Jewish state,' *The New York Times*, January 1, 2014.

'Palestinian leader seeks NATO force in future state,' *The New York Times*, February 2, 2014.

Rufeisen v. Minister of the Interior, PD 16(4) 2428 (1962).

Sabar, G. and E. Tsurkov, *Israel's Policies toward Asylum-seekers: 2002 – 2014* (Rome: Istituto Affari Internazionali, 2015).

Sagi, A., *Tradition vs. Traditionalism: Contemporary Perspectives in Jewish Thought* (New York: Rodopi, 2008).

To Be a Jew: Joseph Chayim Brenner as a Jewish Existentialist (New York: Continuum, 2011).

Sand, S., *The Invention of the Jewish People*, trans. Y. Lotan (New York: Verso, 2010).

How I Stopped Being a Jew, trans. D. Fernbach (New York: Verso, 2014).

The Invention of the Land of Israel: From Holy Land to Homeland, trans. G. Forman, 2nd rev. ed. (New York: Verso Books, 2014).

'How Israel went from atheist Zionism to Jewish state,' *Haaretz*, January 21, 2017.

Sasson, T., M. Shain, S. Hecht, G. Wright, and L. Saxe, 'Does Taglit-Birthright Israel foster long-distance nationalism?' *Nationalism and Ethnic Politics*, 20/4 (2014), 438–54.

Scholem, G., *Continuity and Rebellion – Gershom Scholem in Speech and Dialogue* (Tel Aviv: Am-Oved, 1994).

Schwartz, O., 'What does it mean to be genetically Jewish?' *The Guardian*, June 13, 2019.

Secular Forum, The, 'hadata besifrei halimud.' Website. https://goo.gl/UFpr1d.

Secular Forum, The, 'haforum haḥiloni.' Website. www.hiloni.org.il.

Secular Forum, The, 'hamadrikh lahoreh haḥiloni' Website. www.hiloni.org.il/?p=1025.

Secular Forum, The, 'min hatiqshoret – haforum haḥiloni.' Website. https://goo.gl/UFpr1d.

Shaked, A., Y. Levin, and R. Ilatov, Basic Law proposal: Israel – the nation-state of the Jewish people, The Knesset, Pub. L. No. P/19/1550 (2013).

Shapira, A., *New Jews, Old Jews* (Tel Aviv: Am-Oved, 1997).

'Spiritual rootlessness and circumscription to the 'here and now' in the Sabra world view,' *Israel Affairs*, 4/3–4 (1998), 103–31.

'Whatever became of 'negating exile'?' in A. Shapira (ed.), *Israeli Identity in Transition* (London: Praeger, 2004), pp. 69–108.

Sharon, J., 'Chief Rabbinate admits using DNA tests to help determine Jewish status,' *The Jerusalem Post*, March 6, 2019.

Shavit, J., *The New Hebrew Nation: A Study in Israeli Heresy and Fantasy* (London: Frank Cass, 1987).

Sheleg, Y., *The Jewish Renaissance in Israeli Society: The Emergence of a New Jew* (Jerusalem: Israel Democracy Institute, 2010).

Shenhav, Y., *The Arab Jews: Nationalism, Religion and Ethnicity* (Tel Aviv: Am Oved, 2003).

'Angel-less skies: The debate on religionisation under the canopy of the Protestant ethic,' *Israeli Sociology*, 19/2 (2018), 8–30.

Shiff, A., 'Gafni: hasiʿot haharediyot yasbiʿu neged hoq haleom,' Behadrei haredim, November 21, 2014. https://goo.gl/HsFPVU.

Shils, E., 'Tradition and liberty: Antinomy and interdependence,' *Ethics*, 68/3 (1958), 153–65.

Shimoni, G., *The Zionist Ideology* (Hanover, NH: Brandeis University Press, 1995).

Shoham, H., *Let's Celebrate! Festivals and Civic Culture in Israel* (Jerusalem: The Israel Democracy Institute, 2014).

Shumsky, D., *Beyond the Nation-State: The Zionist Political Imagination from Pinsker to Ben-Gurion* (New Haven, CT: Yale University Press, 2018).

Snir, D., 'Review of Hebrew language reading textbook.' The Secular Forum, https://goo.gl/bkkA1K.

Somfalvi, A. and S. Hai, "ein hinukh hiloni beyisrael': hahorim hahilonim yotz'im lemaavaq,' *Ynet*, May 12, 2016. https://goo.gl/RYBUzV.

State of Israel, 'About the conversion administration,' Prime Minister's Office. https://goo.gl/pHL7yW.

Stern, E., M. Sheetrit, A. Mitzna, D. Tzur, and A. Peretz, 'Basic Law proposal: Israel – the nation-state of the Jewish people,' The Knesset, Pub. L. No. P/19/2883 (2014).

Stern, Y. Z., 'ein leom yisre'eli,' *'Orekh Hadin*, January 2014, 60–61.

Stern, Y. Z., S. Farber, and E. Caplan, *Proposal for a State Conversion Law* (Jerusalem: Israel Democracy Institute and ITIM, 2014).

Sternhell, Z., *The Founding Myths of Israel: Nationalism, Socialism, and the Making of the Jewish State* (Princeton, NJ: Princeton University Press, 1998).

Strenger, C., 'Why nationalist and Jewish orthodoxy are [sic] taking over Israel,' *Haaretz*, January 12, 2017.

Tamarin v. State of Israel, CA 630/70 (1972).

Triandafyllidou, A., 'National identity and the 'other,'' *Ethnic and Racial Studies*, 21/4 (1998), 593–612.

Tsur, M., 'Pesach in the Land of Israel: Kibbutz Haggadot,' *Israel Studies*, 12/2 (2007), 74–103.

Van der Veer, P. (ed.), *Conversion to Modernities* (London: Routledge, 1995).

Vater, R., 'Beyond bi-nationalism? The Young Hebrews versus the 'Palestinian issue," *Journal of Political Ideologies*, 21/1 (2016), 45–60.

Walzer, M., *The Paradox of Liberation: Secular Revolutions and Religious Counterrevolutions* (New Haven, CT: Yale University Press, 2015).

Walzer, M., M. Lorberbaum, N. Zohar, and A. Ackerman (eds.), *The Jewish Political Tradition. Volume 2: Membership* (New Haven, CT: Yale University Press, 2003).

Walzer, M., M. Lorberbaum, N. J. Zohar, and M. Kochen (eds.), *The Jewish Political Tradition. Volume 3: Community* (New Haven, CT: Yale University Press, 2018).

Walzer, M., M. Lorberbaum, N. Zohar, and Y. Lorberbaum (eds.), *The Jewish Political Tradition. Volume 1: Authority* (New Haven, CT: Yale University Press, 2003).

Weiss, Y., 'The Monster and its creator – or how did the Jewish nation-state become multi-ethnic,' *Theory and Criticism*, 19 (2001), 45–70.

Yadgar, Y., *Secularism and Religion in Jewish-Israeli Politics: Traditionists and Modernity* (New York: Routledge, 2011).

   Beyond Secularization: Traditionists and the Critique of Israeli Secularism (Jerusalem: Van Leer Institute/Hakibutz Hameuchad Publishing House, 2012).

   'Tradition,' *Human Studies*, 36/4 (2013), 451–70.

   'Overcoming the 'religion and politics' discourse: A new interpretation of the Israeli case,' *Journal of Religion and Society*, 16 (2014). https://goo.gl/fs8JML.

   'Traditionism,' *Cogent Social Sciences*, 1/1 (2015). https://goo.gl/epMpQo.

   Sovereign Jews: Israel, Zionism, and Judaism (New York: SUNY Press, 2017).

Yakobson, A. and A. Rubinstein, *Israel and the Family of Nations: The Jewish Nation-state and Human Rights* (New York: Routledge, 2009).

Yehoshua, A. B., 'The meaning of Homeland,' in *The A. B. Yehoshua Controversy: An Israel-diaspora Dialogue on Jewishness, Israeliness, and Identity* (New York: Dorothy And Julius Koppelman Institute on American Jewish-Israeli Relations, American Jewish Committee, 2006), pp. 7–13.

Yiftachel, O. and D. Rumley, 'On the impact of Israel's Judaization policy in the Galilee,' *Political Geography Quarterly*, 10/3 (1991), 286–96.

Yiftachel, O. and M. D. Segal, 'Jews and Druze in Israel: State control and ethnic resistance,' *Ethnic and Racial Studies*, 21/3 (1998), 476–506.

Yoʻaz, Y., 'hapraqliṭut: leom ʻyisre'eli ḥoter taḥat hamedina,' *Walla! News*, May 19, 2004.

Yonah, Y., 'Israel's immigration policies: The twofold face of the 'demographic threat,'' *Social Identities*, 10/2 (2004), 195–218.

Zerubavel, Y., *Recovered Roots: Collective Memory and the Making of Israeli National Tradition* (Chicago: University of Chicago Press, 1995).

Zisenwine, D., 'Jewish education in the Jewish state,' *Israel Affairs*, 4/3–4 (1998), 146–55.

Index